MW01640369

CENTIFOLIA

CENTIFOLIA

by Stuart Immonen

Entire contents copyright © 2008 Stuart Immonen unless otherwise noted.

Pages 53–59: "Slightly Related" copyright © 2006 Kathryn Immonen & Stuart Immonen. "Slightly Related" originally appeared in *Guernica Variaciones Gernika*, 2006.

Page 109: Paul, Angela, and the Power Glove copyright © 2008 Chris Duffy.

All rights reserved.

No part of this publication may be reproduced or stored in a retrieval system, or transmitted in any form or by any means, electronic, mechanical, recording or otherwise, without written permission of the Author, except for purposes of review. Any similarity between names, characters, persons or institutions portrayed in this work to any names, characters, persons or institutions living or dead without satirical purpose is unintentional.

For more books, visit www.adhousebooks.com

AdHouse Books | 1224 Greycourt Avenue | Richmond, VA 23227

Printed in Canada

6 5 4 3 2

ISBN 978-1-9352331-3-8

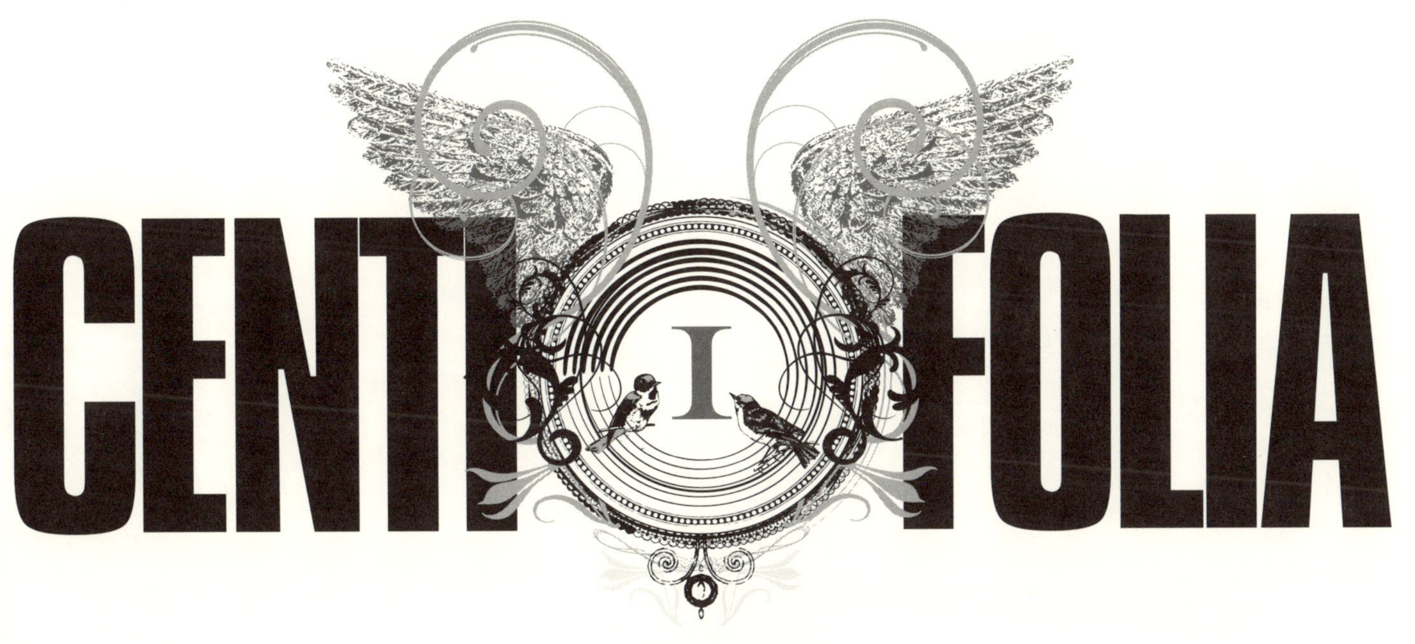

CENTIFOLIA I

STUART IMMONEN

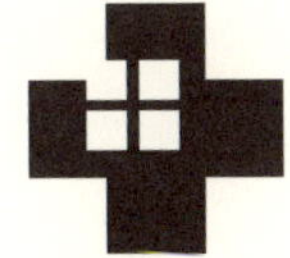

AdHouse Books Richmond VA

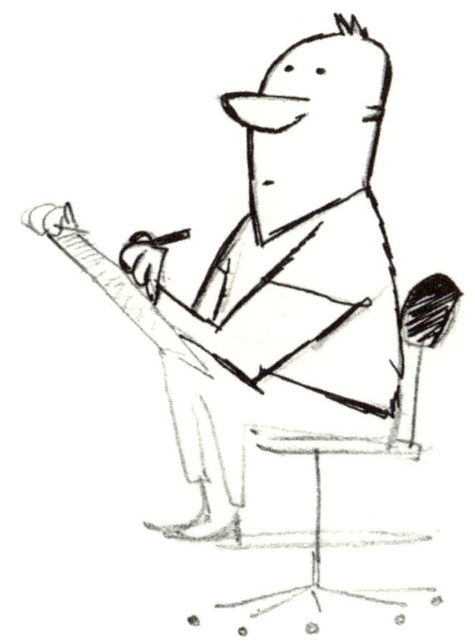

Look.

I'm going to be honest. I don't draw every day. Not the way I should.

Not for fun.

Mr. Pate, my high school art teacher, warned me, actually. He told me that if art became my job, I might not want to do it on my own time, too. Or words to that effect. This is the kind of career advice doled out at a rural learning institution back in the dark ages.

A long string of jobs followed; bowling lane pinsetter, maintenace mechanic, busboy, waiter, record store clerk, floor supervisor, art supply salesperson, comic book retailer; during that period, I drew a lot, and while it was with purpose (namely getting into comics), it wasn't my job.

But whether by the power of suggestion or fate or (lack of) will, Mr. Pate's prediction came to pass. When I began freelancing, all my energy went into the page to be printed, and I developed the questionable habit of working almost every day, leaving little time for personal projects. In fact, I didn't even begin keeping a sketchbook until 2002, more than 10 years into my professional career as a picture-maker, and even then, only because I thought I was supposed to have one. I wasn't very dedicated to it, though; after a day in the comicbook salt mines, there are any number of things I would rather do than pick up the pencil I just put down.

And yet, here are a hundred and twenty pages or so of drawings I've made for no other purpose than for "fun", drawings otherwise without a home, and it's frankly somewhat embarrassing. Turn to a random page, and you're as likely to find an unfinished comic, or a half-attempted illustration technique as you are likely to find something genuinely of note. For me, it's so different from my other published work, that for the longest time, I didn't know what to do with it. It seems to me that publishing the contents of five years of sketchbooks is rather like giving one's houseguests a tour of the closets; here's the dustpan, the toilet brush, the towels and sheets. I guess some people like that.

I hope you're one of them.

Stuart Immonen, March 2008

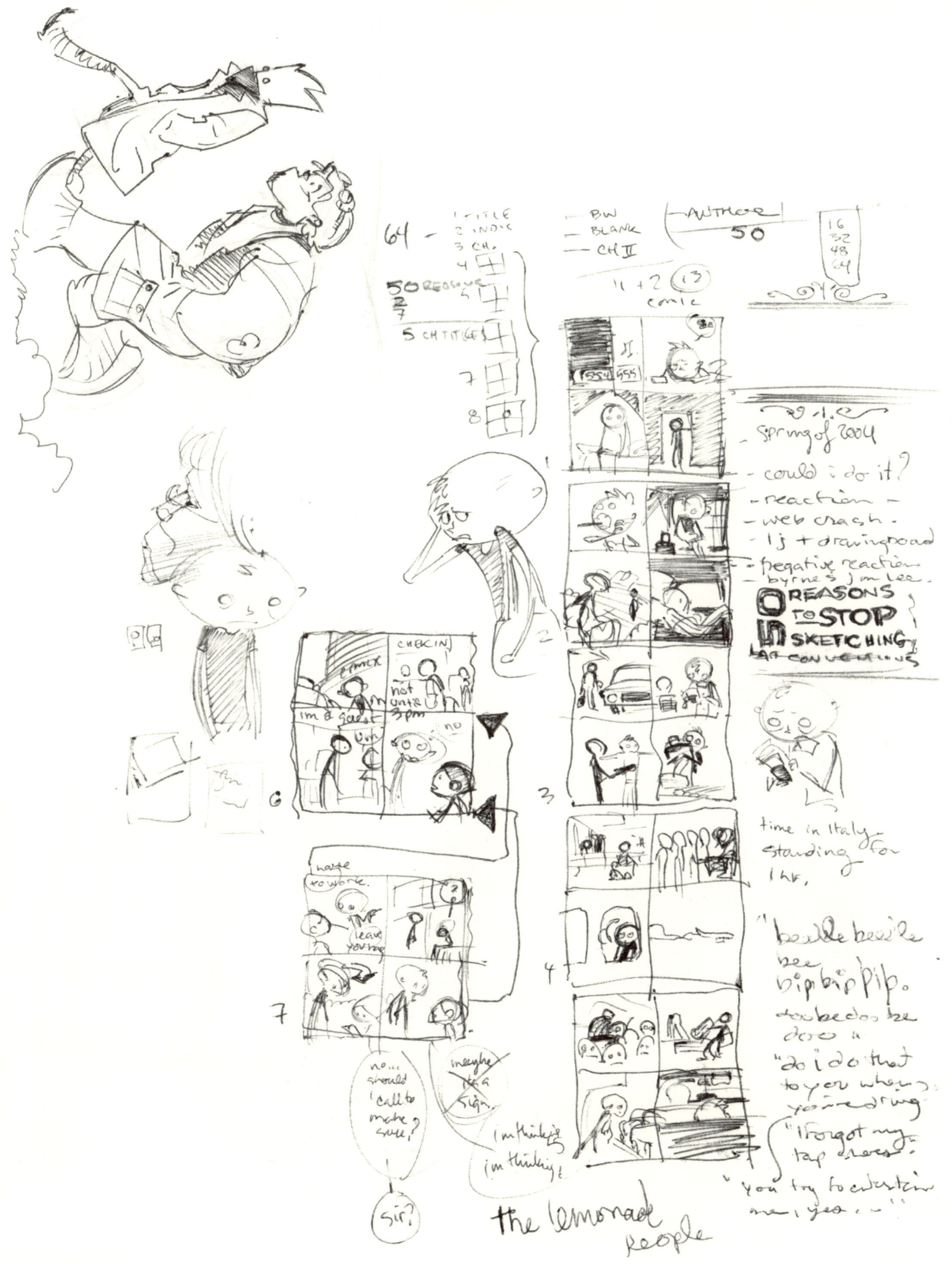
64
1 TITLE
2 INDIC
3 CH.
B/W
BLANK
CH II
AUTHOR
50
16
32
48
64
50 REASONS
5 CH TITLES
11 + 2 13
comic
CHECKIN
not until 3pm
im a guest
no
spring of 2004
could i do it?
reaction
web crash
lj + drawingboard
negative reaction
byrnes jim lee
REASONS
TO STOP
SKETCHING
time in Italy
standing for
have to work.
leave your bag
no... should i call to make sure?
sir?
im thinking
im thinking
the lemonade people
"do i do that to you when you're driving
"I forgot my tap shoes"
"You try to entertain me, yea..."

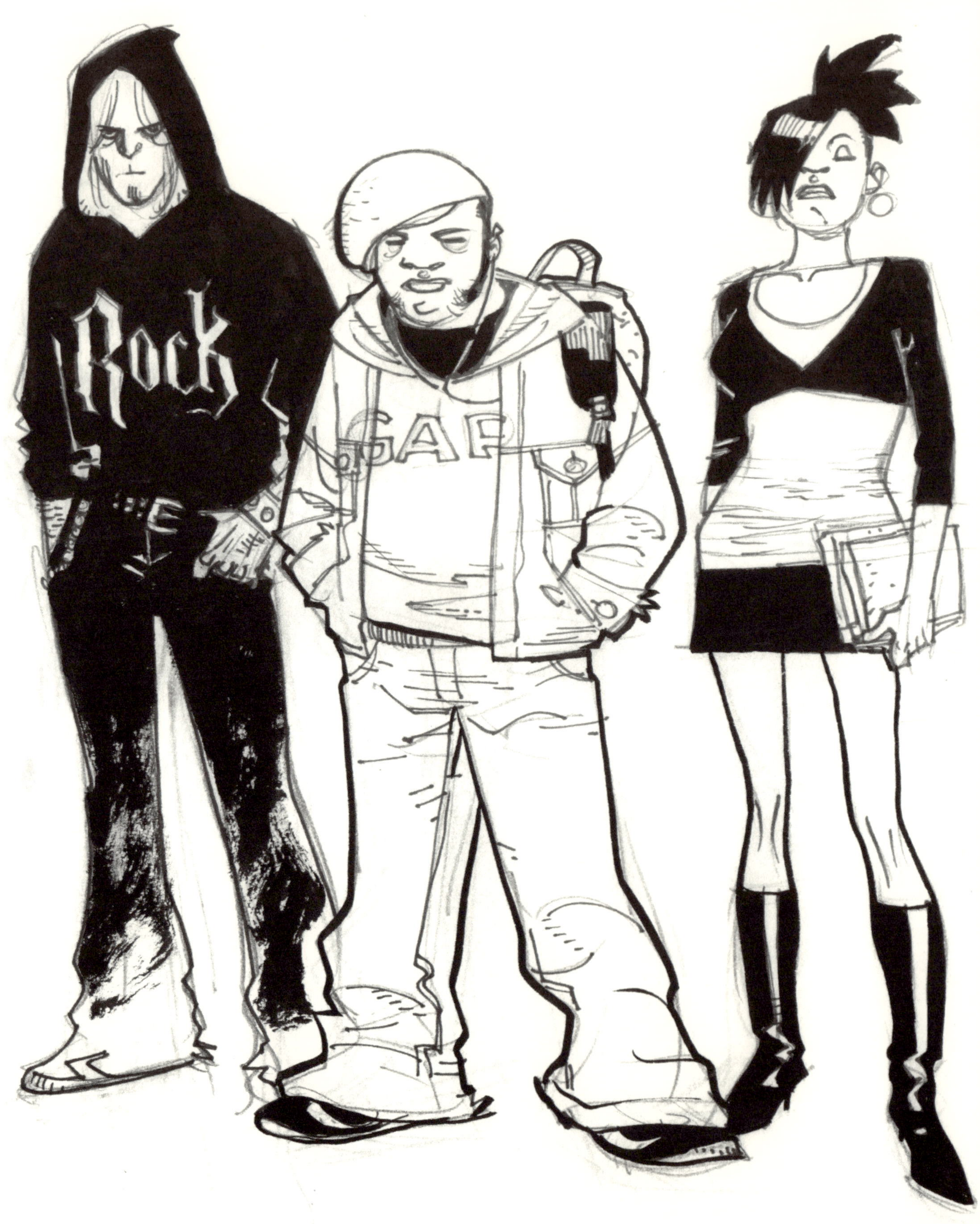
Rock
GAP

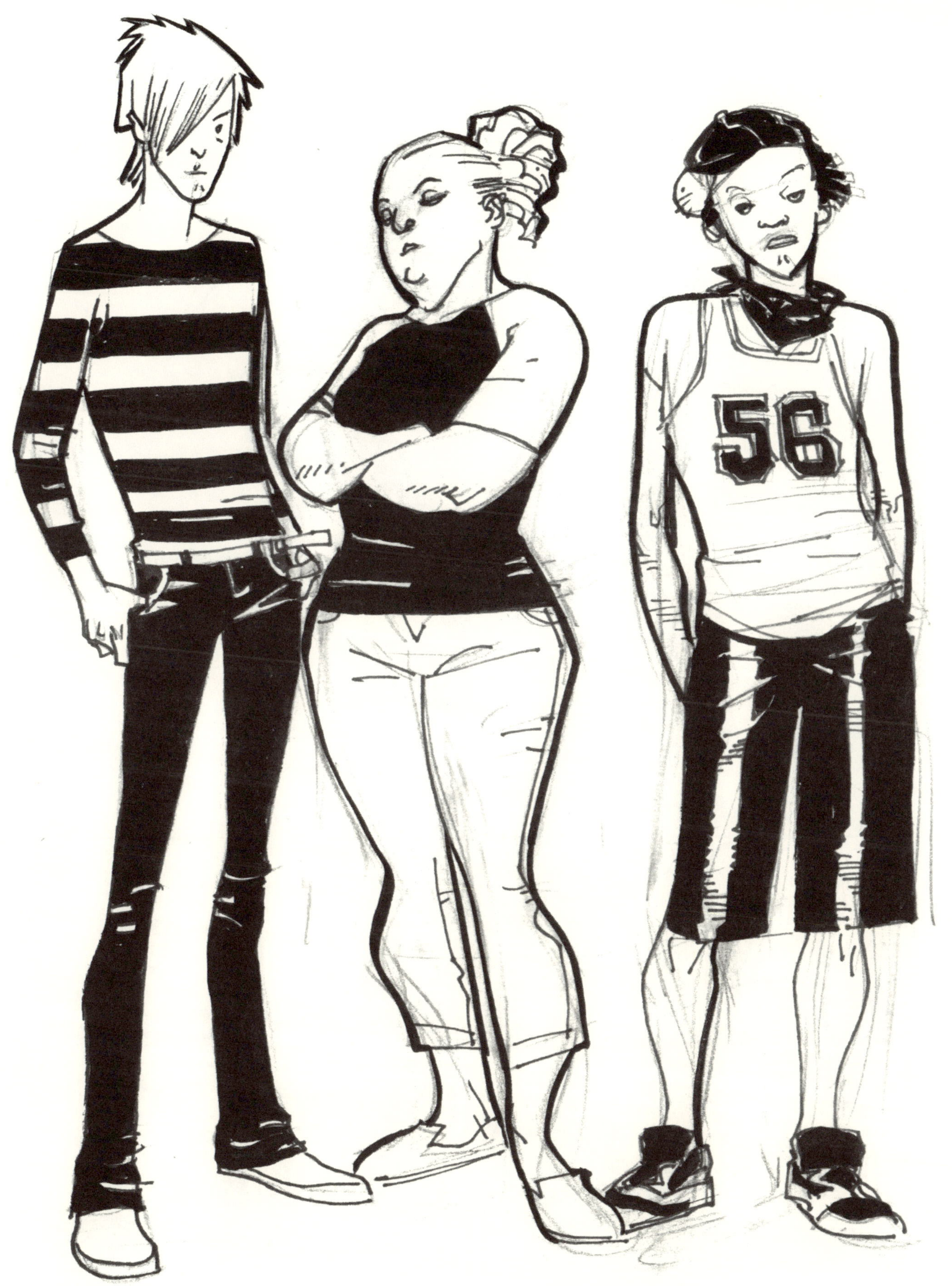
56

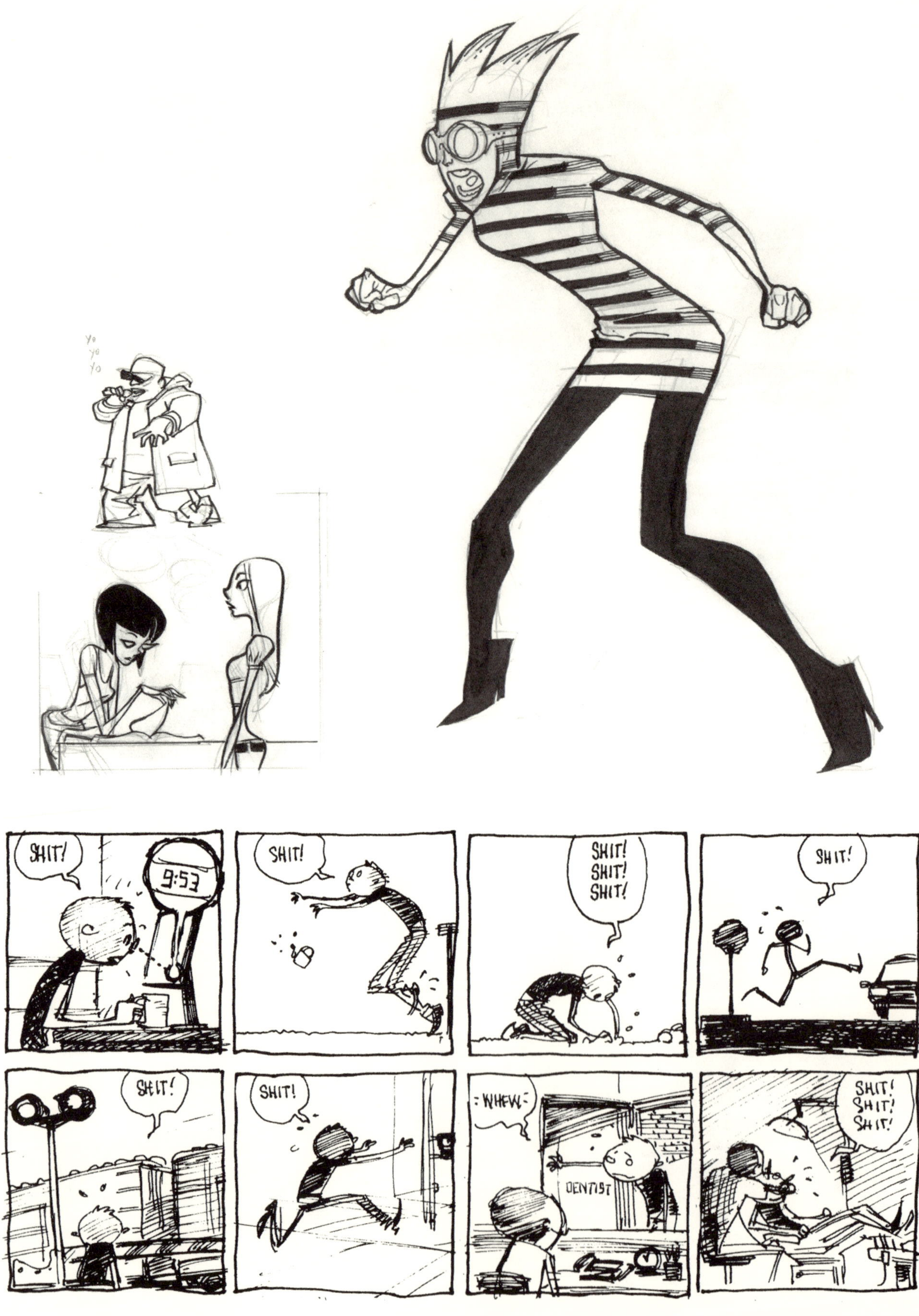
yo
yo
yo
SHIT!
9:53
SHIT!
SHIT!
SHIT!
SHIT!
SHIT!
SHIT!
SHIT!
WHEW
DENTIST
SHIT!
SHIT!
SHIT!

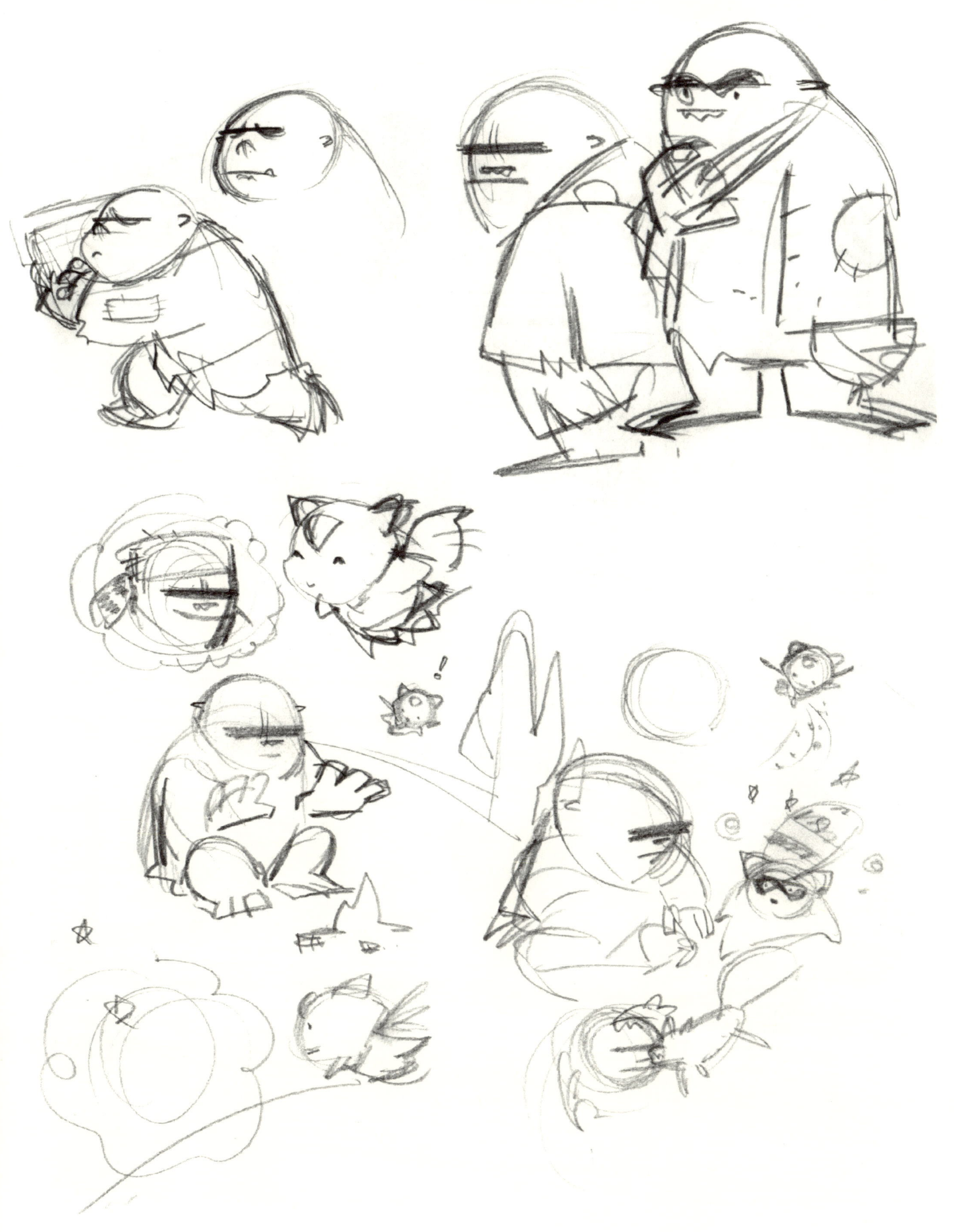

LAX AFTERNOON

After a 16-hour flight from Auckland, NZ, the scheduled three hour wait in Los Angeles didn't appeal.

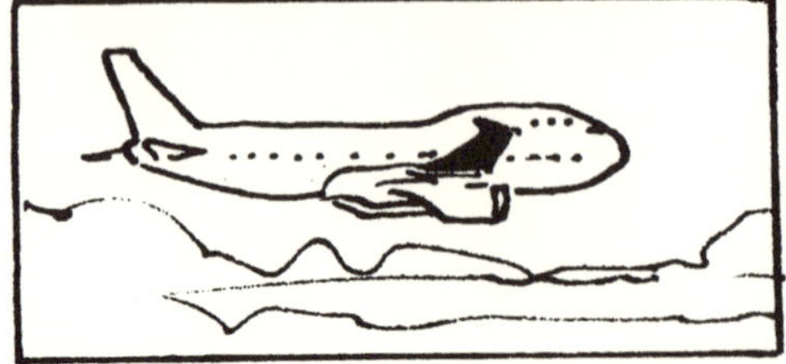

But there was a short delay with the bags...

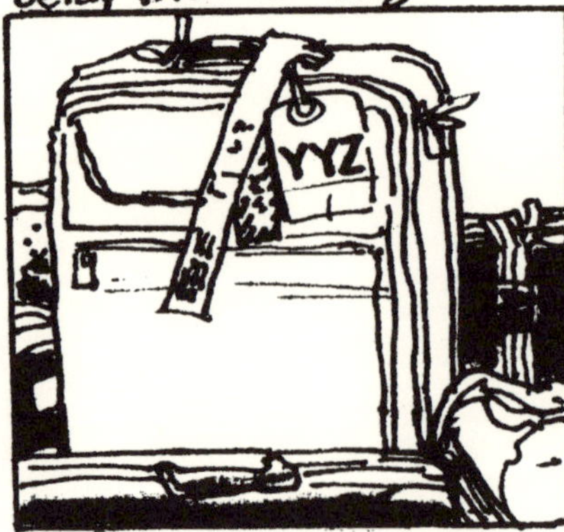

And a long line at border control.

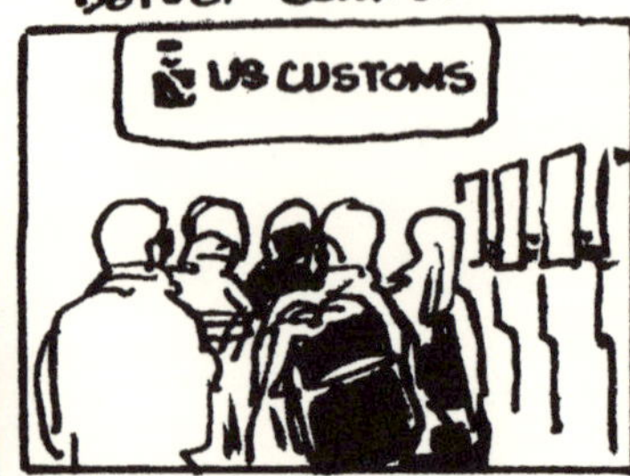

On line, I tried to guess how much time I might need to reschedule my flight itinerary.

But there were too many distractions, including a run-in with an Agriculture Detector Dog who wanted the apple I'd thrown out minutes before.

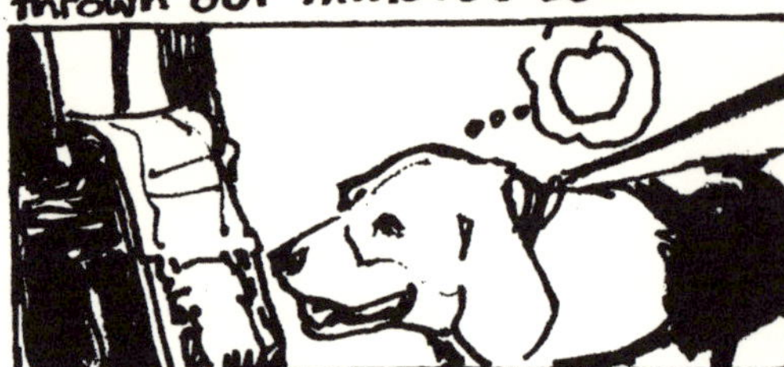

LAX isn't a confusing airport, but you're never presented with many options to deviate.

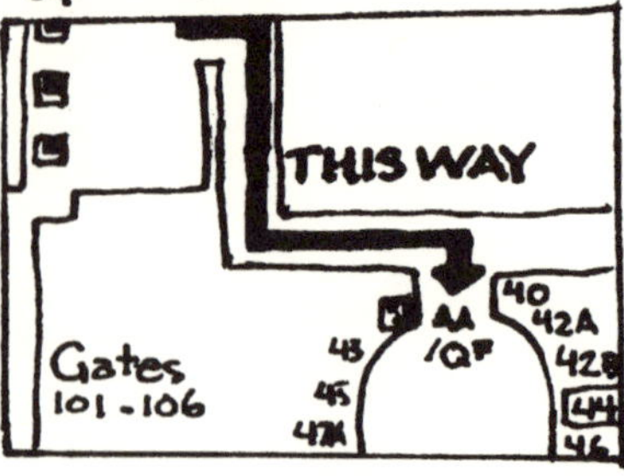

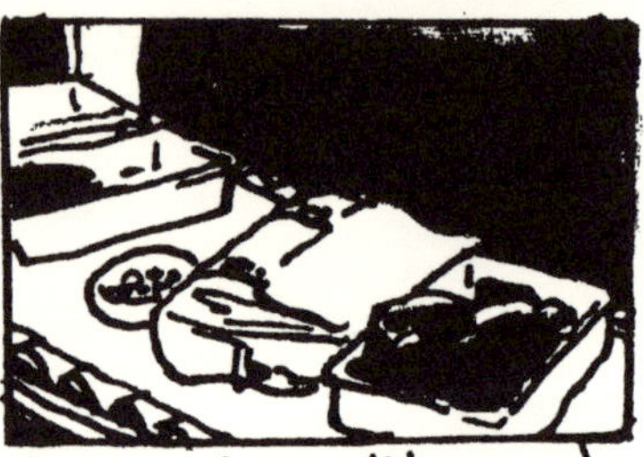

By the time I'd passed the final security check I was resigned to the wait, and found a seat where I could draw.

1

The final few hours of a trip are so often the most difficult to get through.

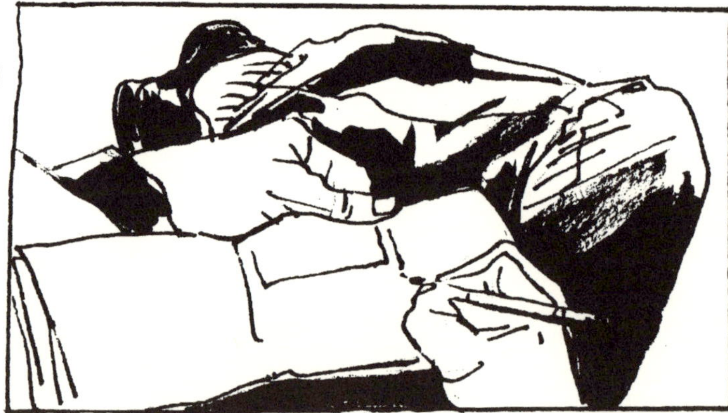

I was shuttled through so many lineups on arrival I never had the chance to possibly change my flight.

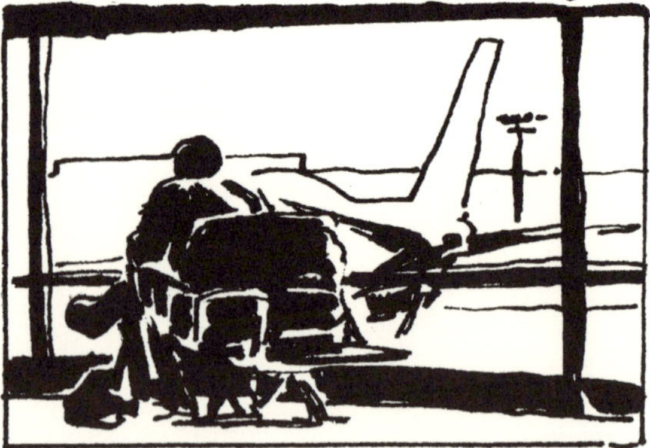

Sketching airport vehicles was only fun for so long. With more than two hours until boarding I'd have to think of something else to do. A tour of the facility seemed an appropriate way to waste time.

I first made sure I knew my gate.

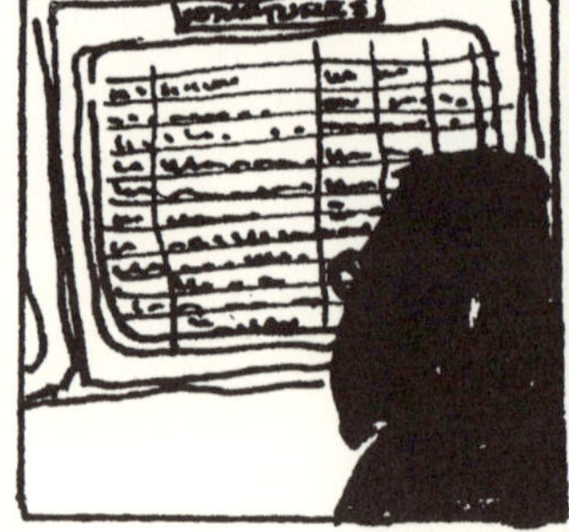

The shops looked promising.

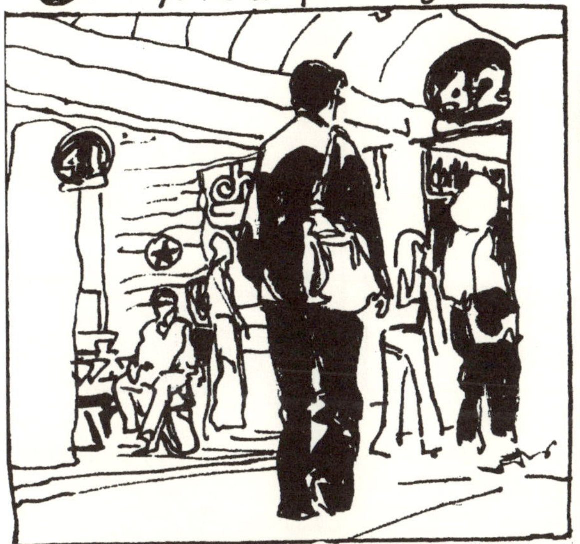

But it's always the same junk, no matter what airport you're in.

The newspapers lacked any interesting headlines, thank goodness, but a few magazines caught my eye.

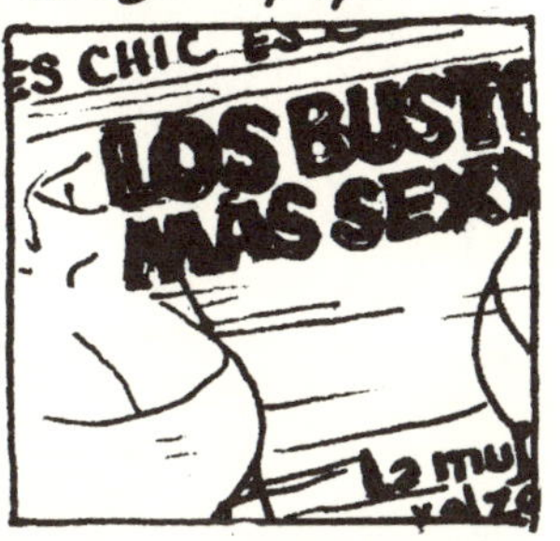

Nothing actually worth buying of course.

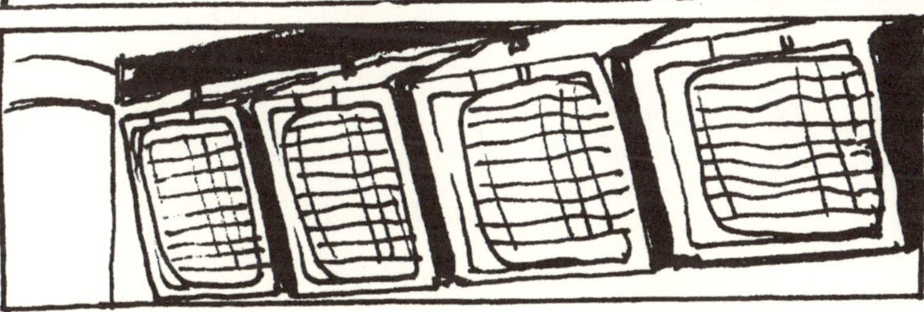

I came across another bank of terminals and looked for my flight — new gate.

3

A few hours left — I really timed it badly — so I exchange some NZ$ for greenbacks.

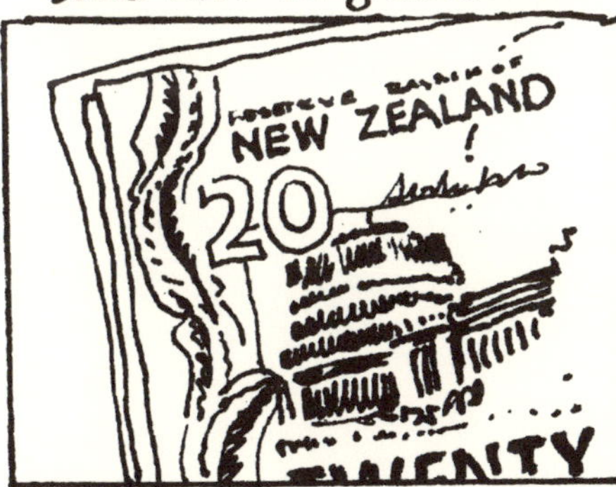

Which I used to buy an evil coffee drink.

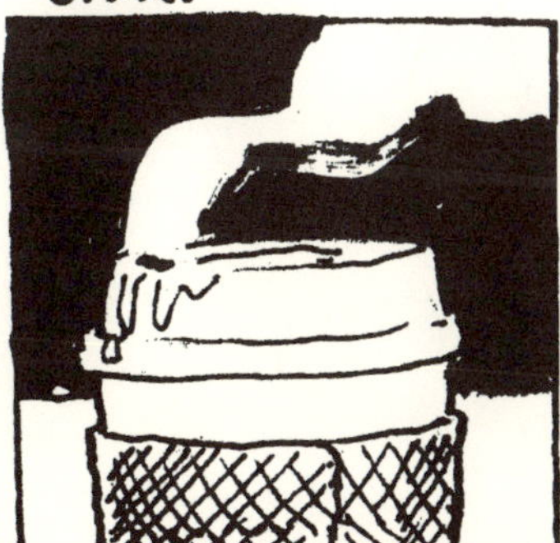

The sugar and caffeine gave me shooting pains behind my right eye, but I'd already maxed on ASA.

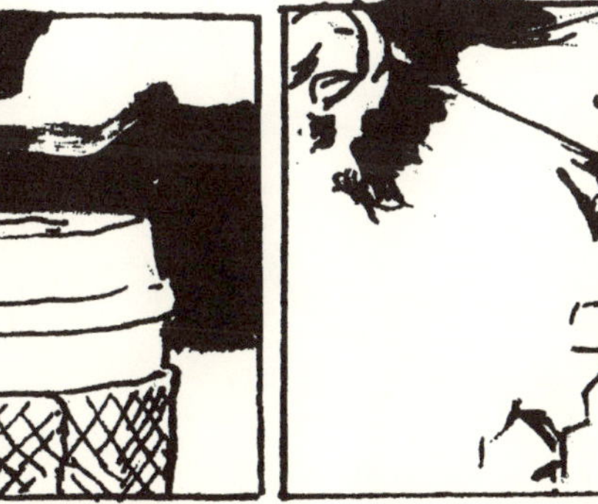

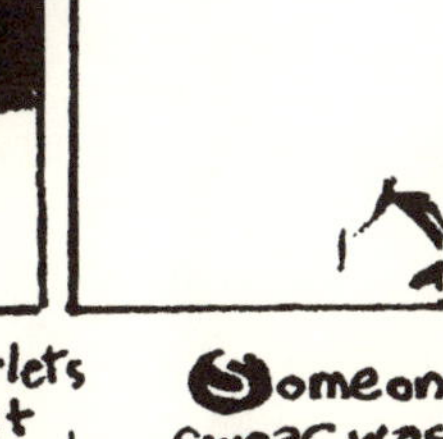

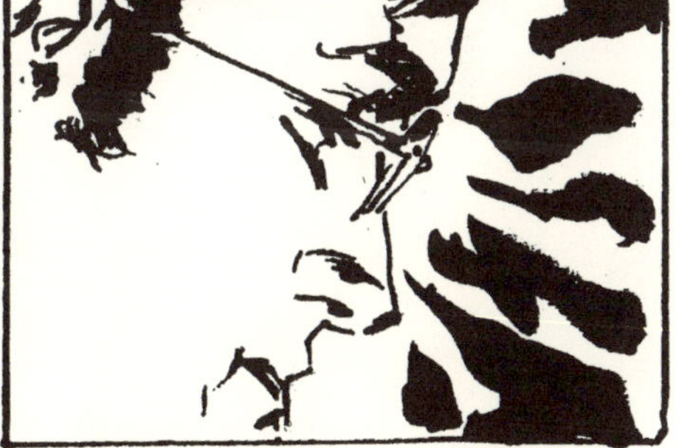

It just won't go away. I can't do any work. I can't even sit and read. All I can do is watch the crowds.

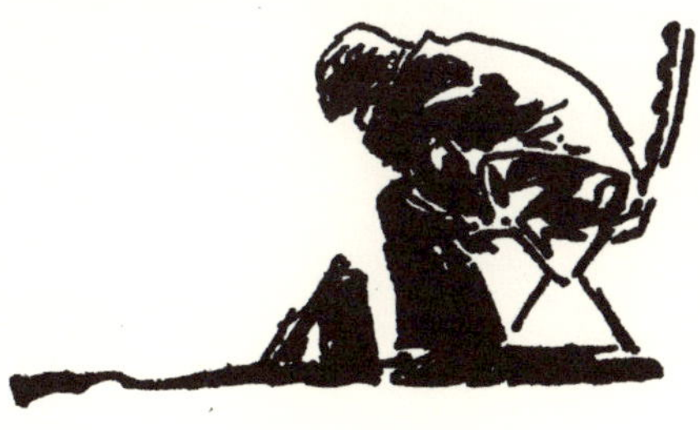

A couple of starlets in strappy starlet stilettos paused nearby.

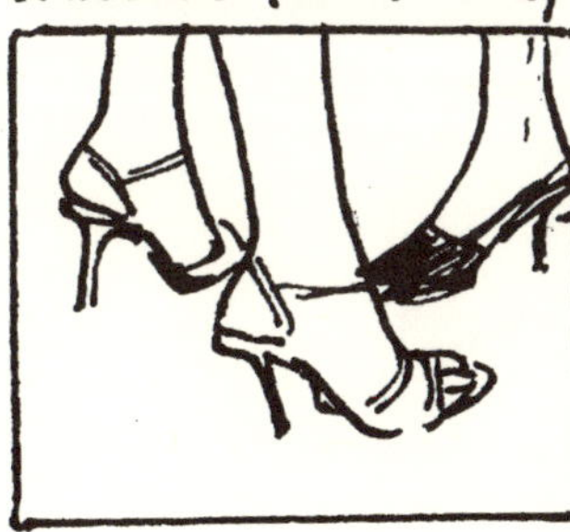

Someone I swear was Julie Delpy passed in trenchcoat and red Converse hi-tops. She also wore an enormous mobile phone headset, right out of the Apollo missions

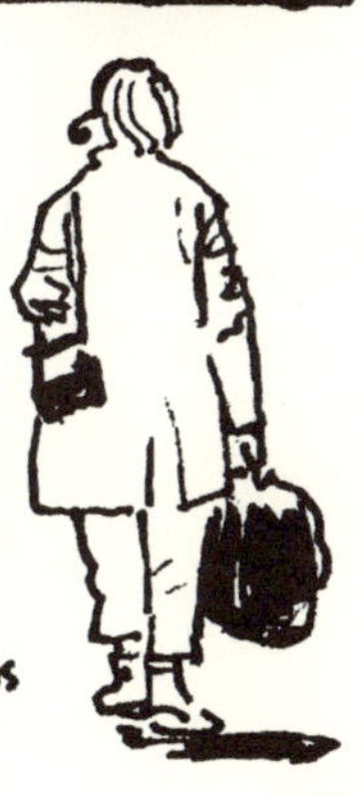

4

When I realized that I'd be sitting for another five hours, so I'd better get up and walk.

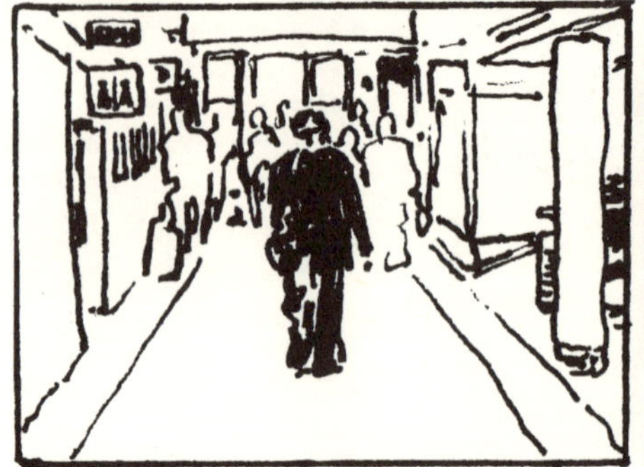

Unfortunately, there wasn't that far to go. I looked in each shop three times or more.

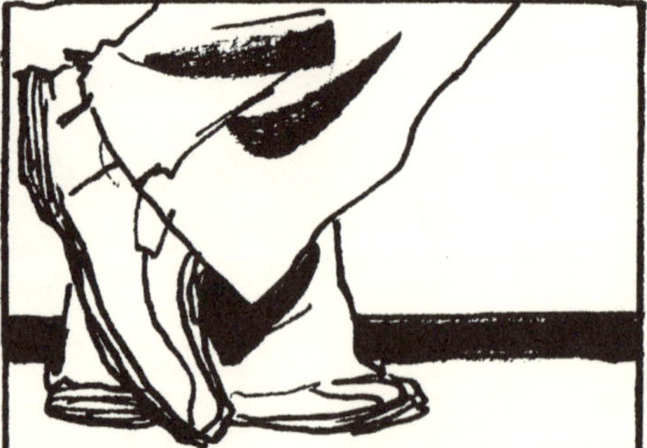

Another gate change. I thought: I'm going crazy, maybe.

Well that was it. I wasn't moving until I saw 'Toronto' come up behind the ticket counter.

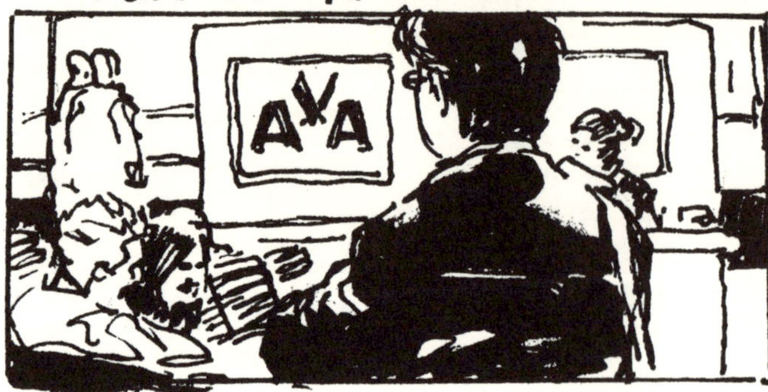

Happily, my headache subsided just as I realized that I'd be on board a 737 with only about fifty others, which meant the trip home might be the best part of the travelling afterall.

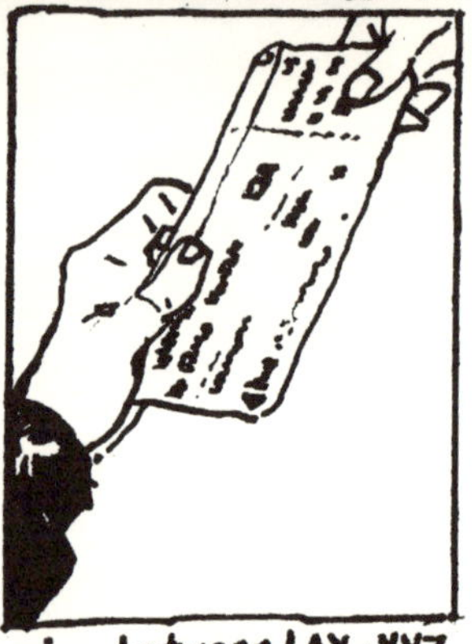

sai - between LAX+YYZ
09/28/04

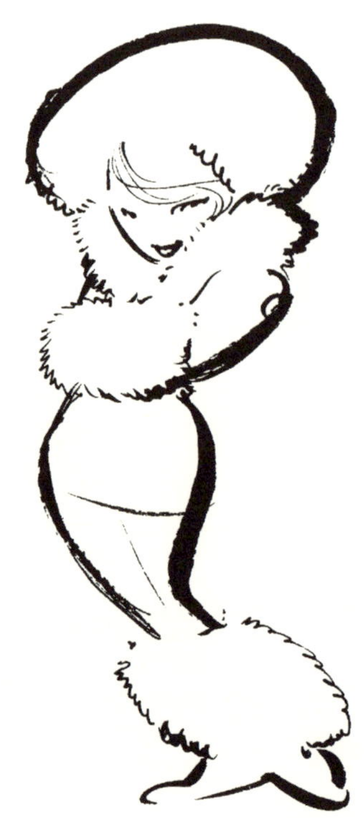

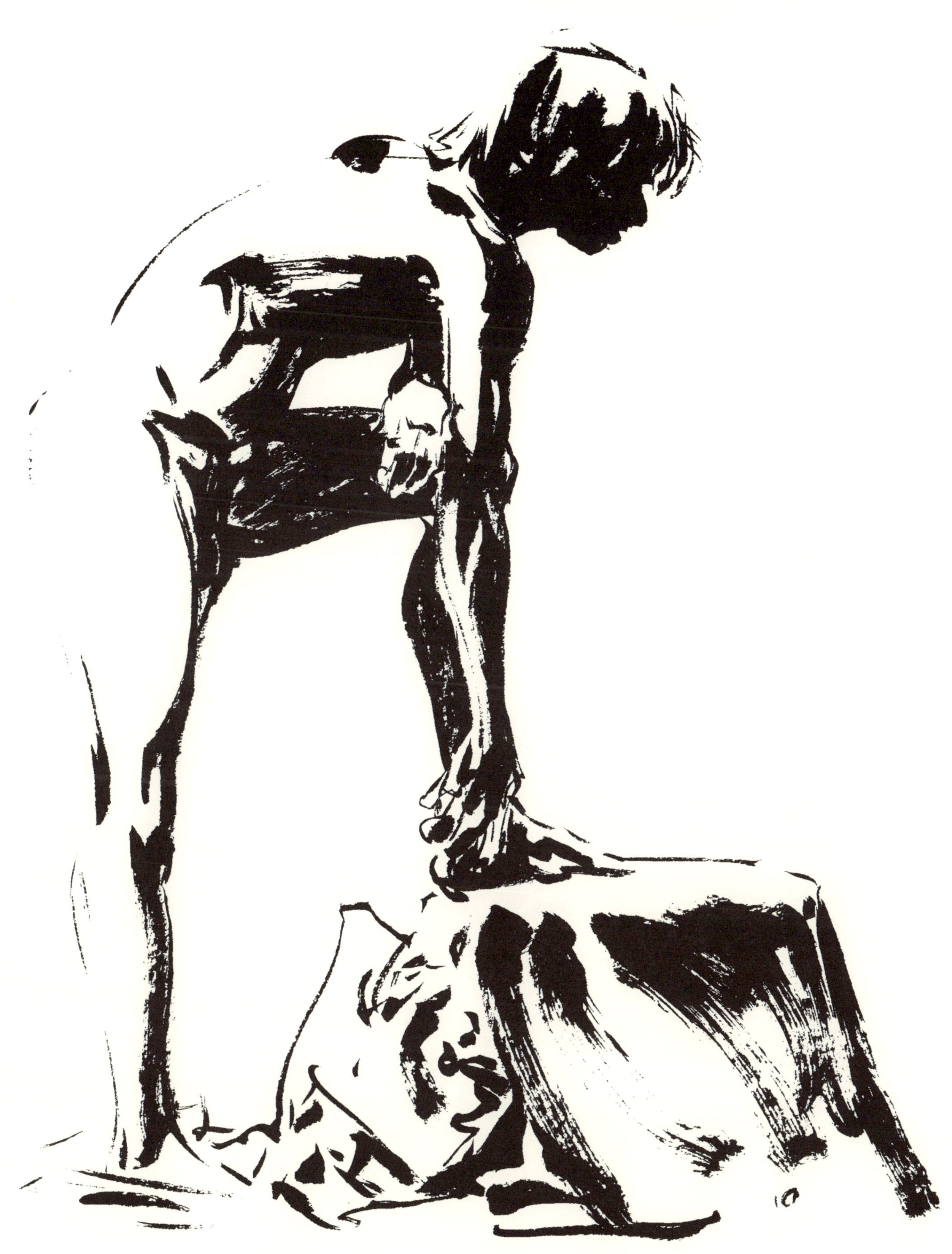

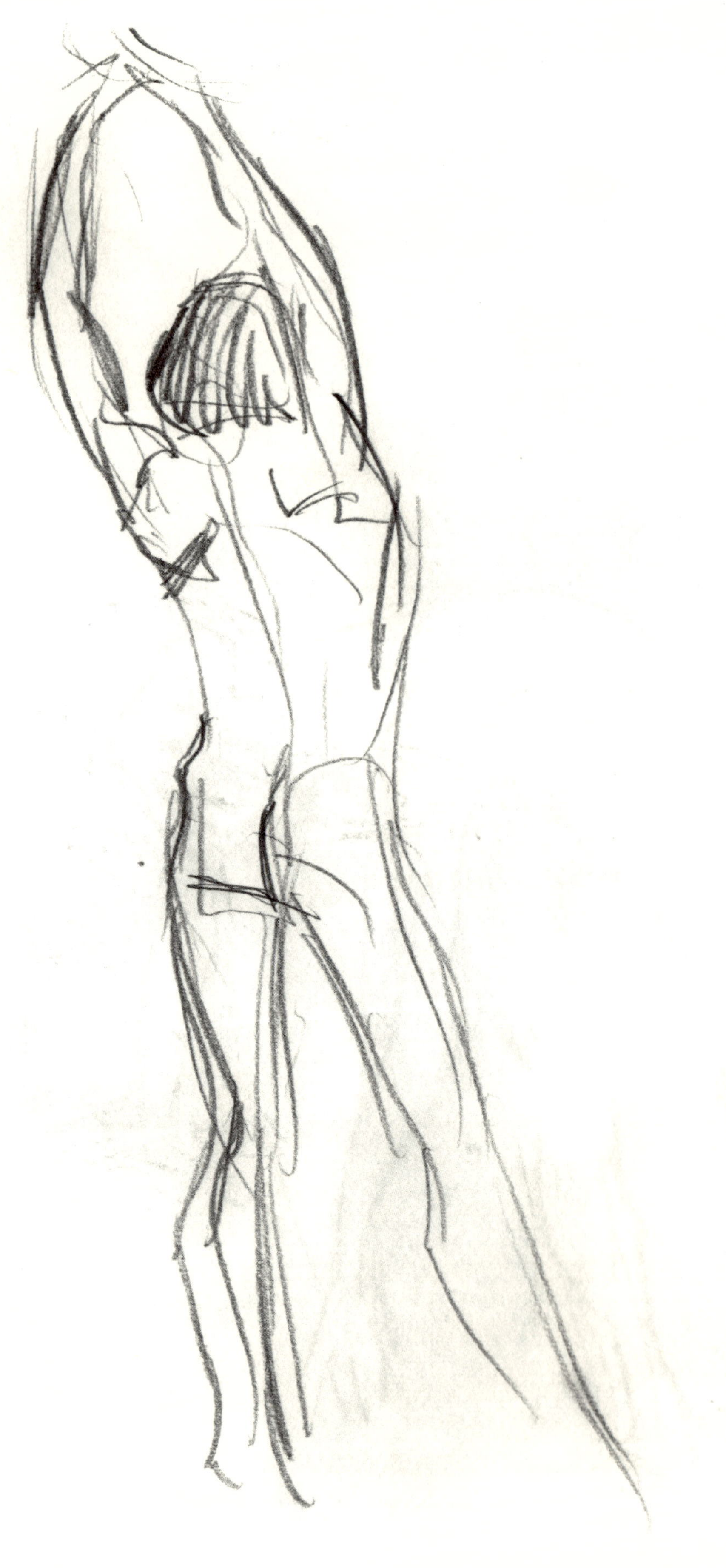

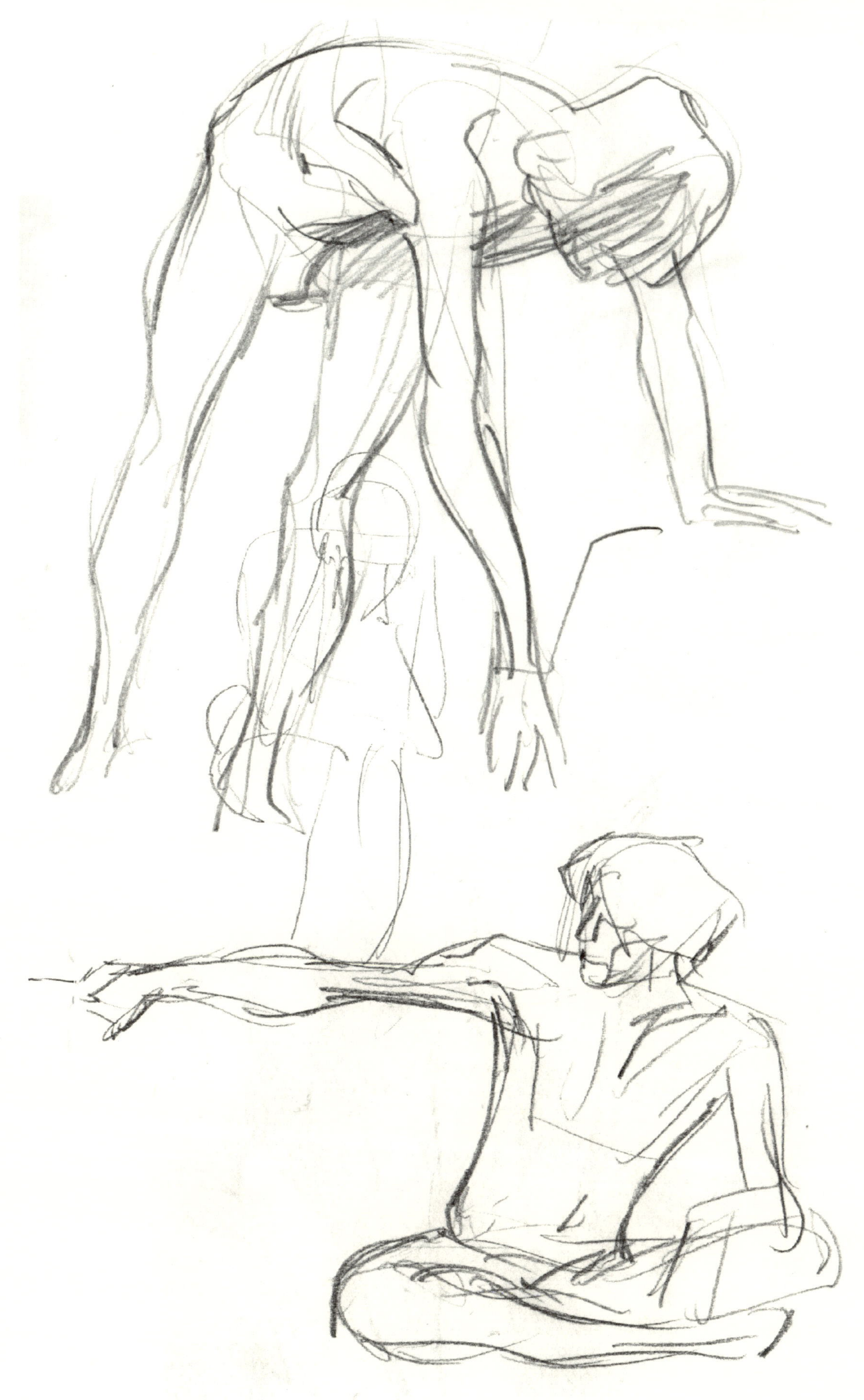

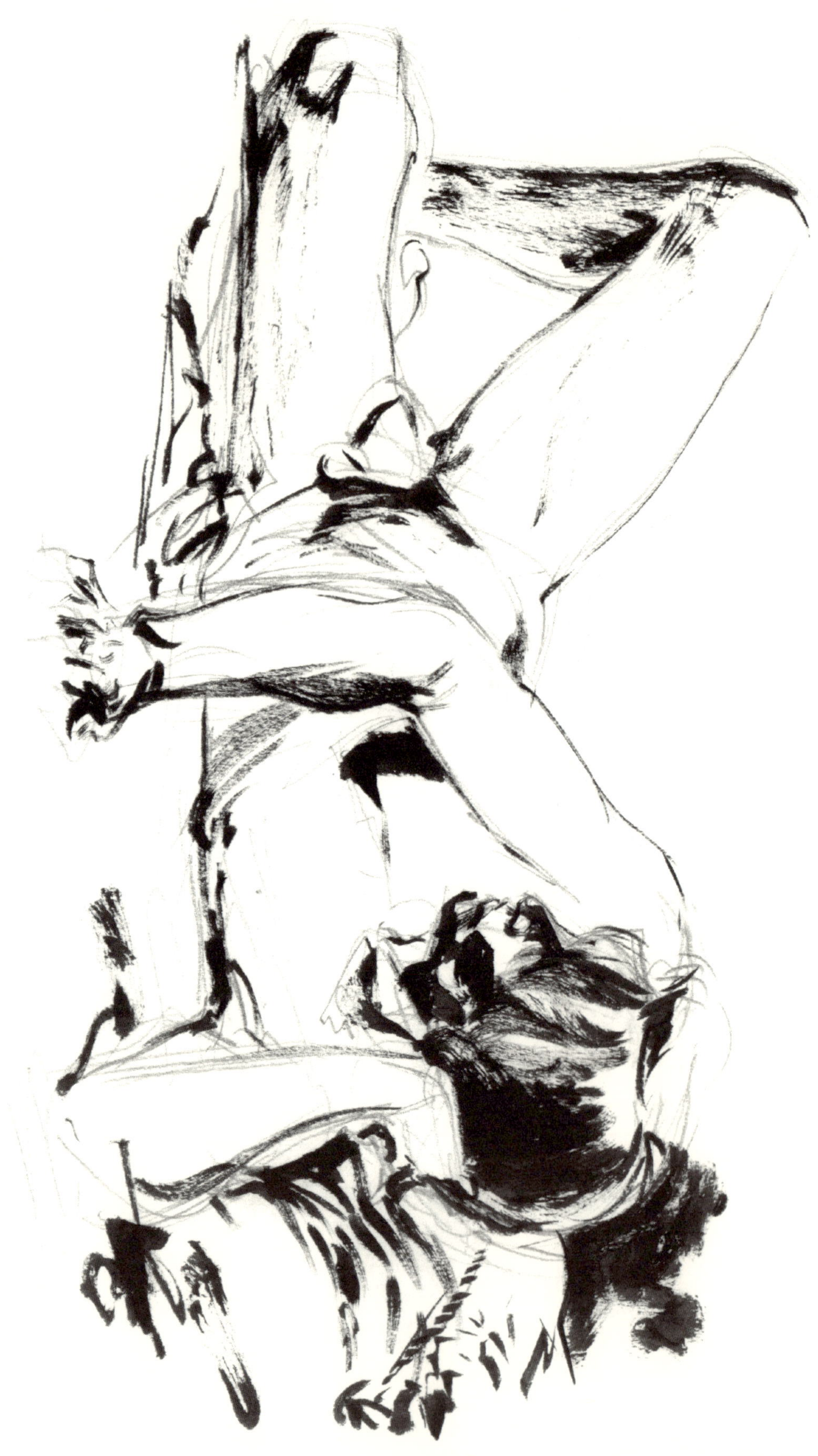

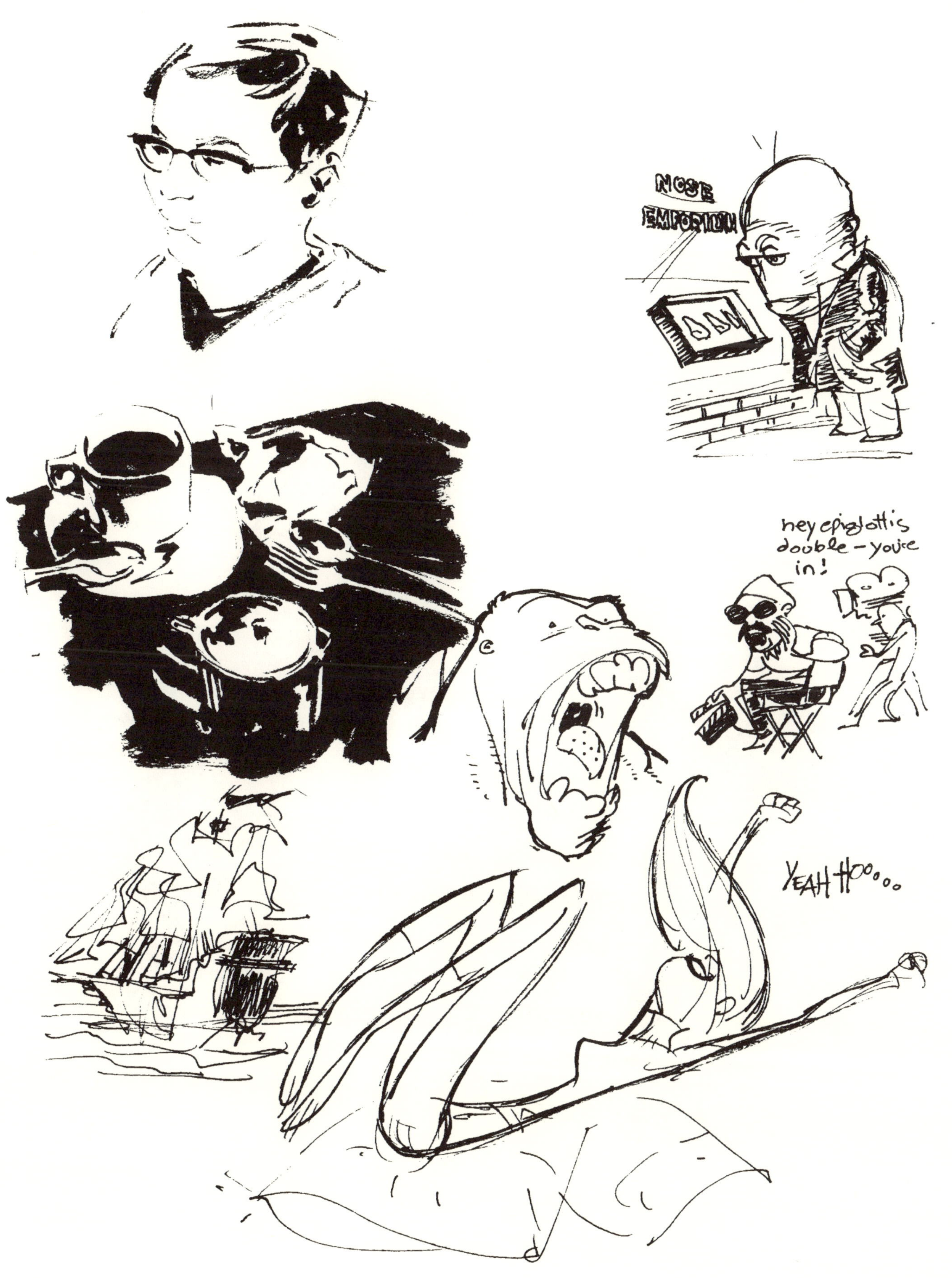
NOSE
EMPORIUM
hey epiglottis
double - you're
in!
YEAH HOooooo

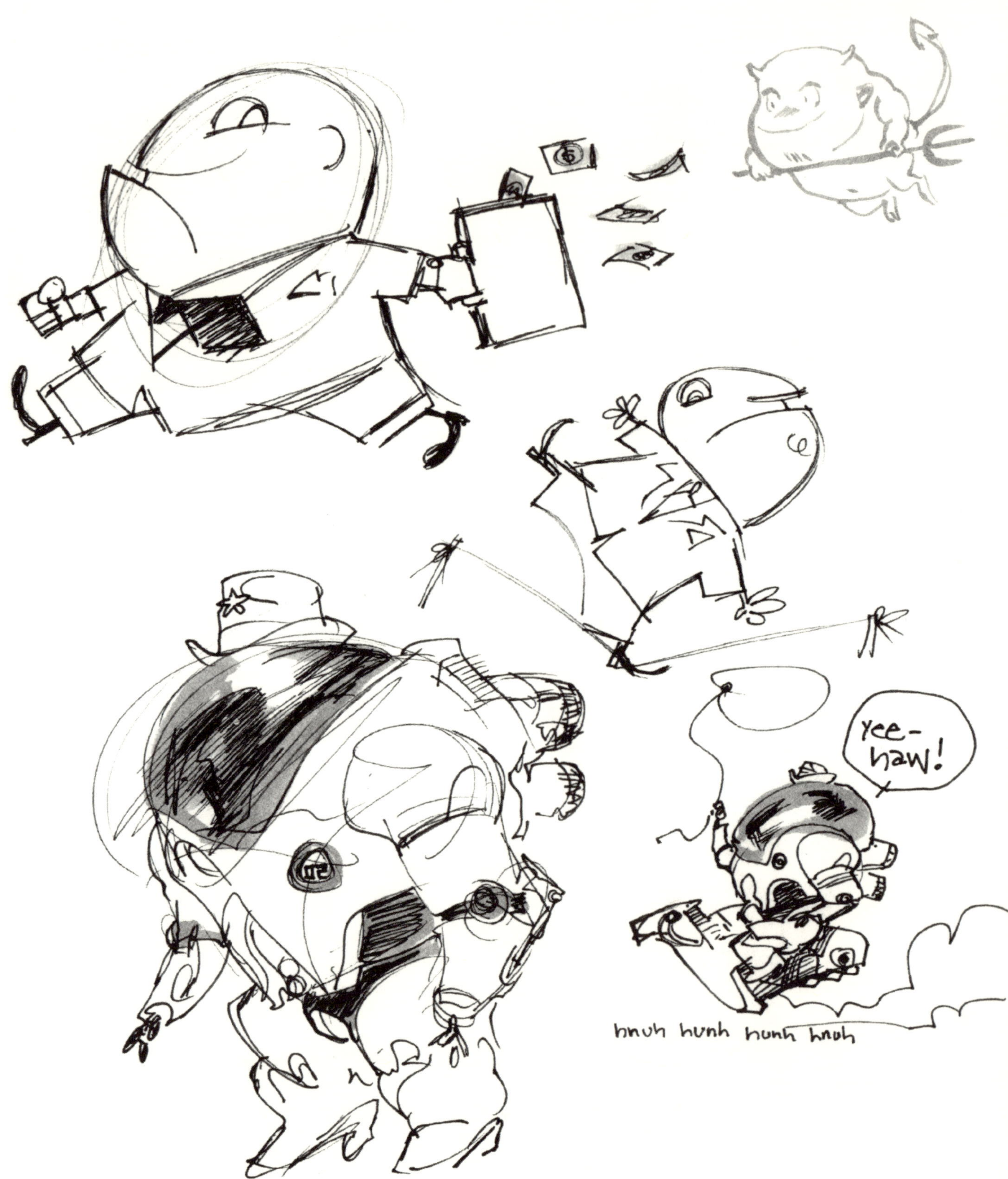
yee-
haw!
hnuh hunh hunh hnuh

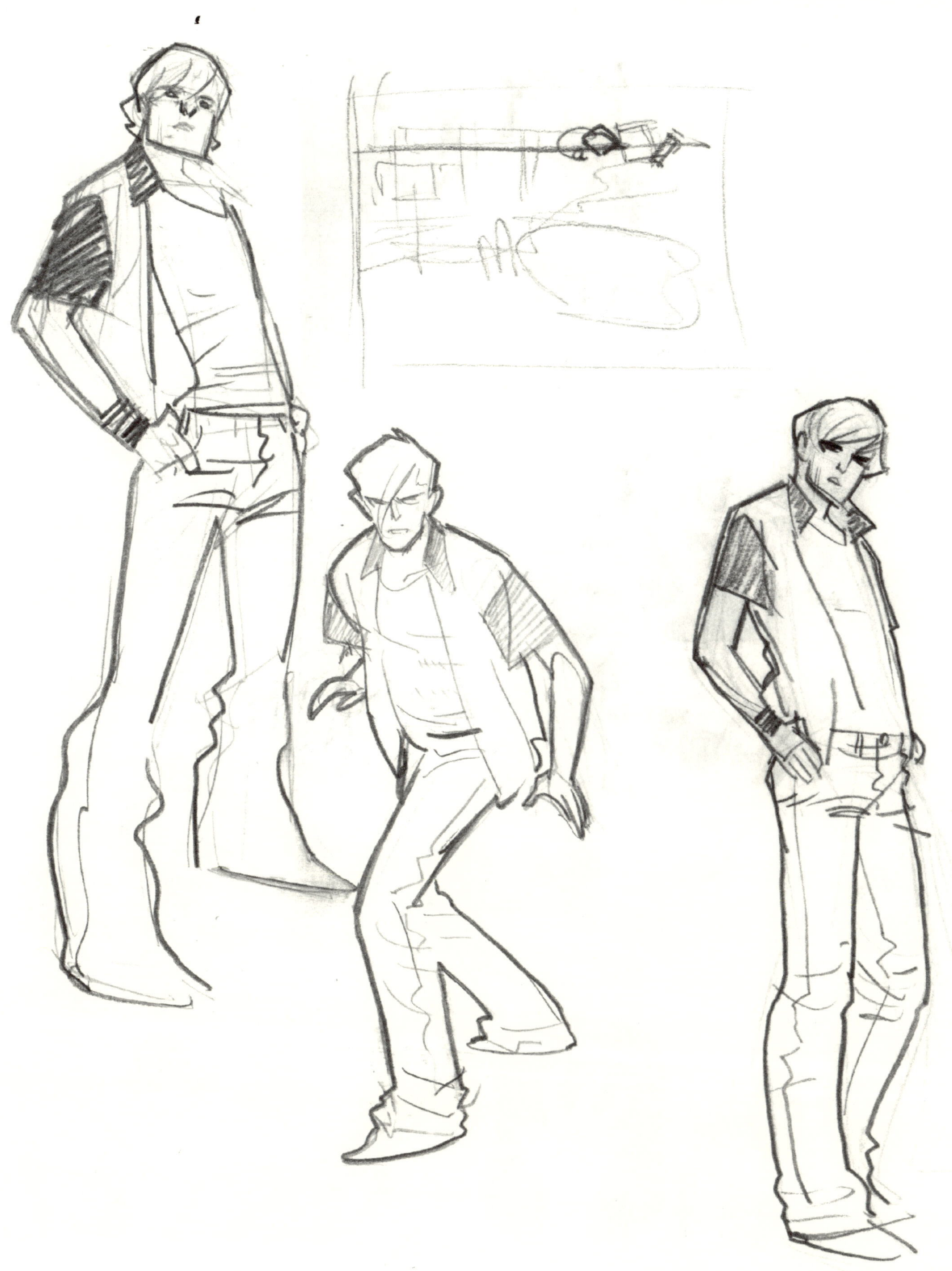

Auld Acquaintance

This summer, we drove to a nearby town where we met my editor and his parents for dinner.

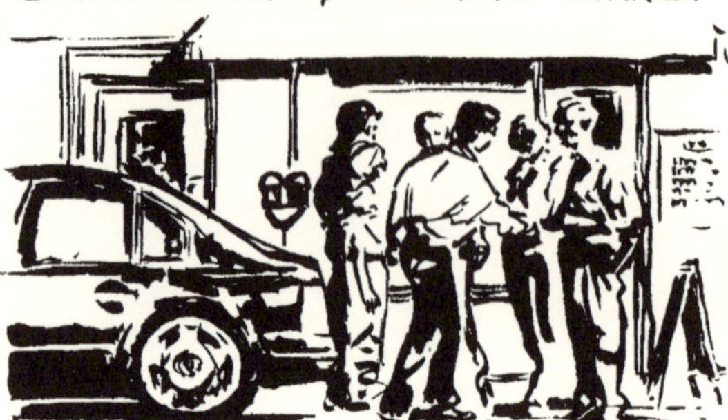

During main course, Dad employs military tactics, Flanking me conversationally.

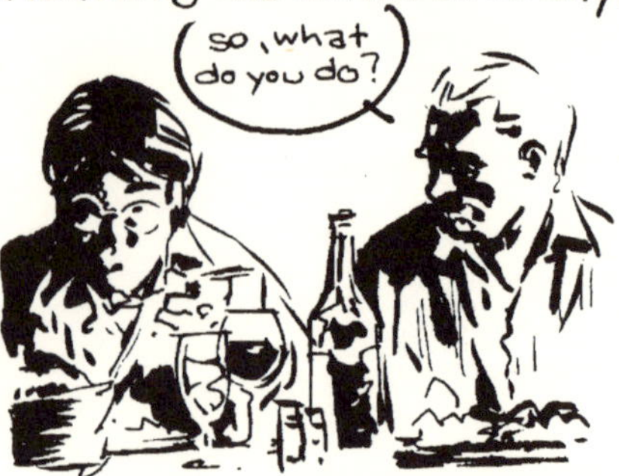

I jokingly stammer out something about 'work', but he only wanted to talk golf, a subject I know a little of.

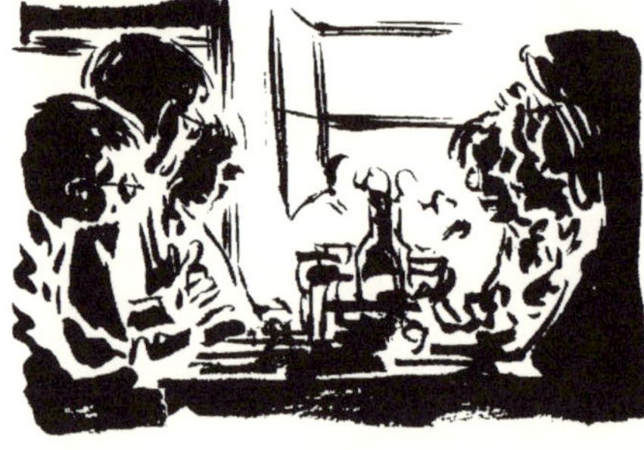

The local mythology is rich, including a tale of a secret hidden course at which Sean Connery supposedly duffs.

och.
i've lost my wey.

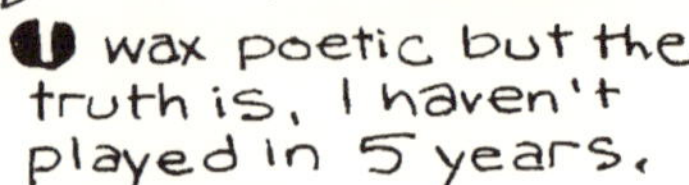

I wax poetic but the truth is, I haven't played in 5 years.

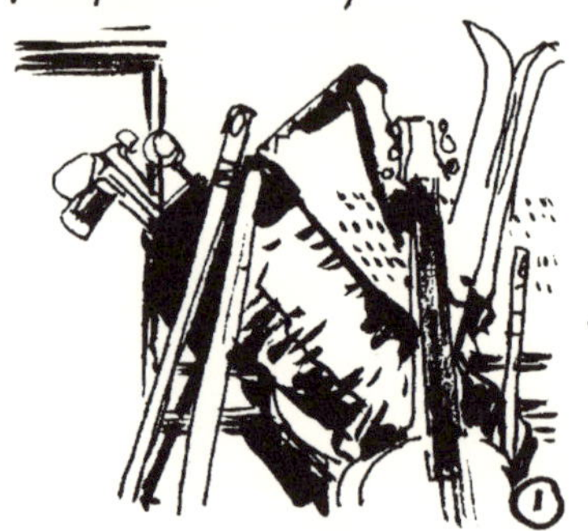

At first, I told everyone (including myself) that I was too busy with work.

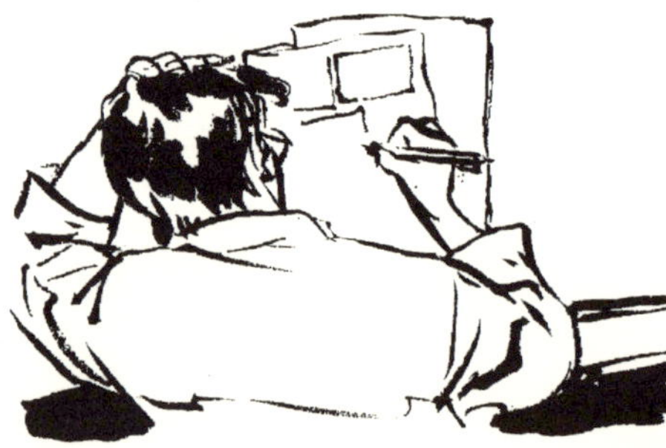

But it's hard to find a partner when you're not that good and it's no fun alone.

The last time I played, my pal snickered as my first drive went straight... down the wrong fairway.

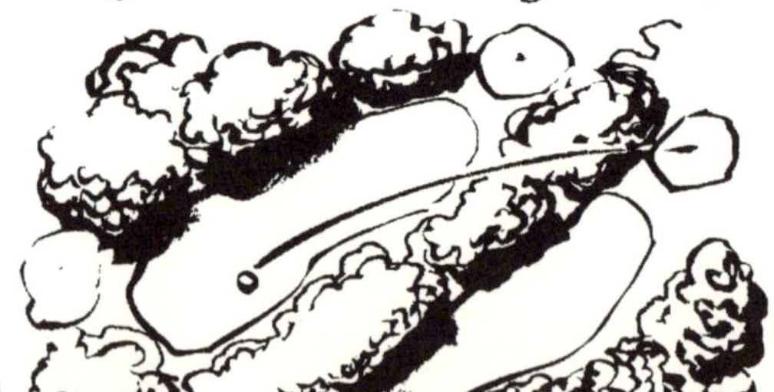

So my hand-me-down clubs languished in the basement.

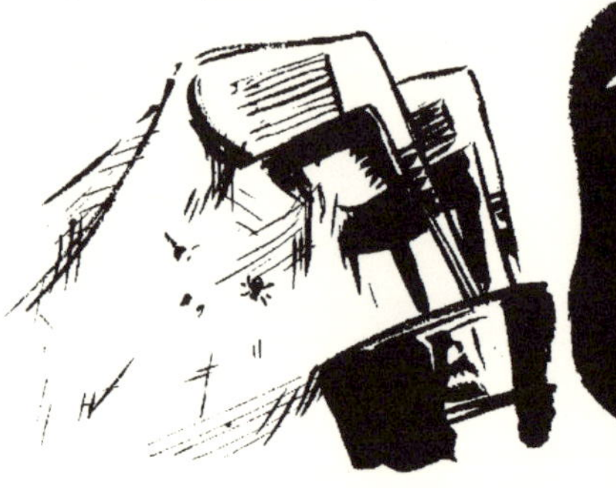

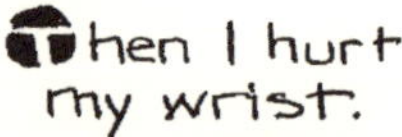

Then I hurt my wrist.

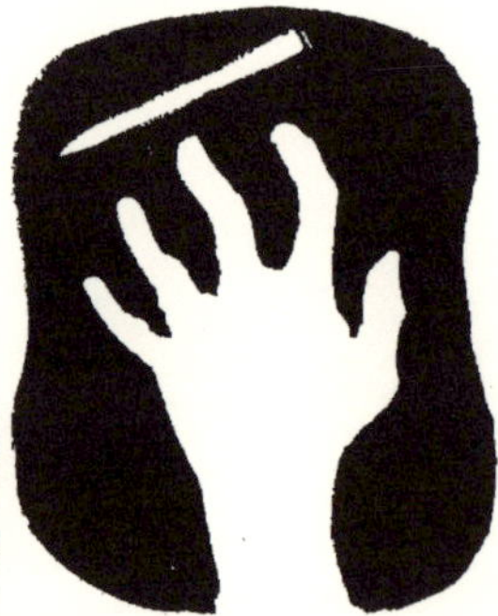

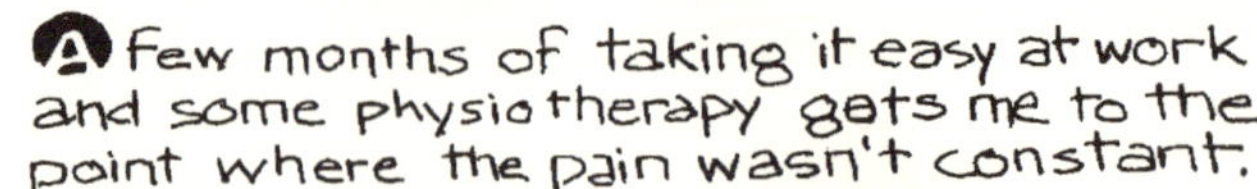

A few months of taking it easy at work and some physiotherapy gets me to the point where the pain wasn't constant.

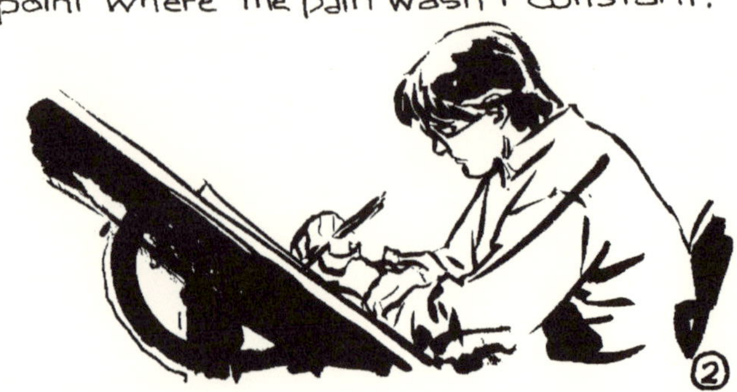

Not to mention my new drawing accessory.

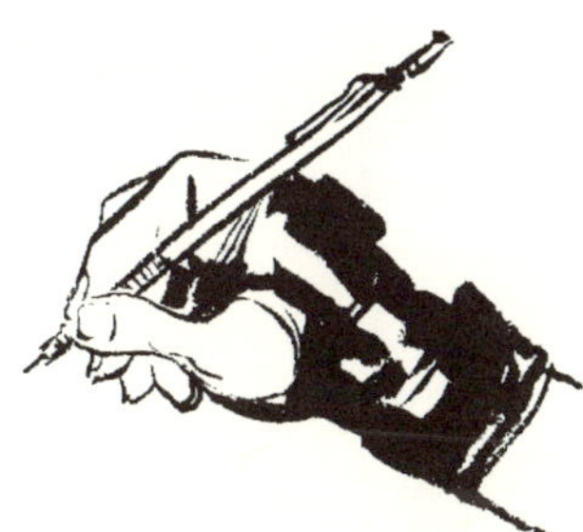

I muse aloud in the sporting goods department at Wal-Mart:

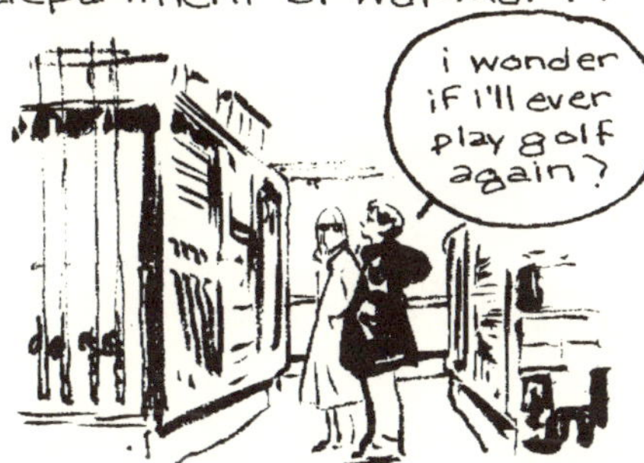

Girl answers definitively – it would be foolish to try – and I agree.

A visit to the basement reveals the clubs are rusted, mouldy and beyond keeping.

Girl puts them out unceremoniously.

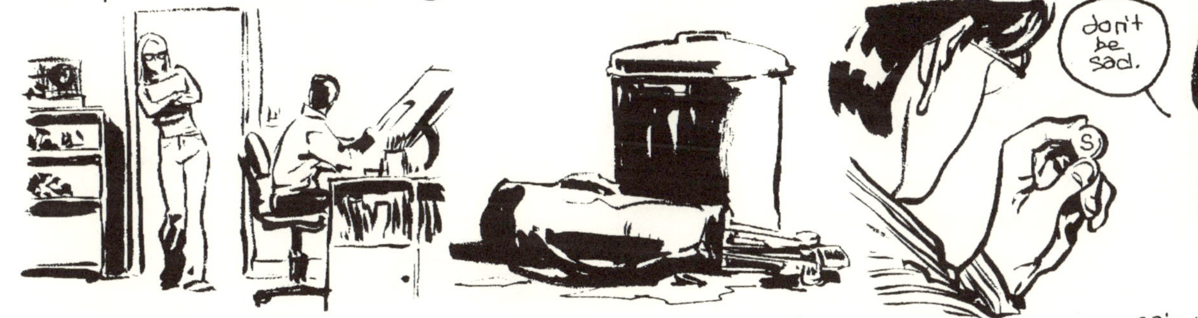

Weeks later, on my birthday, I receive a personalized ball marker in the mail.

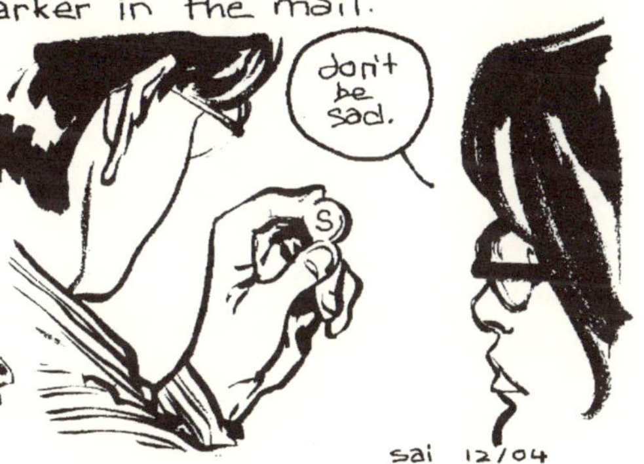

sai 12/04

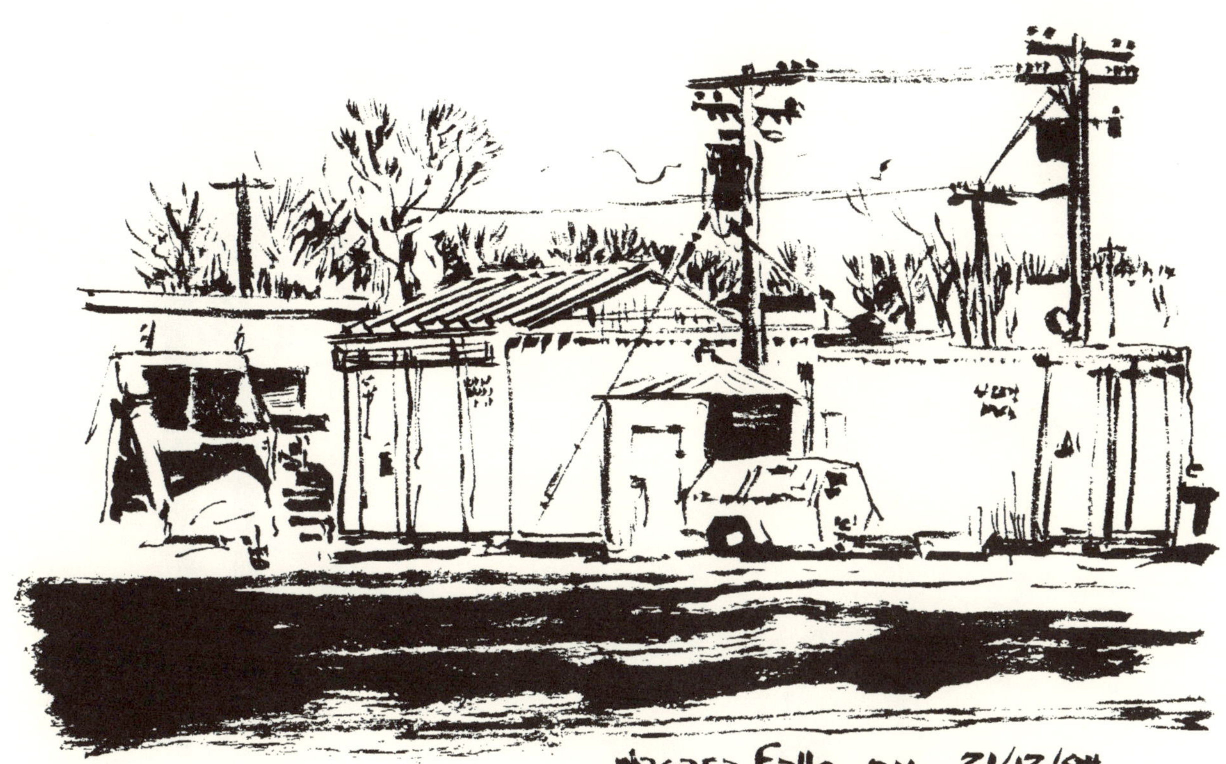

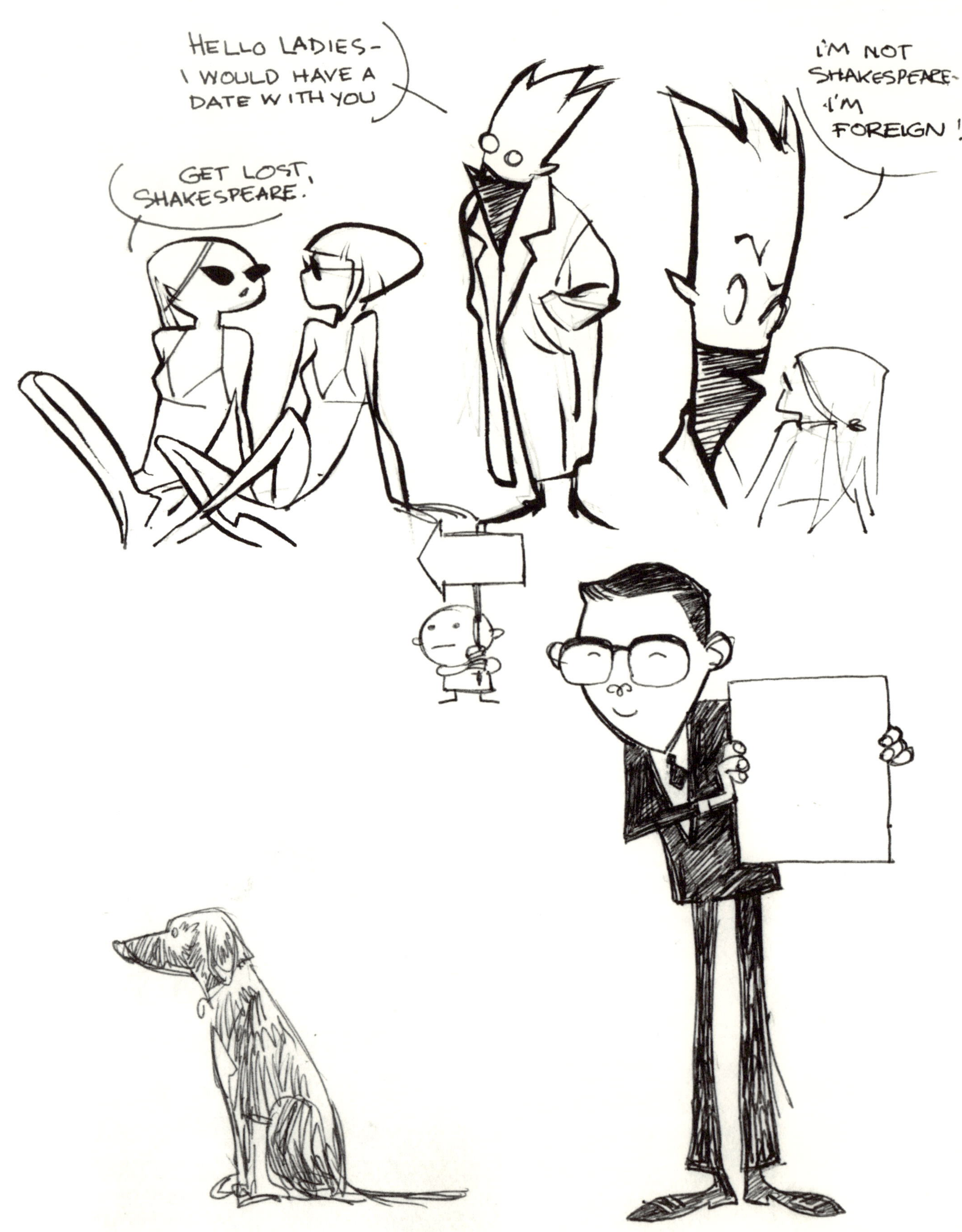
GET LOST, SHAKESPEARE!
HELLO LADIES-
I WOULD HAVE A
DATE WITH YOU
I'M NOT
SHAKESPEARE-
I'M
FOREIGN!

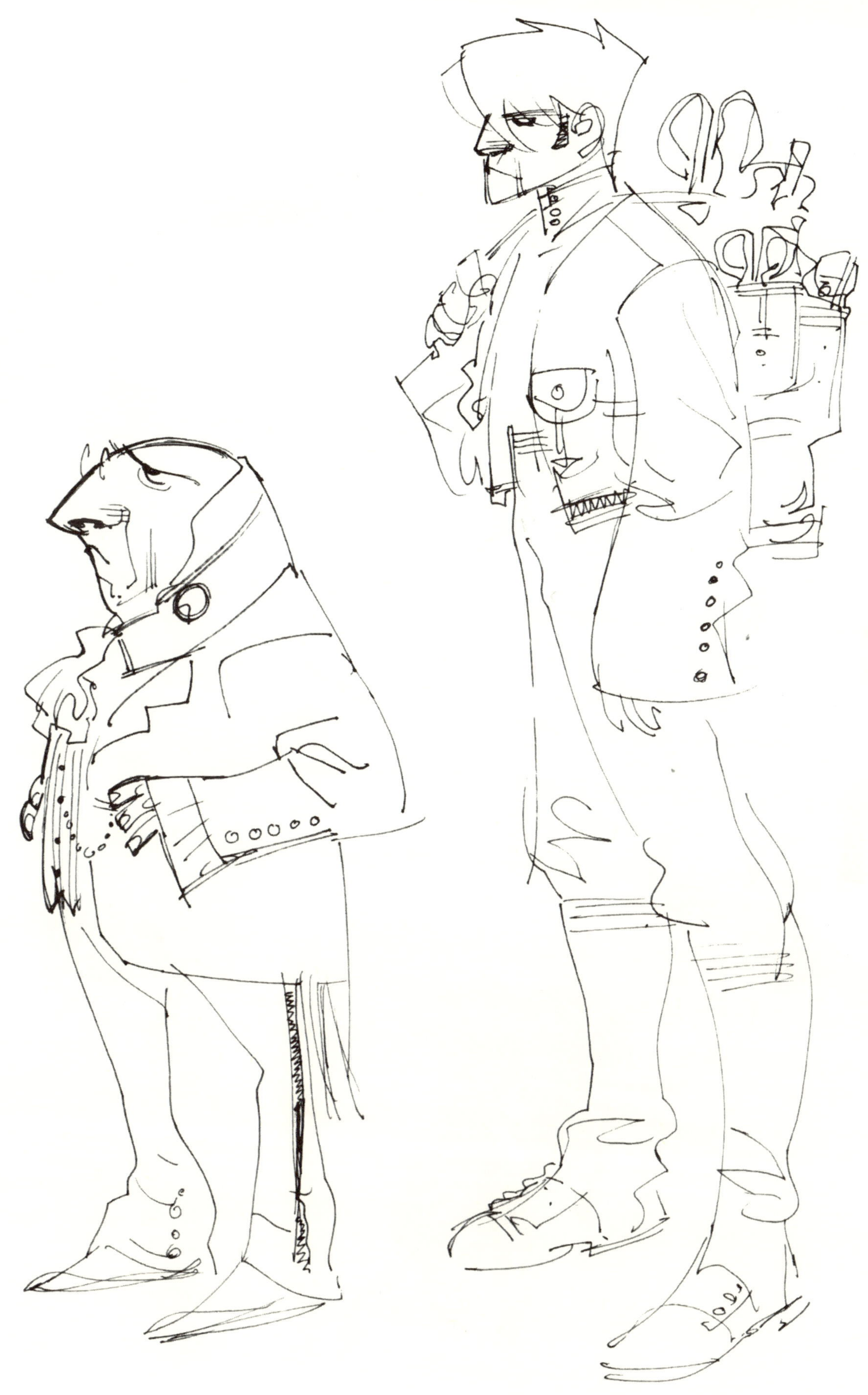

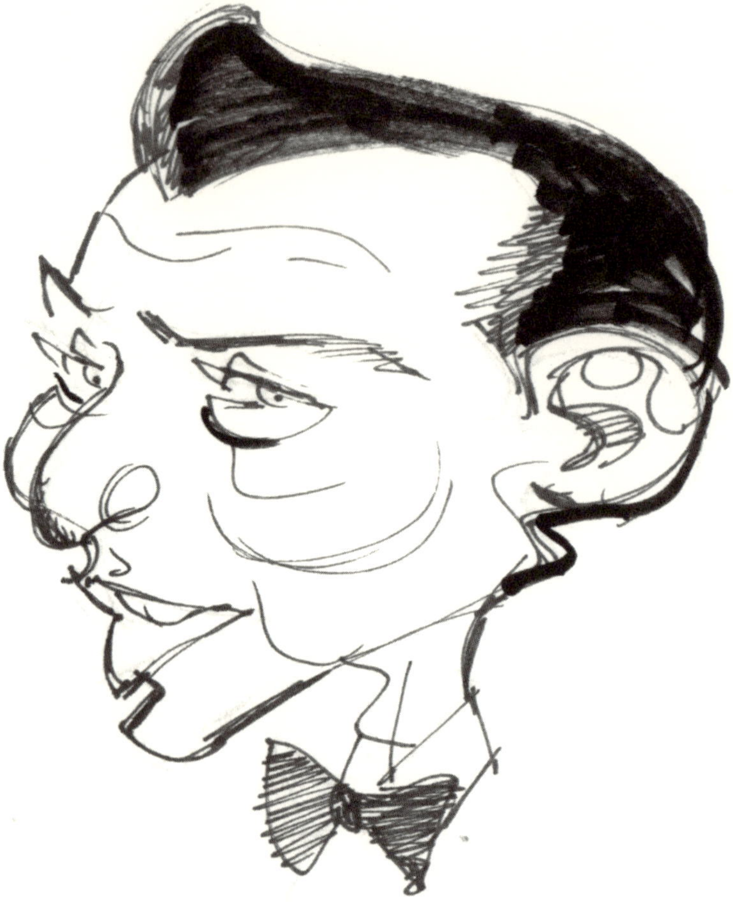

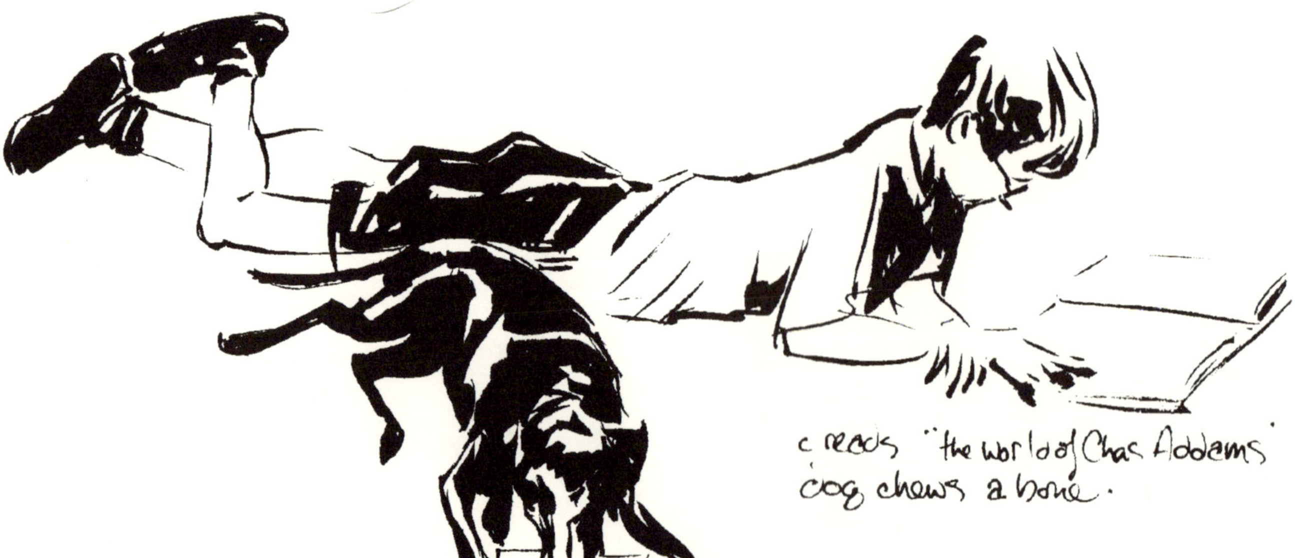
c reads "the world of Chas Addams"
dog chews a bone.

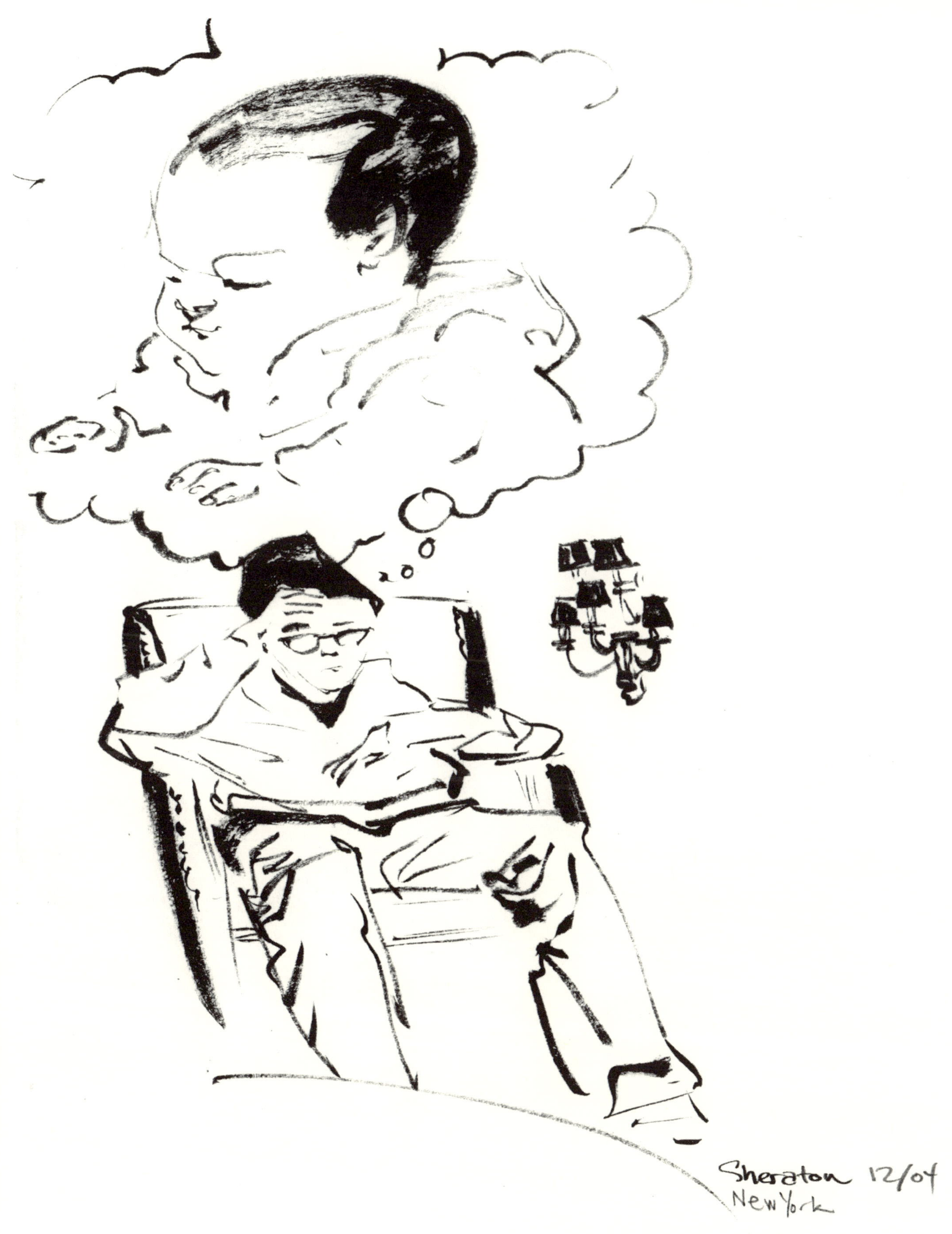
Sheraton 12/04
New York

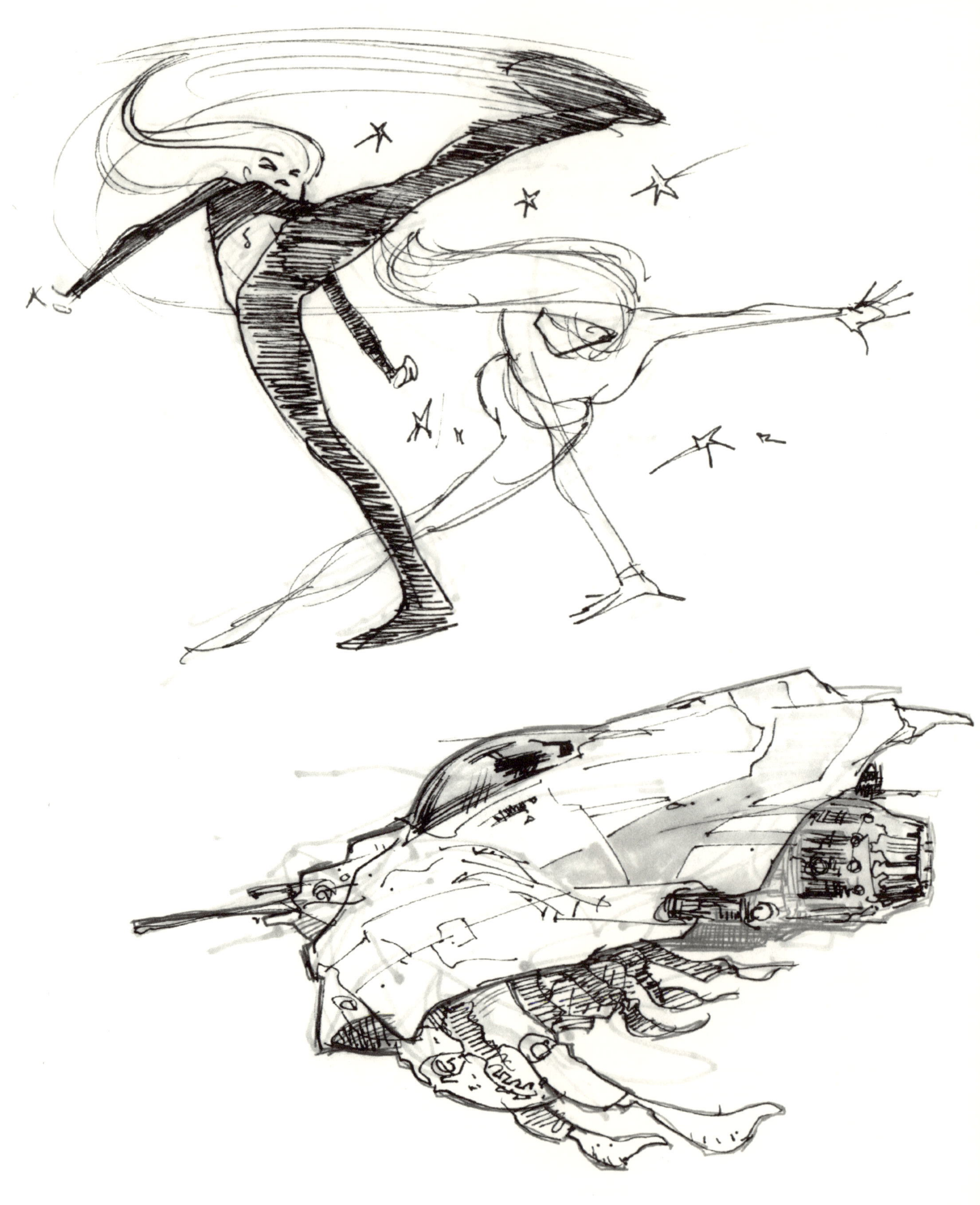

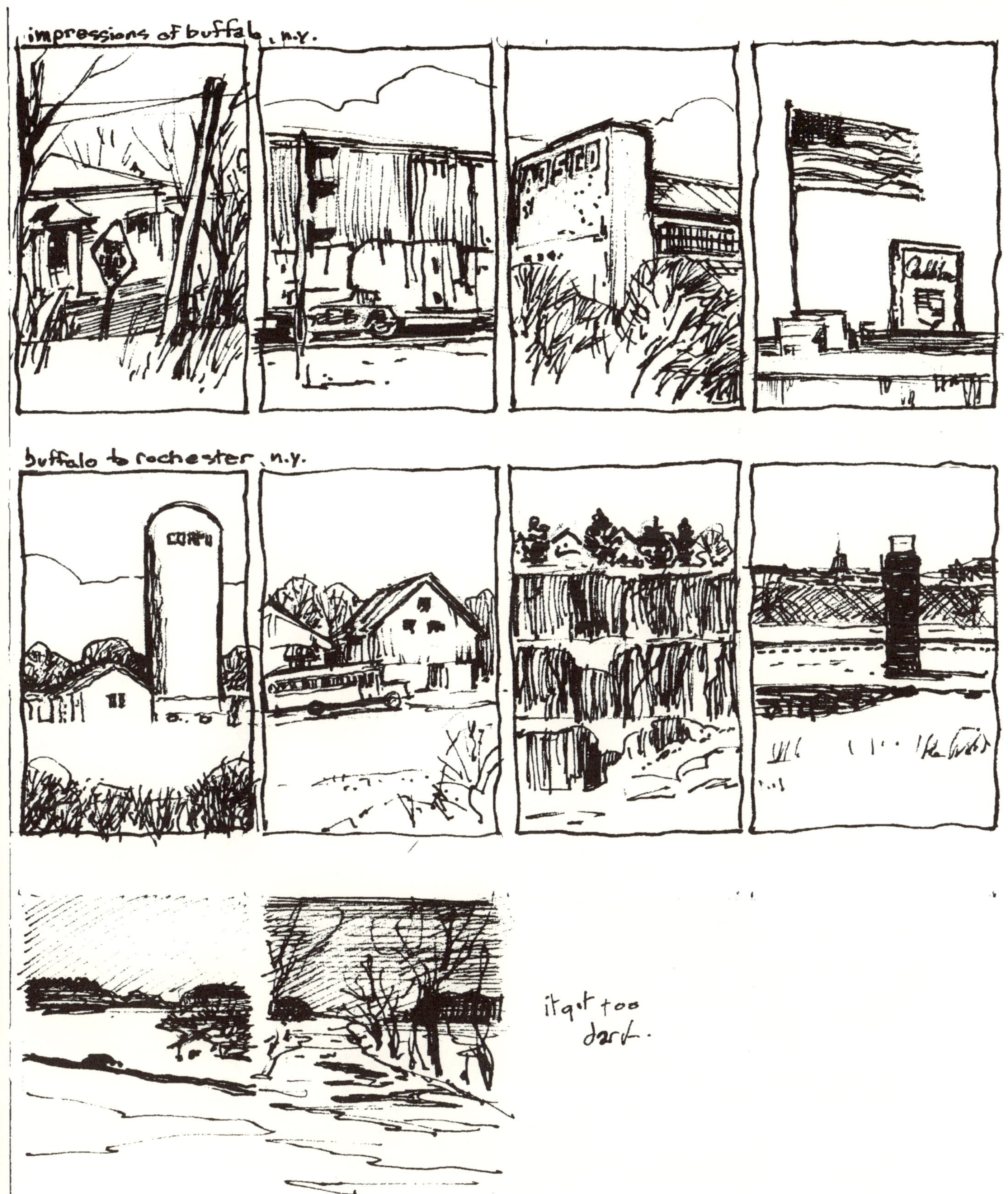
impressions of buffalo, n.y.
buffalo to rochester, n.y.
it got too dark.

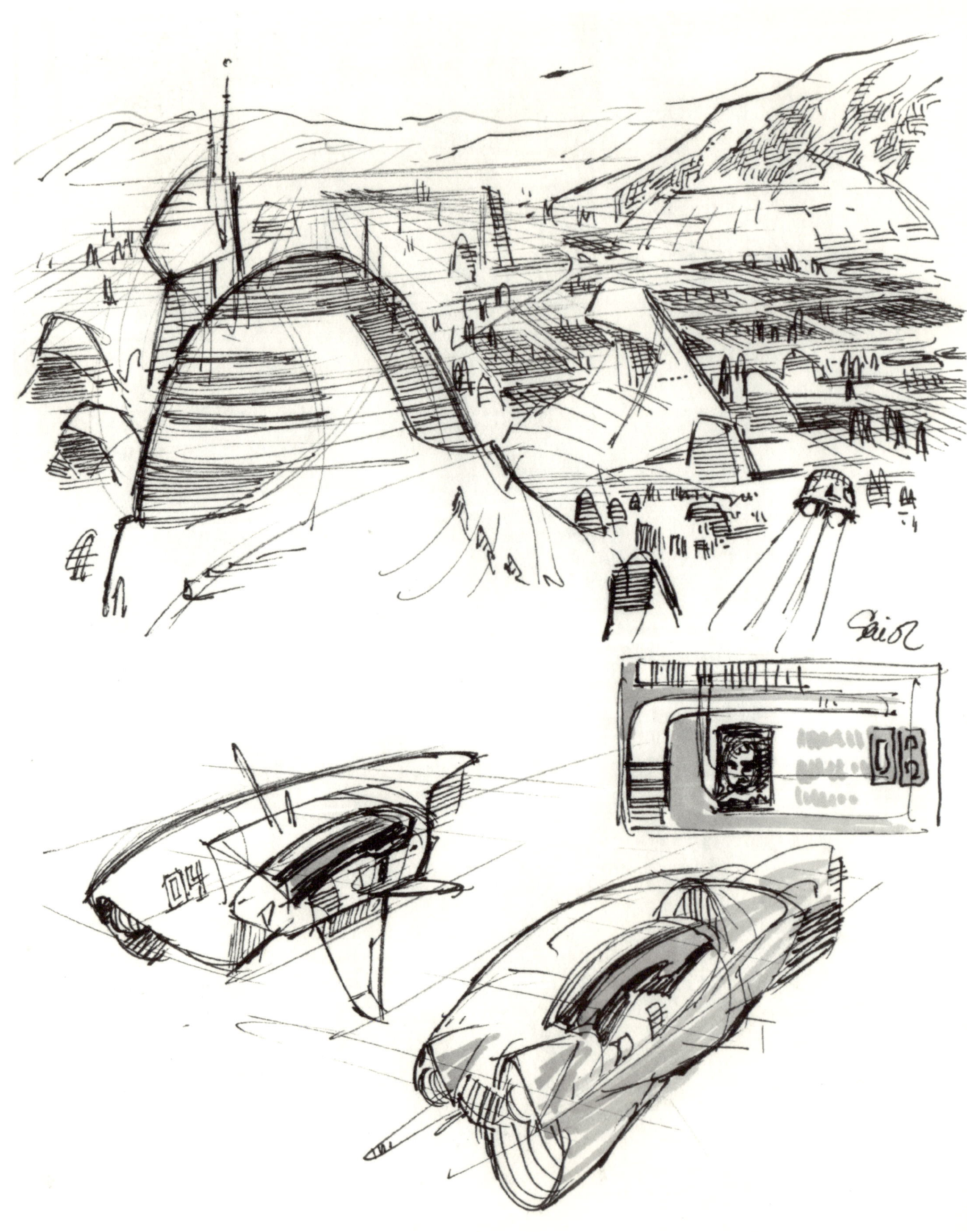
04
03

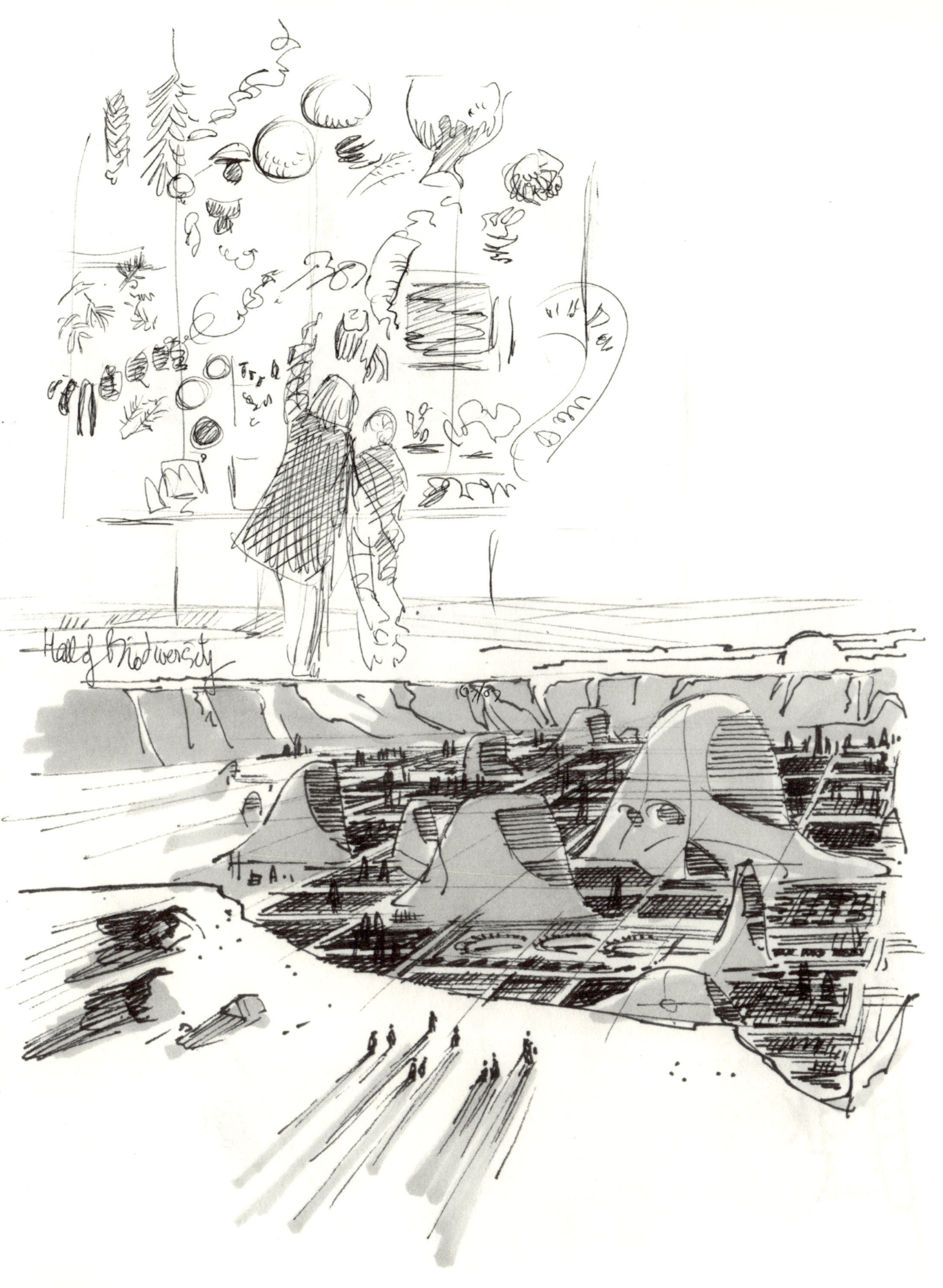
Hall of Biodiversity

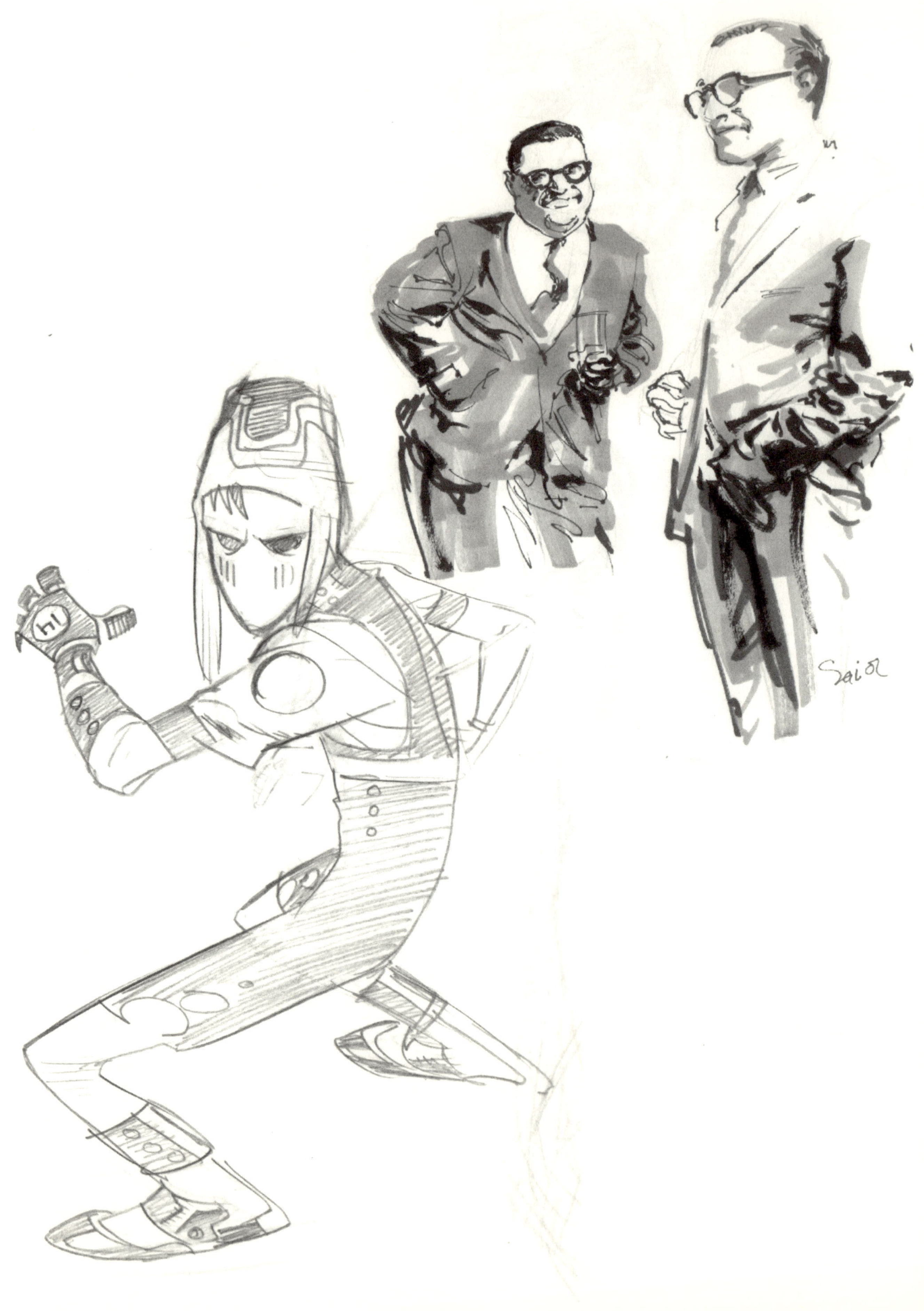
hi

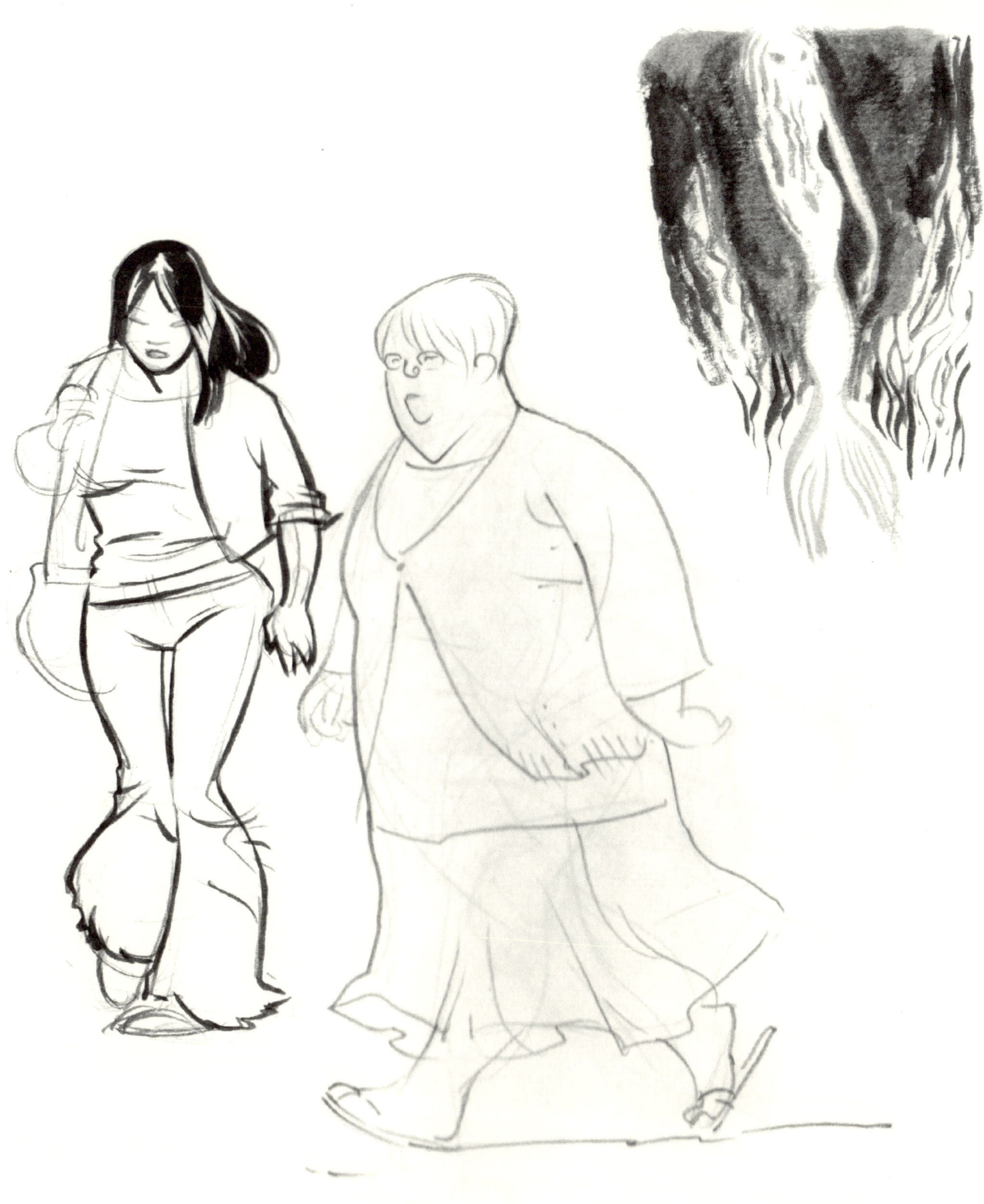

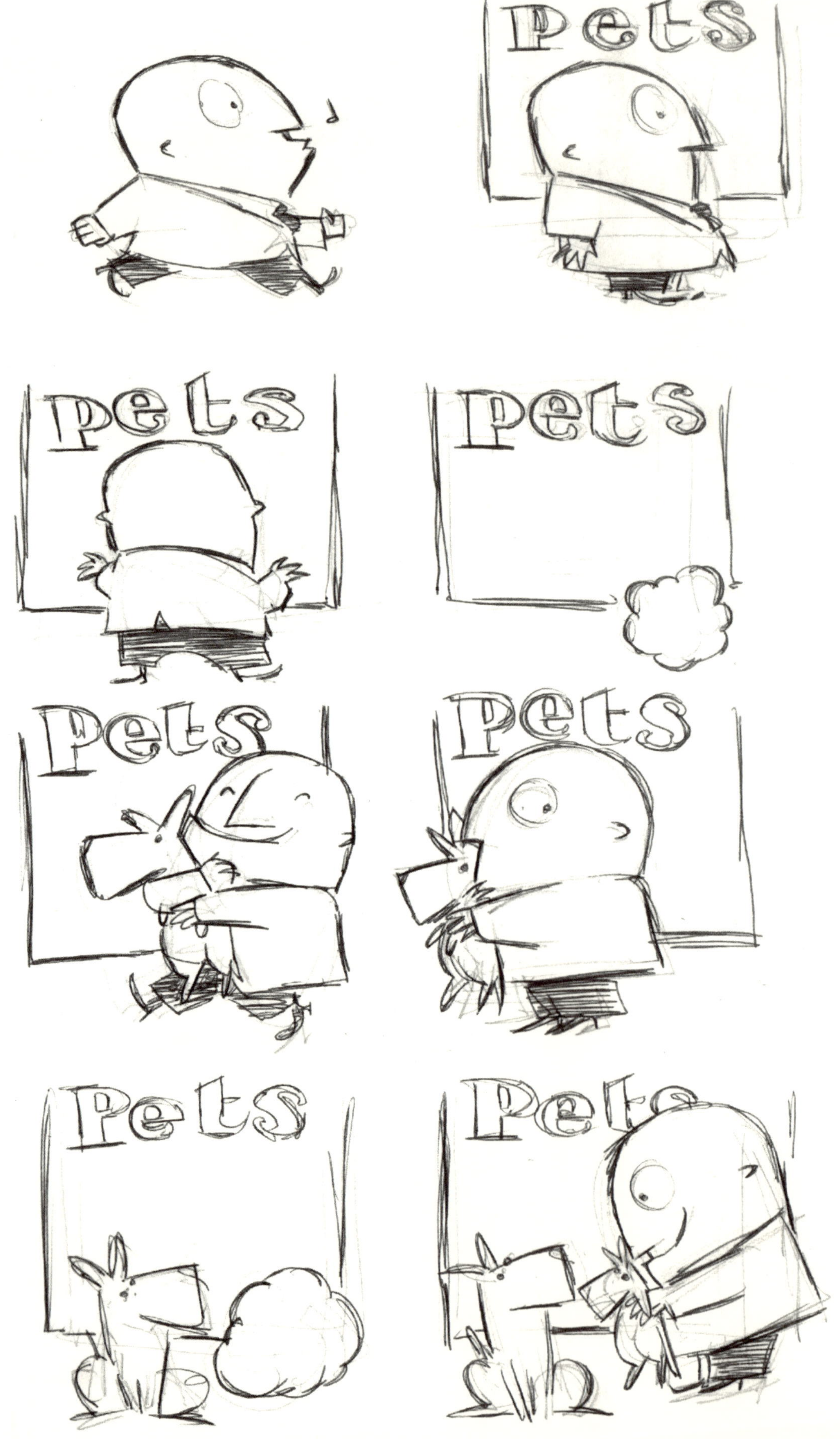
Pets
pets
pets
Pets
Pets
Pets
Pets

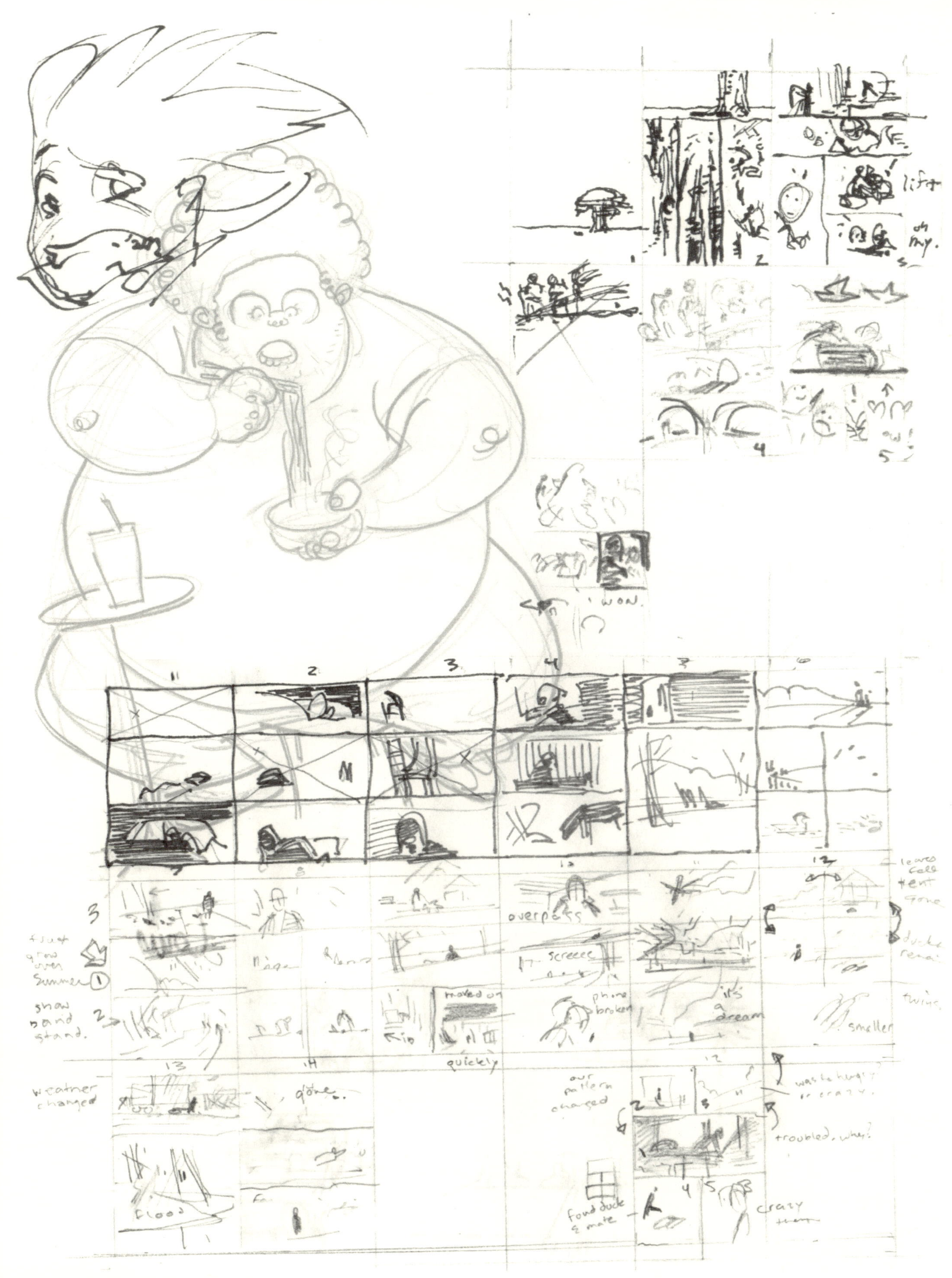
lift
oh my.
won.
overpass
screeee
phone broken
it's a dream
moved on
quickly
smaller
twins
show band stand.
weather changed
gone.
flood
our pattern changed
troubled, why?
found duck & mate
crazy

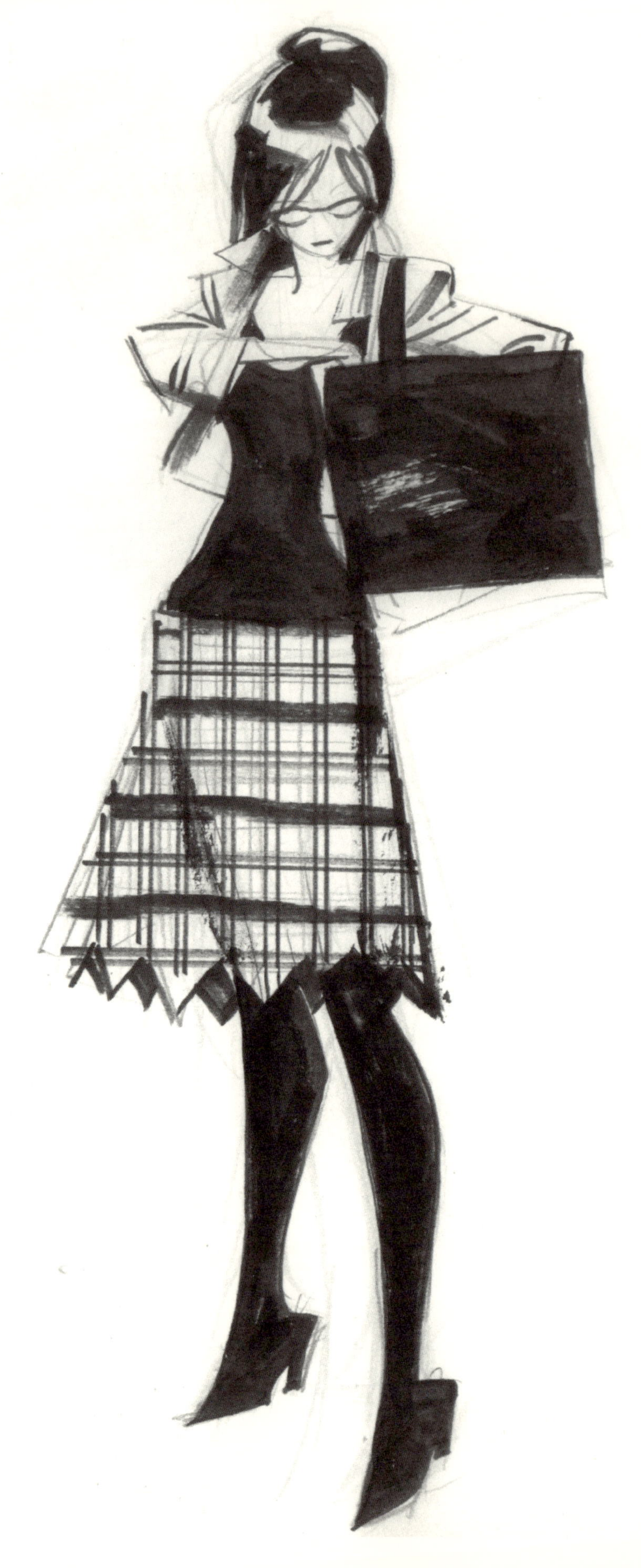

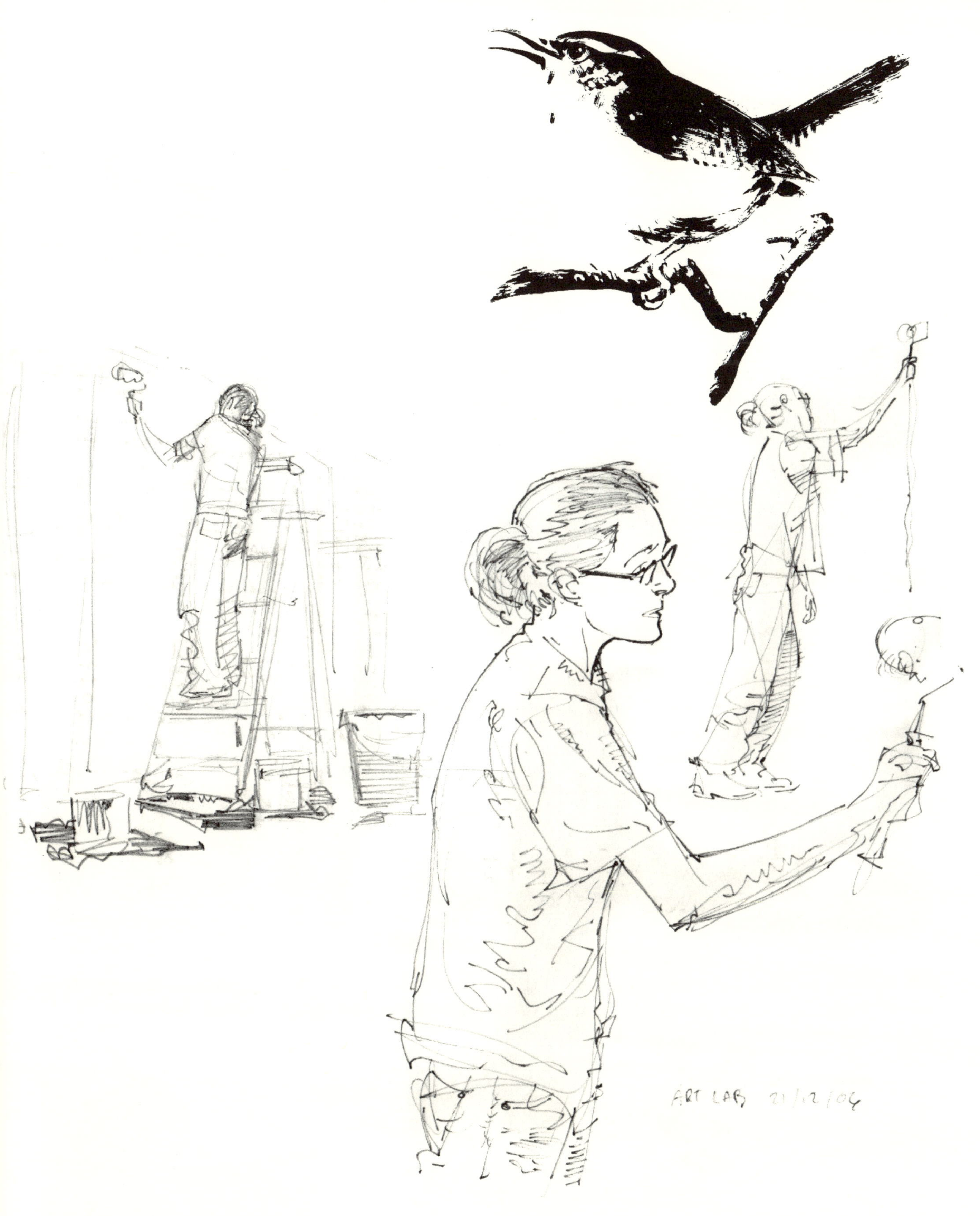
ART LAB 21/12/04

November 21, 2004 – Enrico Casarosa's **sketchcrawl day** and I'm going to draw up a storm.

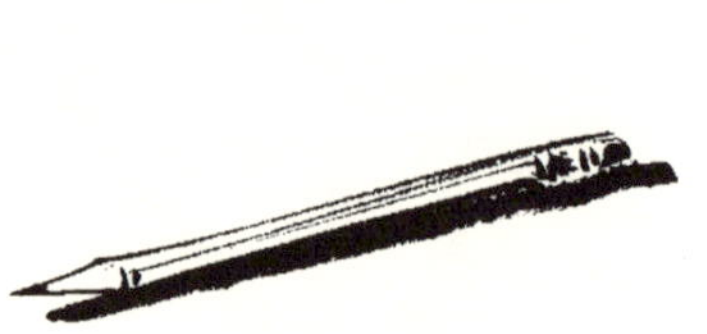

I'm ready to go bright & early. Girl volunteers to model in bed. It's hard to turn her down.

Out the door before succumbing to temptation.

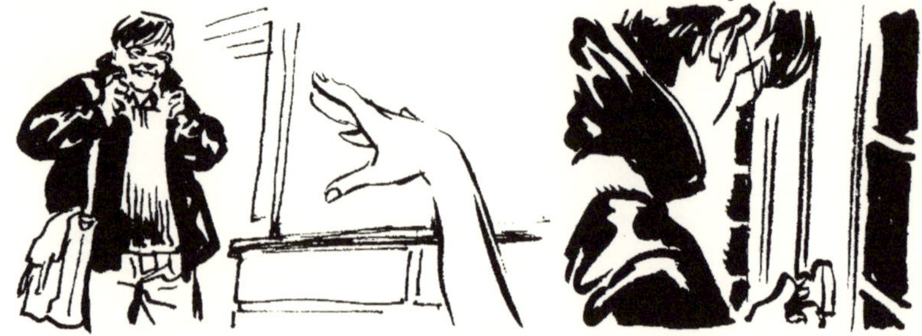

I'm excited – I'll see the city anew, walk all the way downtown, visit the museum, and record it all with my new paints – whoops! forgot water.

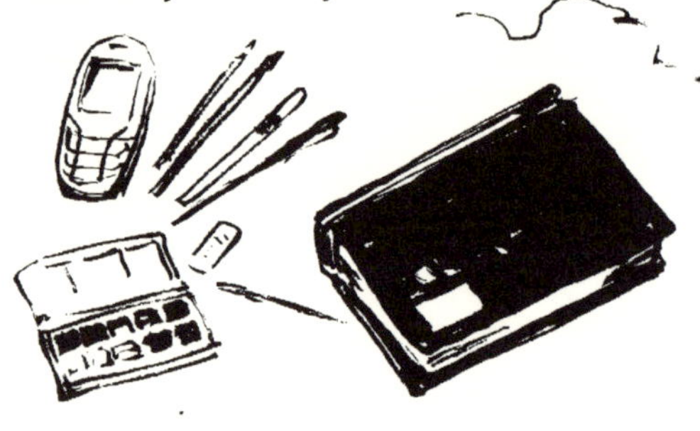

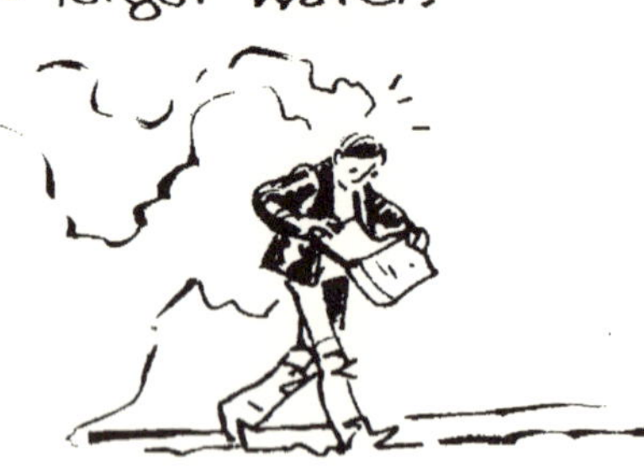

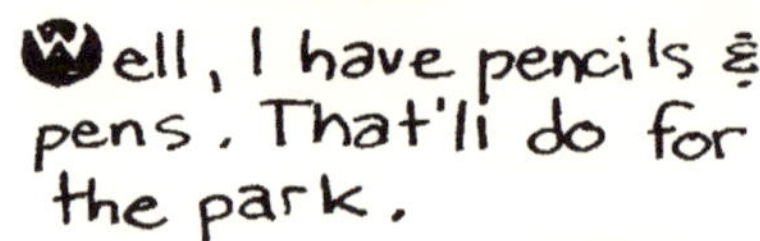

Well, I have pencils & pens. That'll do for the park.

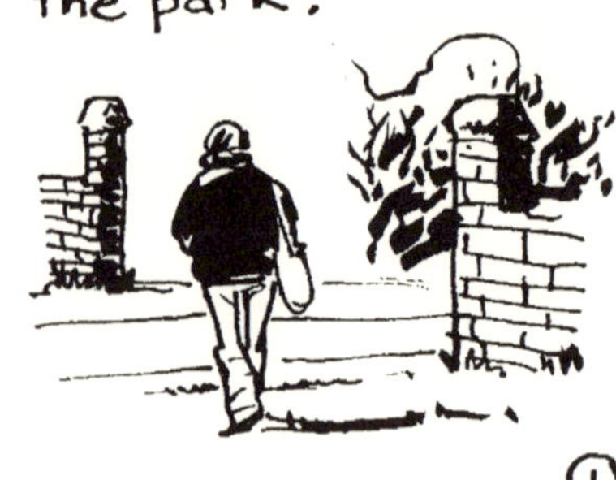

(1)

What to draw first? An interesting fallen limb in a culvert catches my eye.

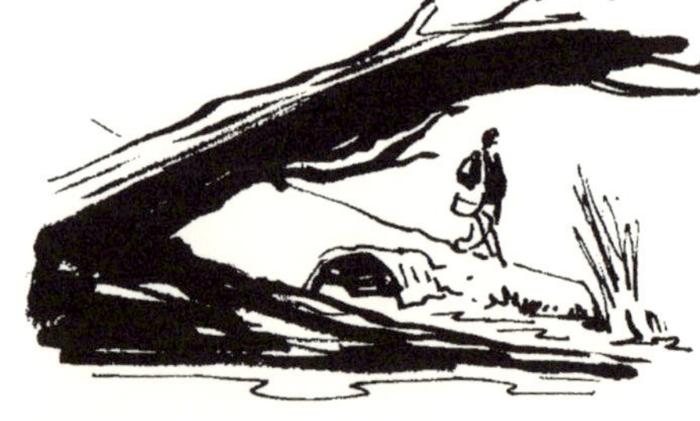

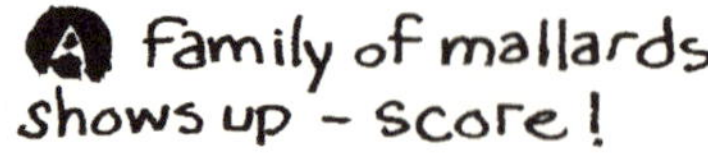

A family of mallards shows up – score!

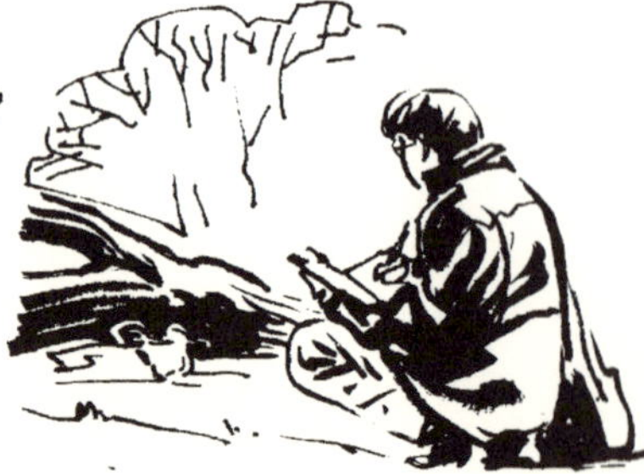

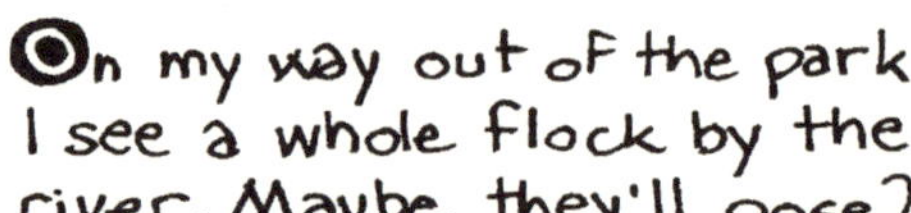

On my way out of the park I see a whole flock by the river. Maybe they'll pose?

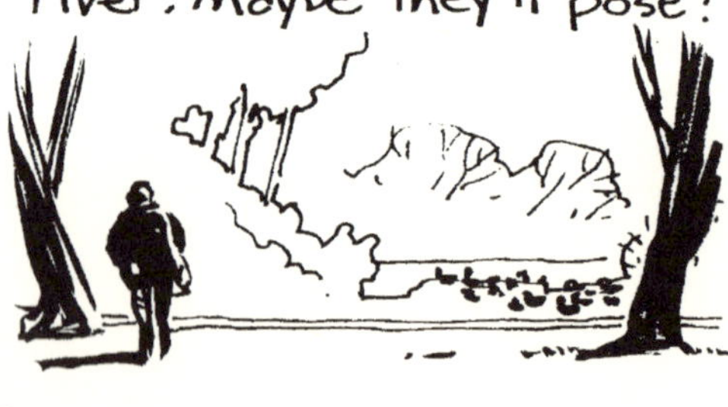

A puddle in the riverside rock wall means I can paint! I drop my bag and set up.

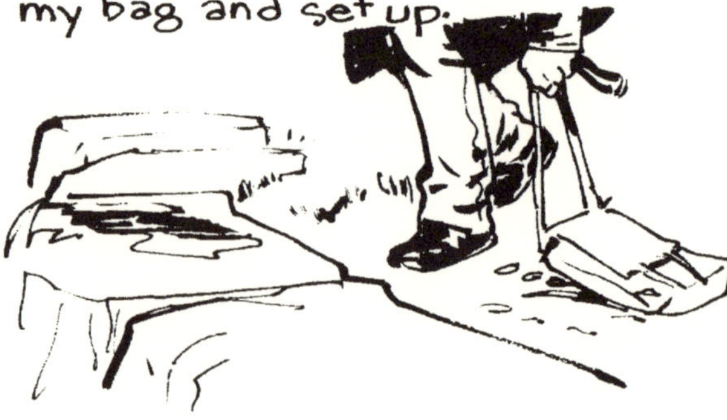

The waterfowl do their part – the painting is OK, but it's cold and I need to pack up.

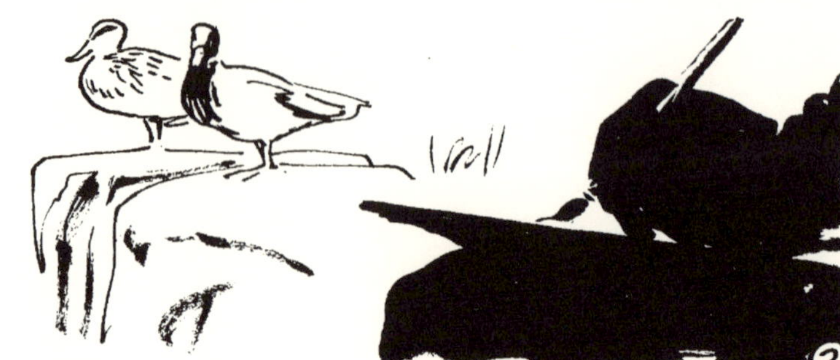

(2)

I sling the bag over my shoulder ...and I quickly discover it's been sitting in dogshit.

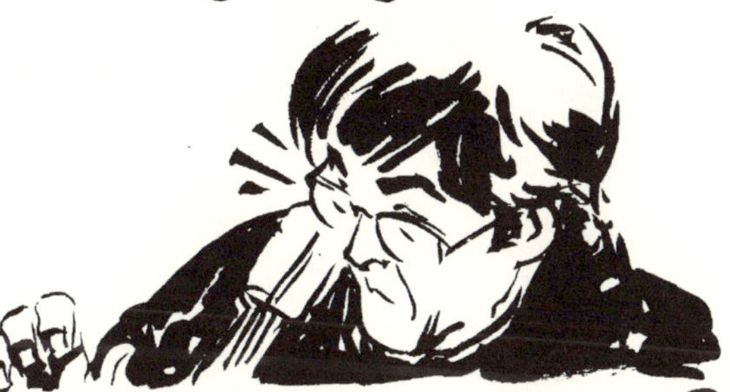

It's vile — I mean VILE. Suddenly it's on everything. I try scrubbing the bag in the river. It doesn't really help.

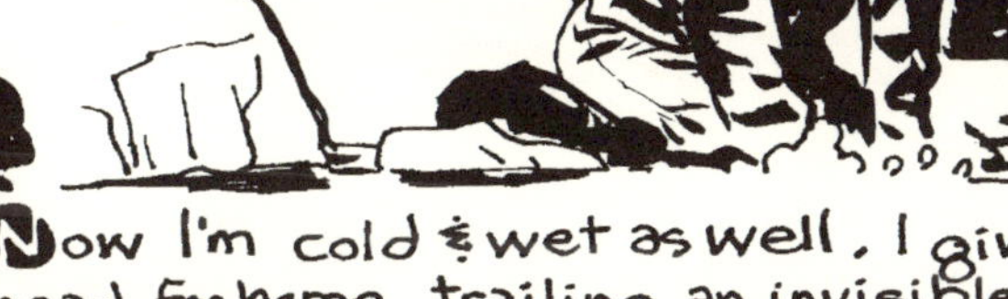

My whole kit reeks of dog – including my sketchbook.

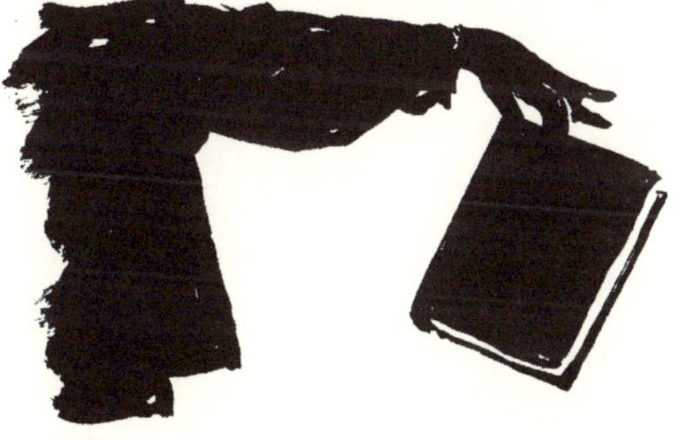

Now I'm cold & wet as well. I give up and head for home, trailing an invisible cloud of hatred and foul odour. I curse all dogs.

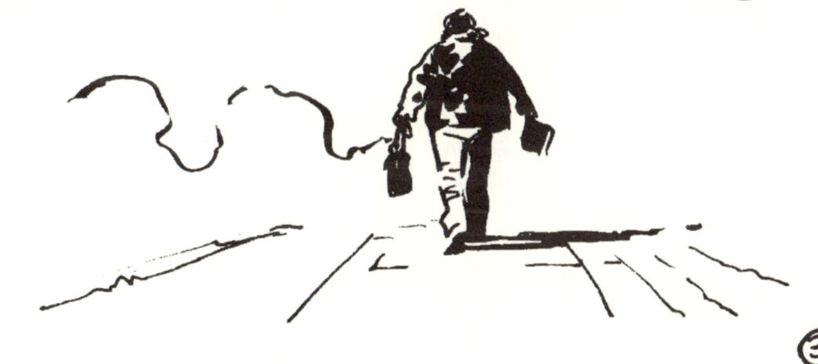

③

On the way past the garage, I throw the book in the trash.

In the laundry room, I shake out the bag and strip off anything offensive.

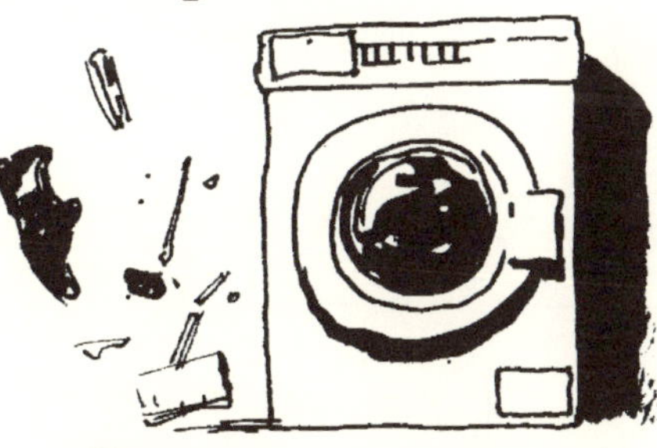

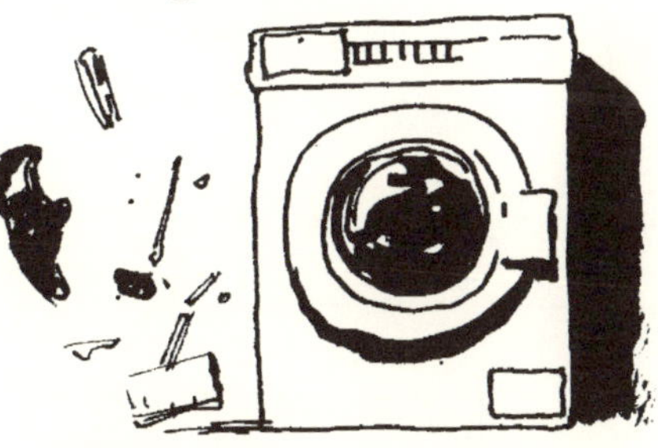

It's more difficult to shake off my anger & frustration.

I lock horns with girl who didn't even know I'd left already. It's all so regrettable.

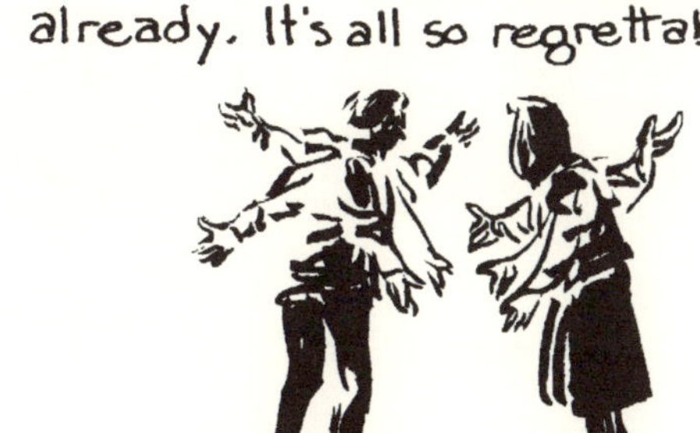

It ends in tears and a cup of coffee.

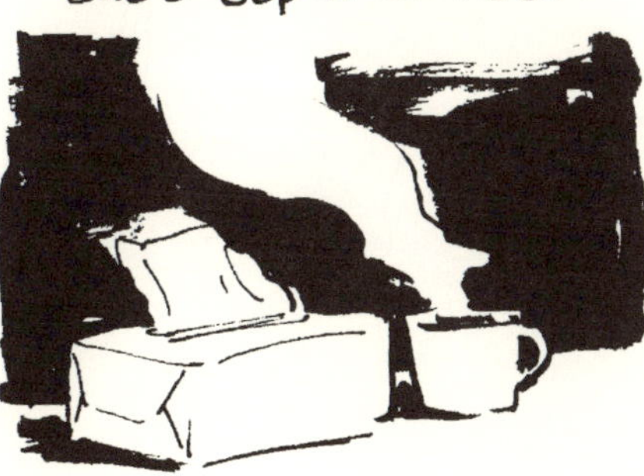

Same time next year, I guess.

©sai 21/11/04

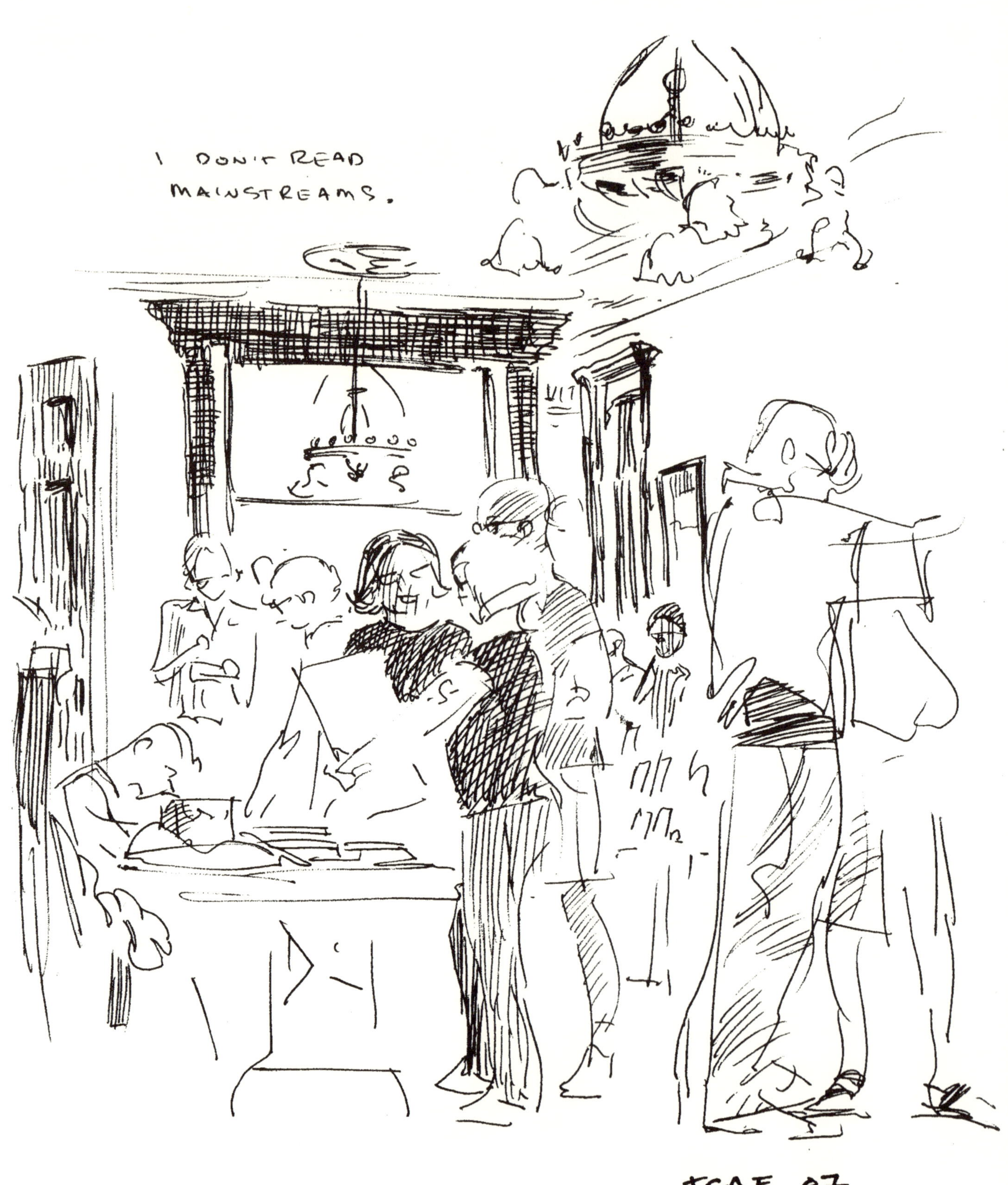
I DON'T READ
MAINSTREAMS.
TCAF 07

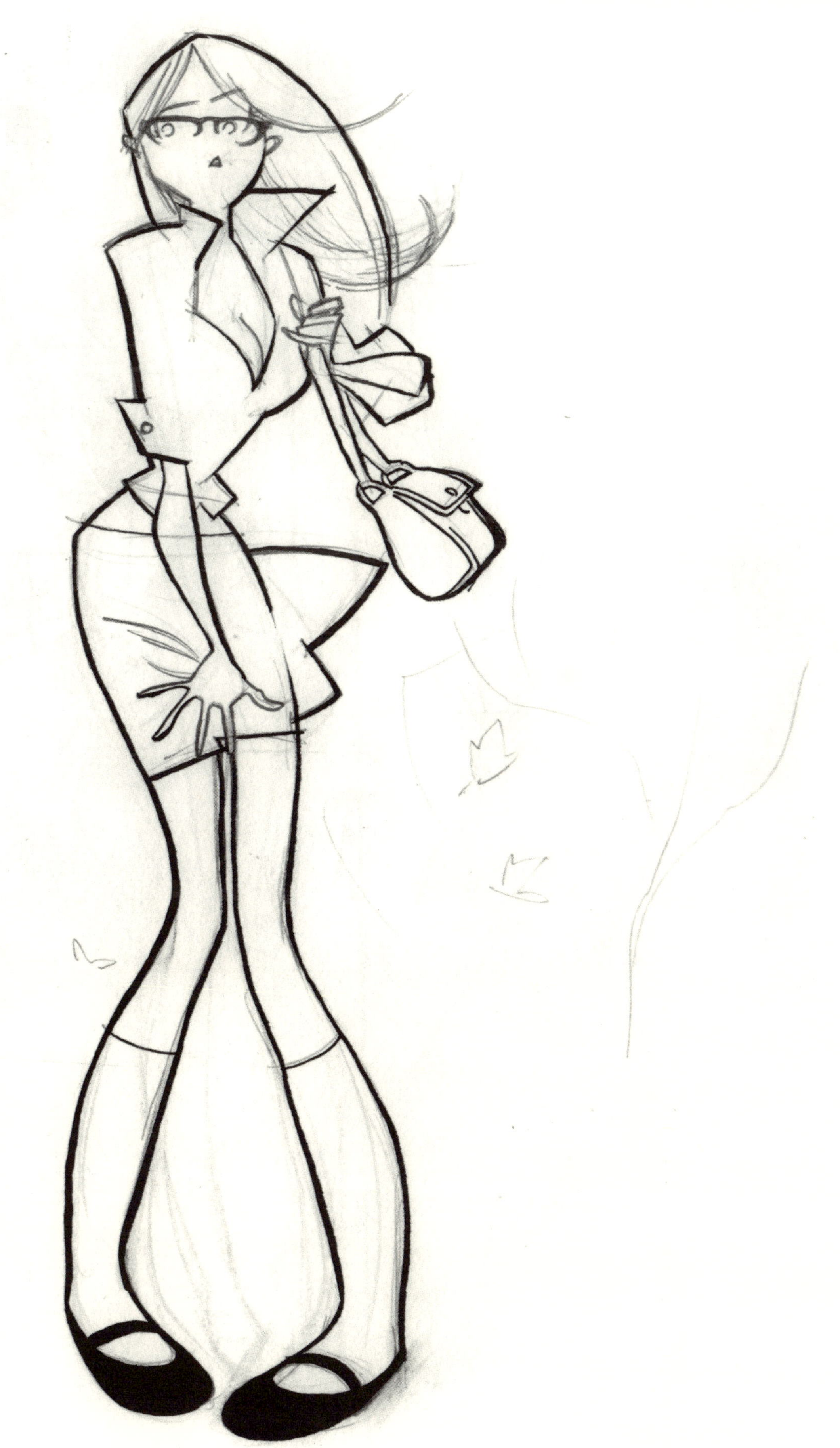

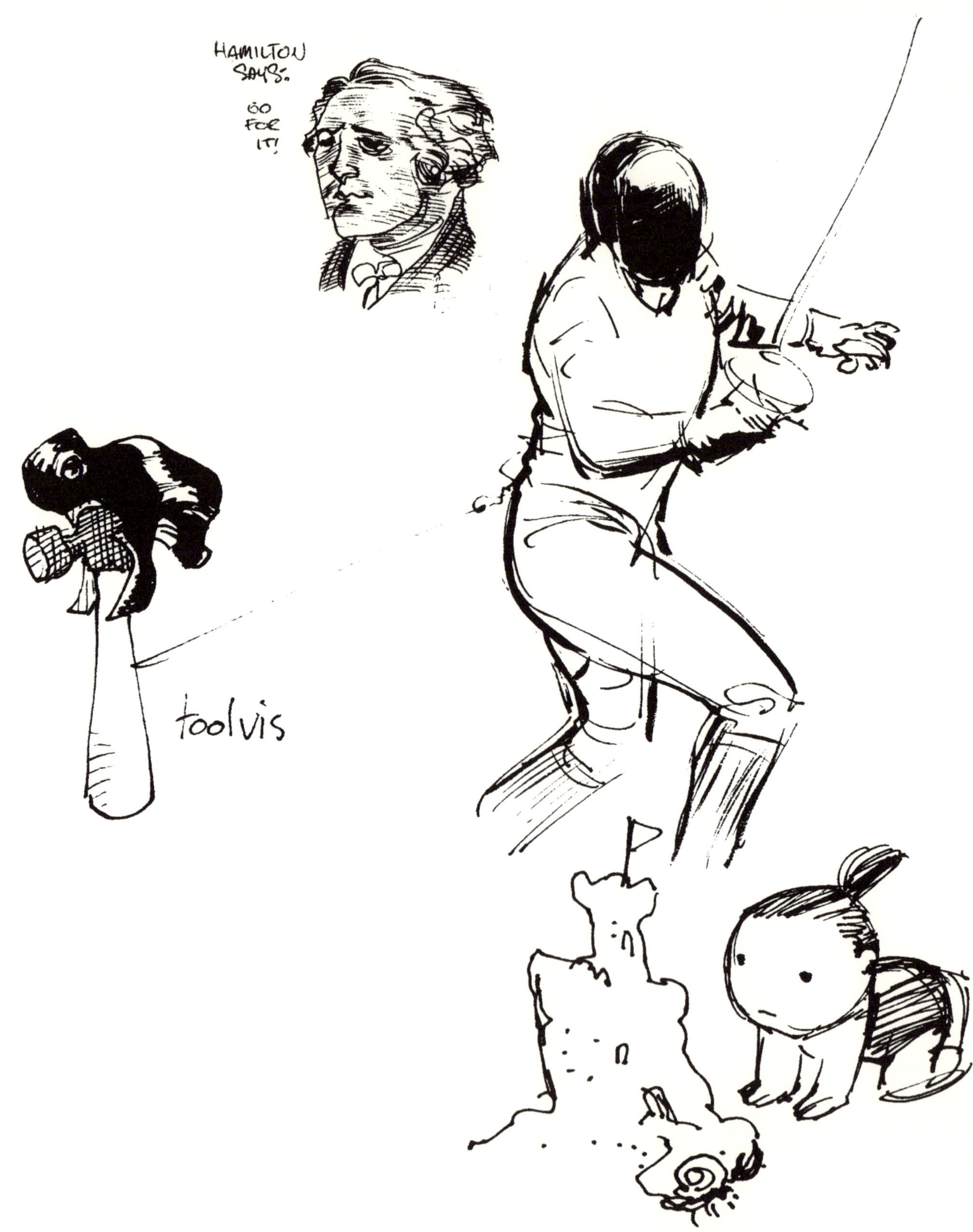
HAMILTON SAYS:
GO FOR IT!
toolvis

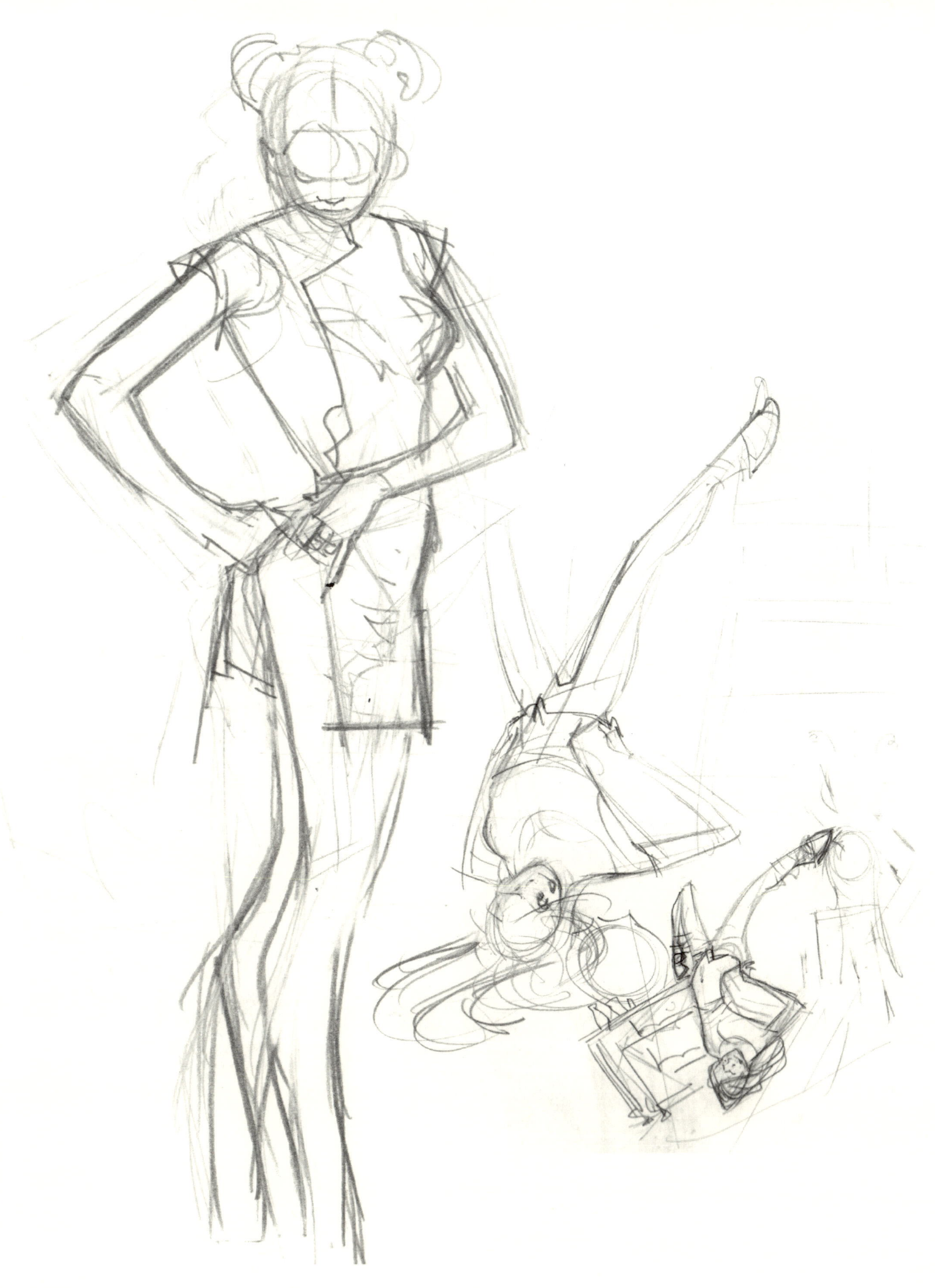

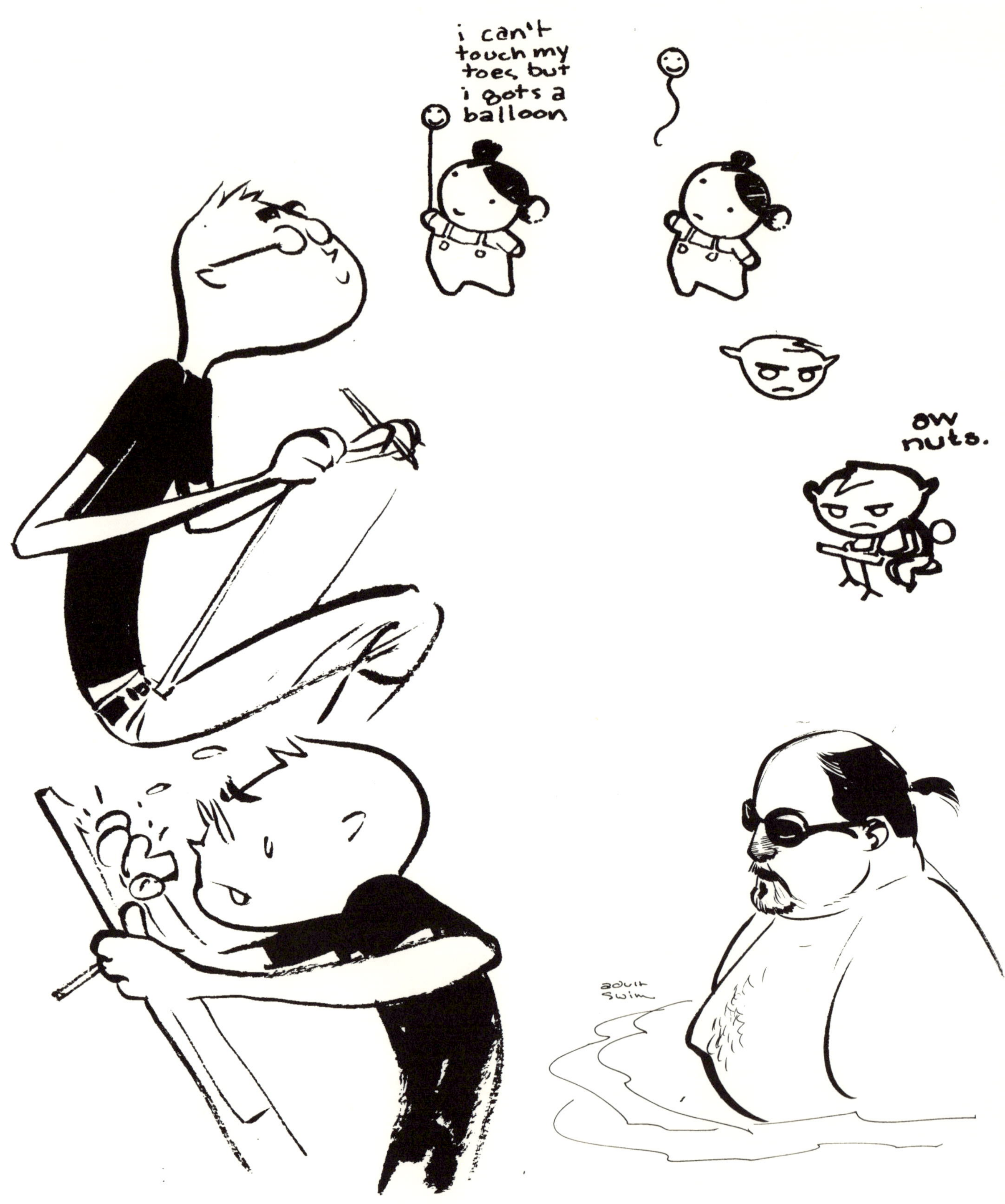
i can't touch my toes but i gots a balloon
aw nuts.
adult swim

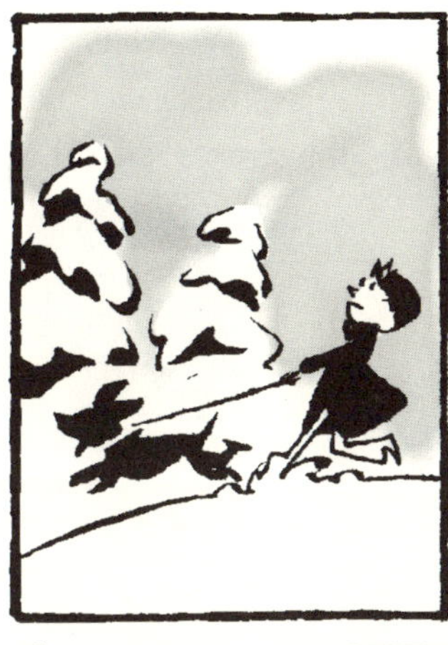

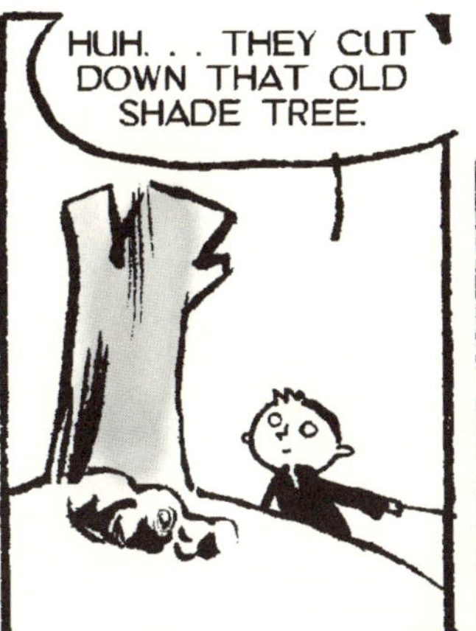
HUH. . . THEY CUT DOWN THAT OLD SHADE TREE.

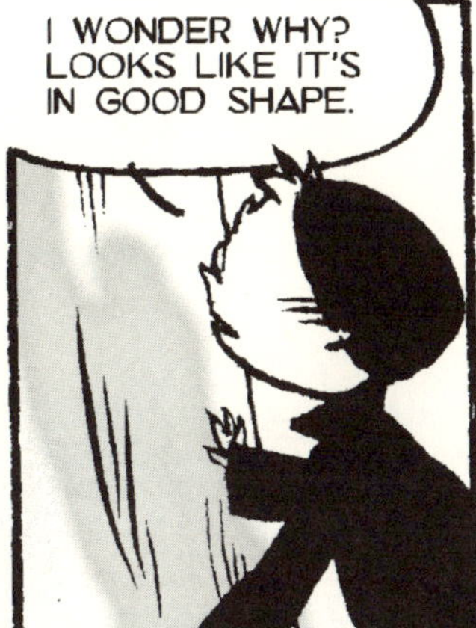
I WONDER WHY? LOOKS LIKE IT'S IN GOOD SHAPE.

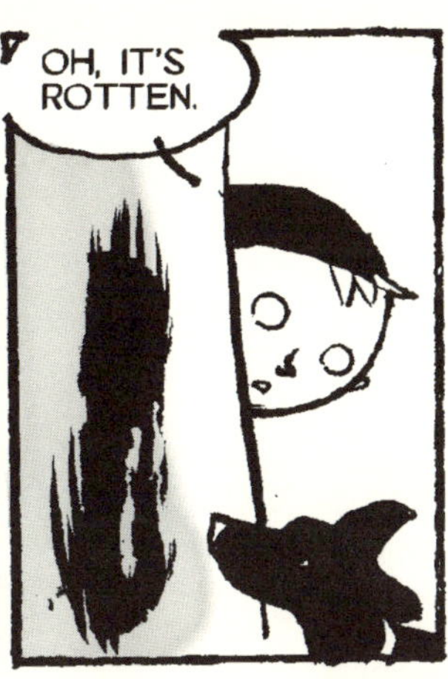
OH, IT'S ROTTEN.

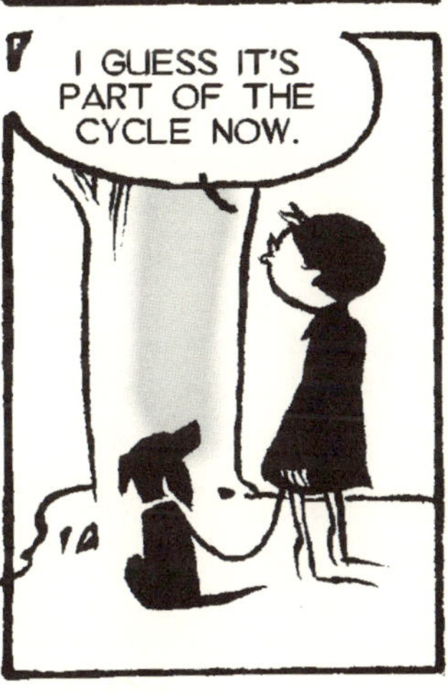
I GUESS IT'S PART OF THE CYCLE NOW.

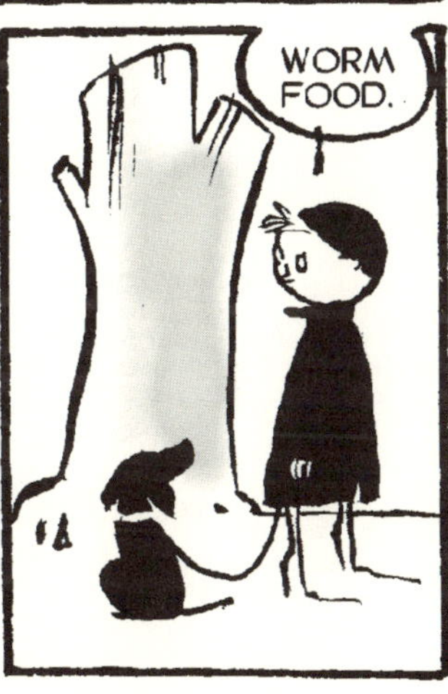
WORM FOOD.

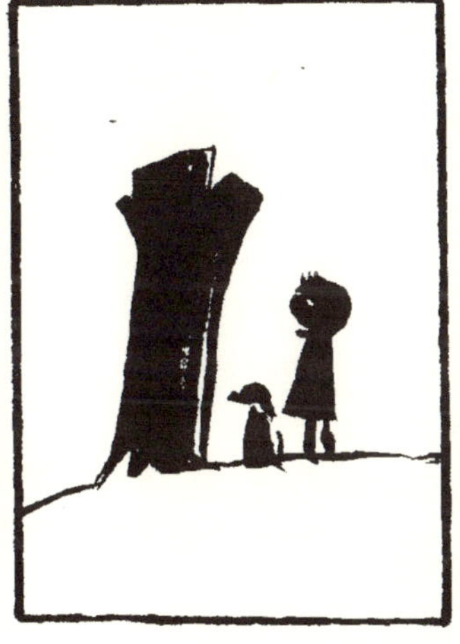

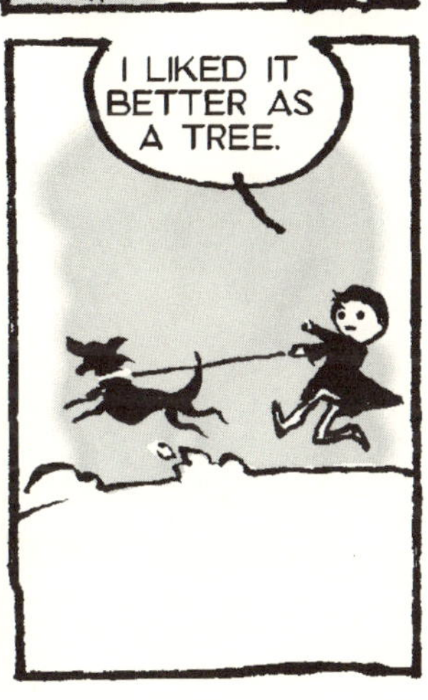
I LIKED IT BETTER AS A TREE.

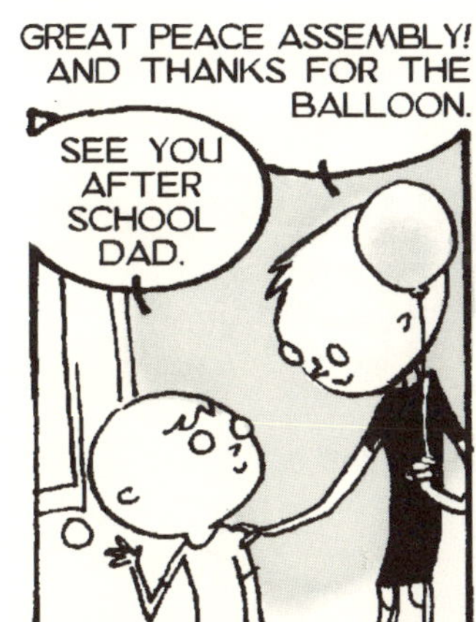
GREAT PEACE ASSEMBLY! AND THANKS FOR THE BALLOON.
SEE YOU AFTER SCHOOL DAD.

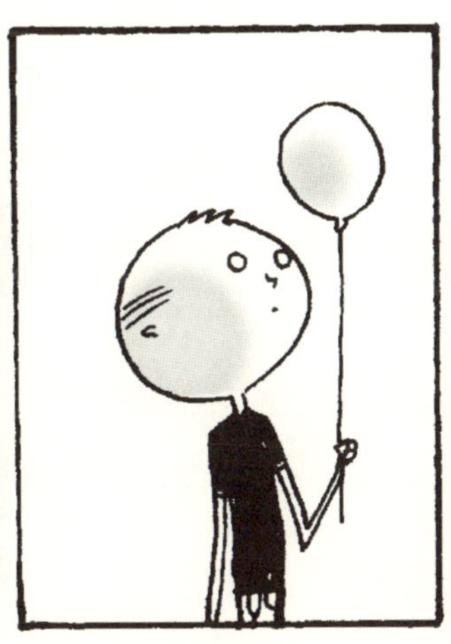

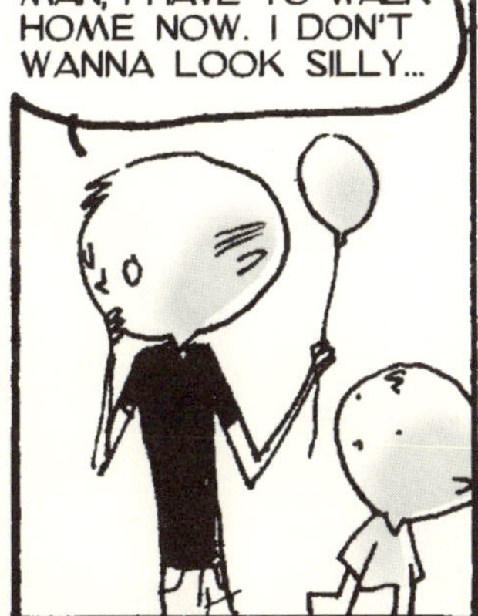
MAN, I HAVE TO WALK HOME NOW. I DON'T WANNA LOOK SILLY...

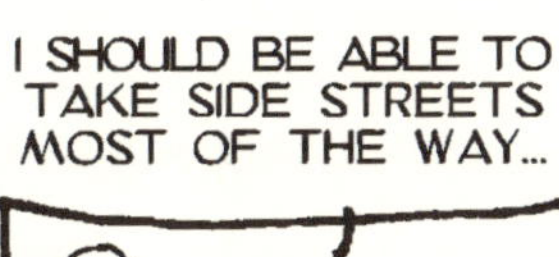
I SHOULD BE ABLE TO TAKE SIDE STREETS MOST OF THE WAY...

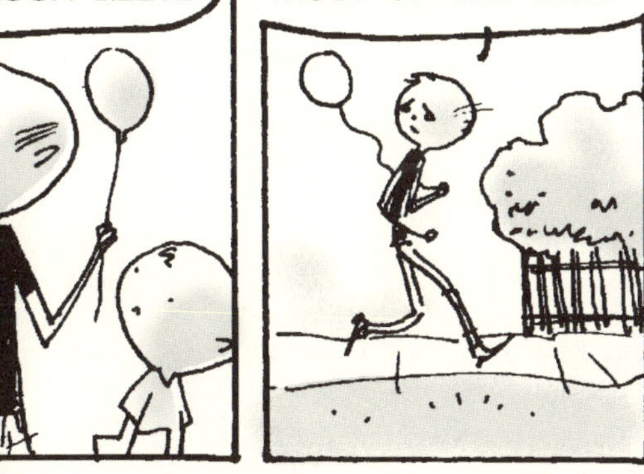

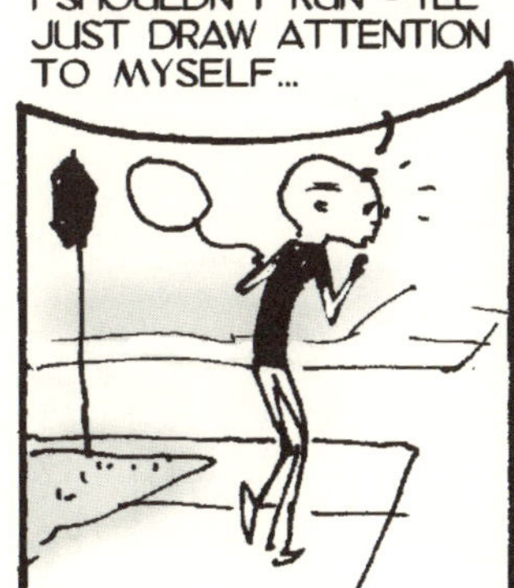
I SHOULDN'T RUN - I'LL JUST DRAW ATTENTION TO MYSELF...

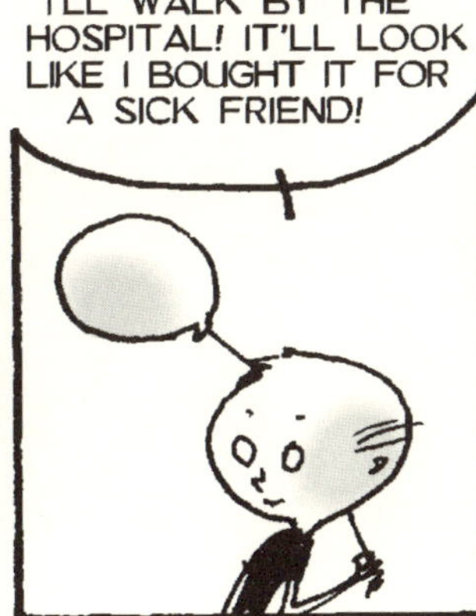
I'LL WALK BY THE HOSPITAL! IT'LL LOOK LIKE I BOUGHT IT FOR A SICK FRIEND!

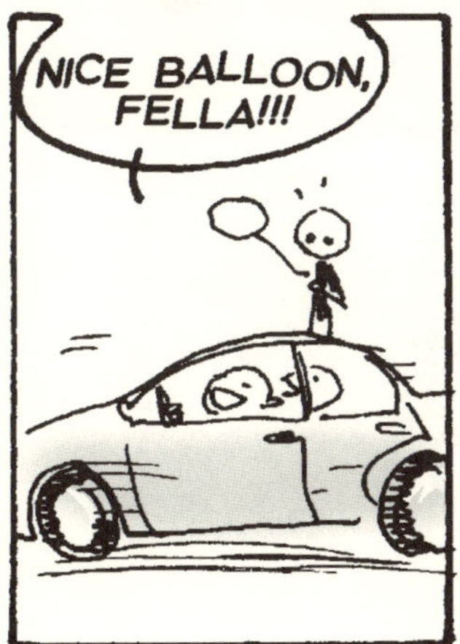
NICE BALLOON, FELLA!!!

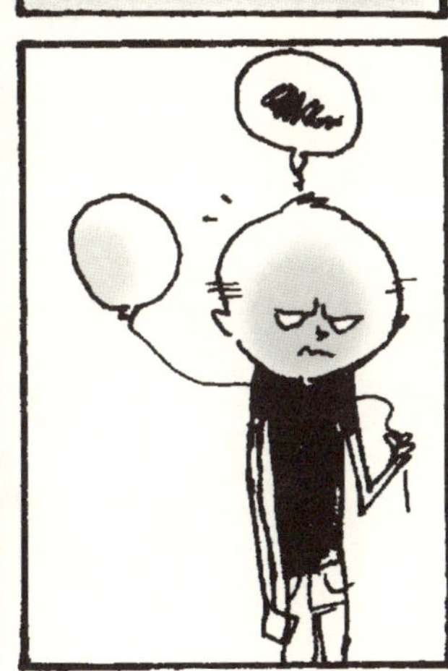

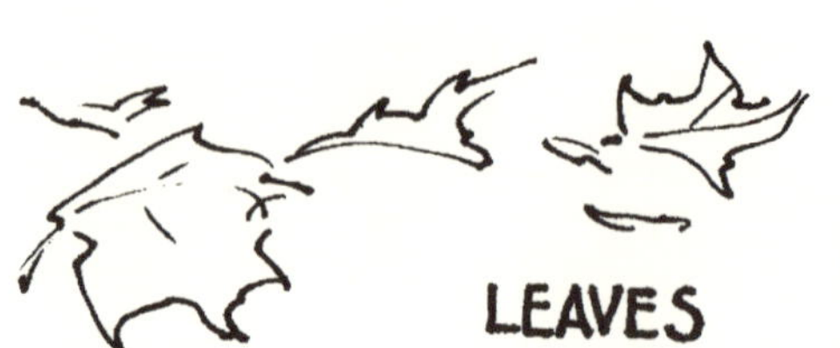

Saturday, after waking in the grim pre-dawn of late October, I enjoy coffee and a book in bed.

So does girl.

A yawn and a stretch later and I head to the garden.

We raked an acre of leaves last week. Nature vengefully filled the vacuum with that many again and more.

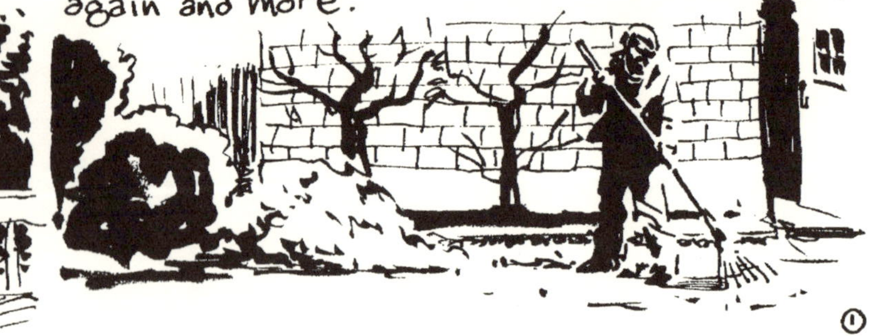

①

It's unseasonably warm, so I'm quick to shed my coat.

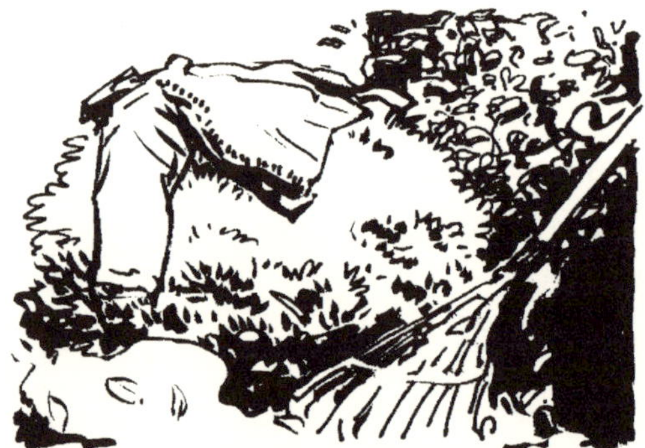

I unearthed little treasures: a snail,

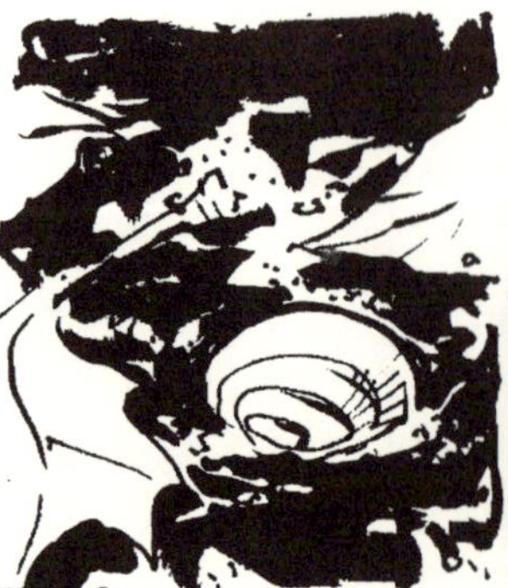

Grubs.

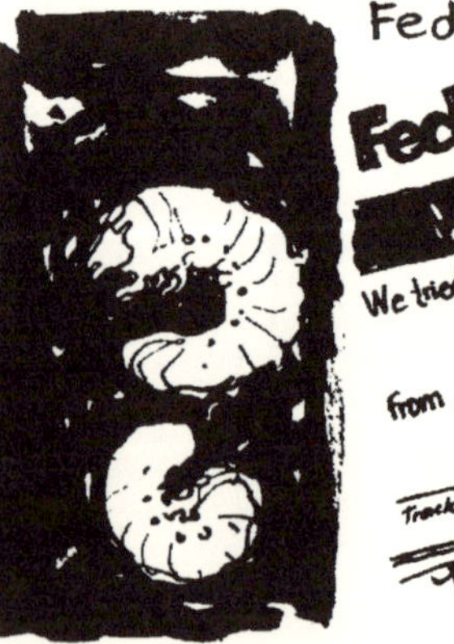

An old note from Federal Express.

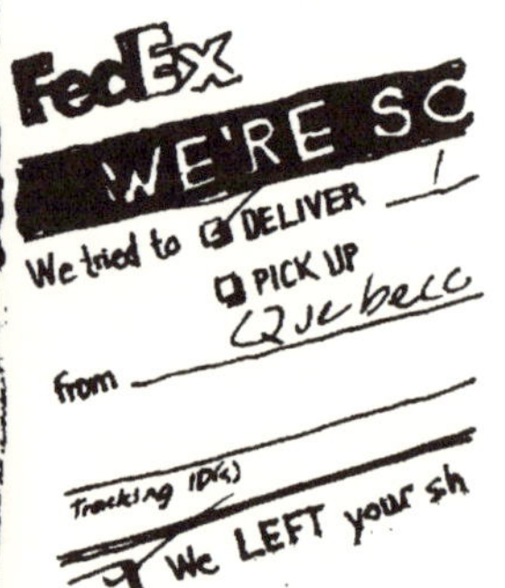
FedEx
WE'RE SC
We tried to DELIVER
PICK UP
Quebec
from
Tracking ID(s)
We LEFT your sh

As usual, the magnolia is holding onto every leaf, meaning more work in spring.

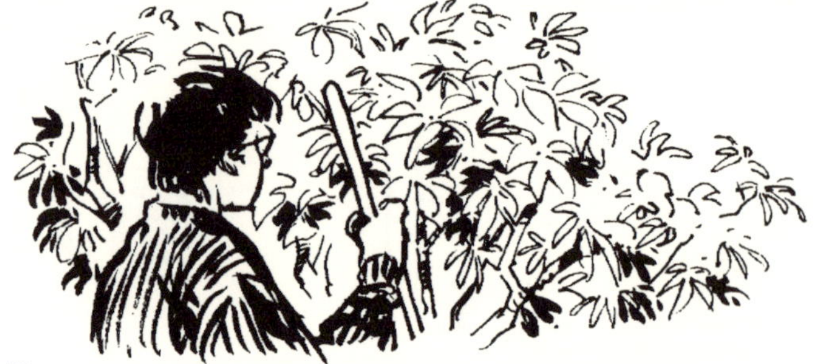

The norwegian maple also refuses to relenquish its bounty.

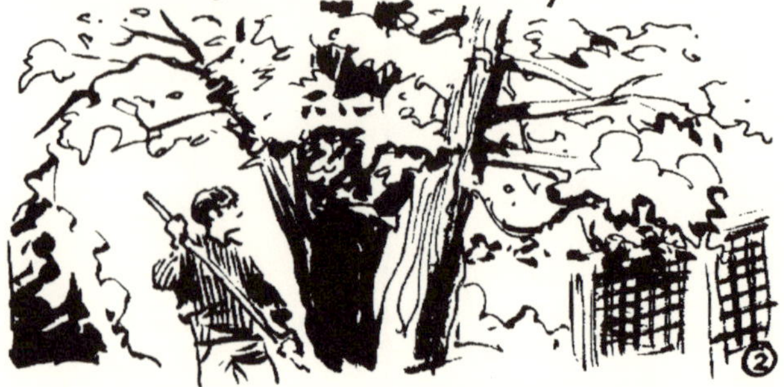

②

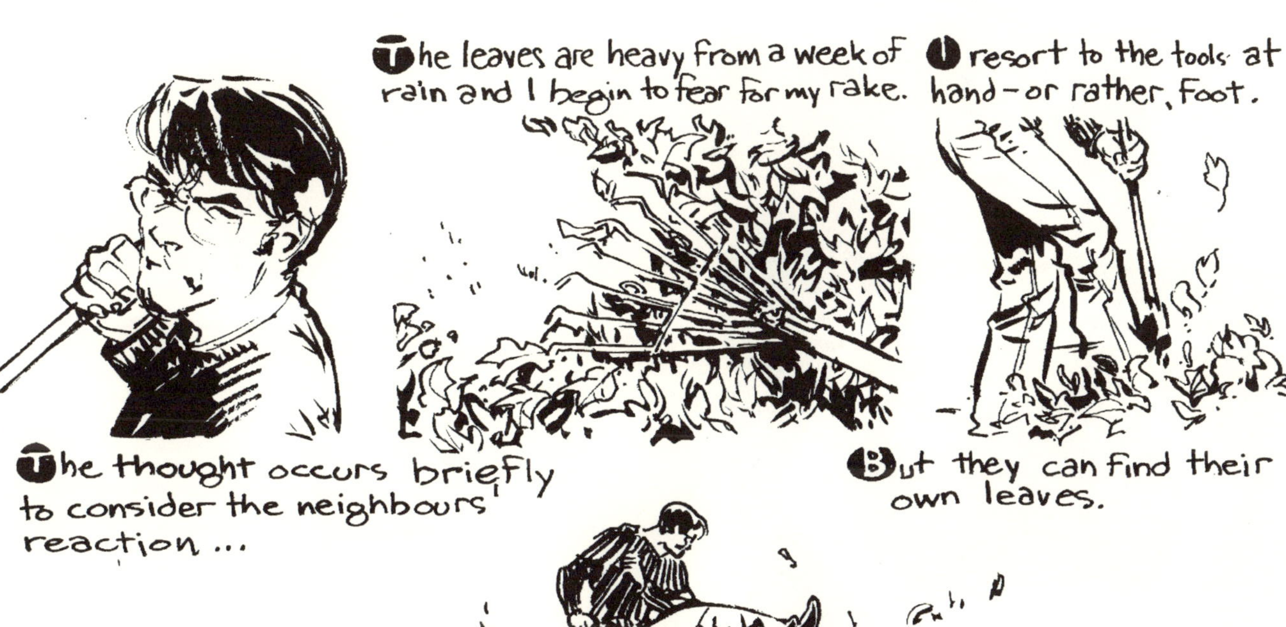
The leaves are heavy from a week of rain and I begin to fear for my rake.
I resort to the tools at hand - or rather, Foot.
The thought occurs briefly to consider the neighbours' reaction ...
But they can find their own leaves.
sai 11/04

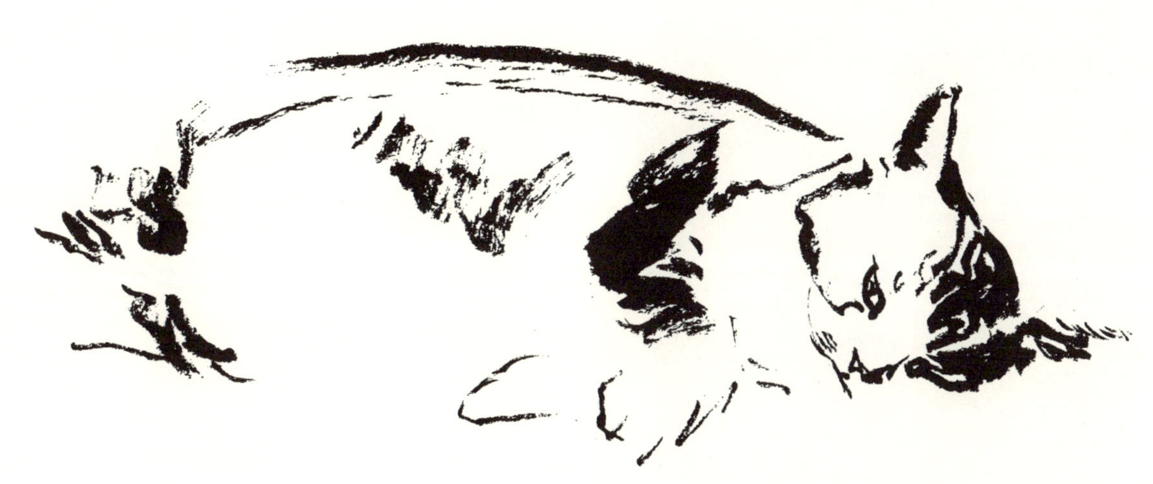

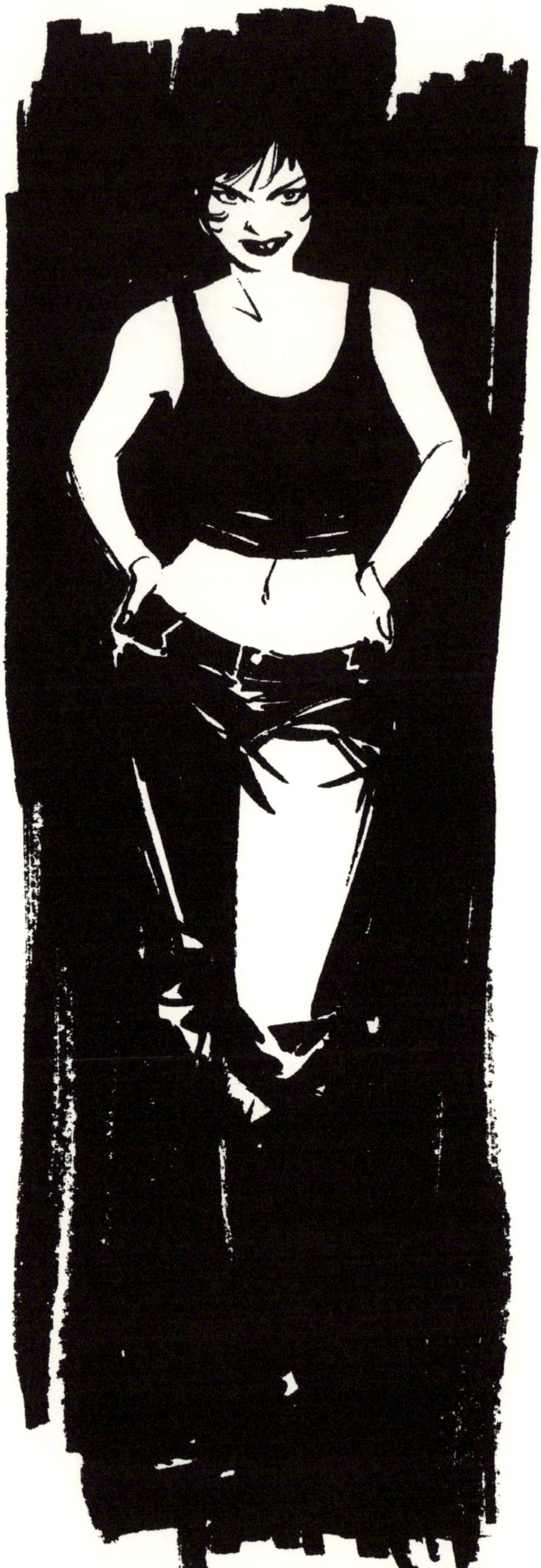

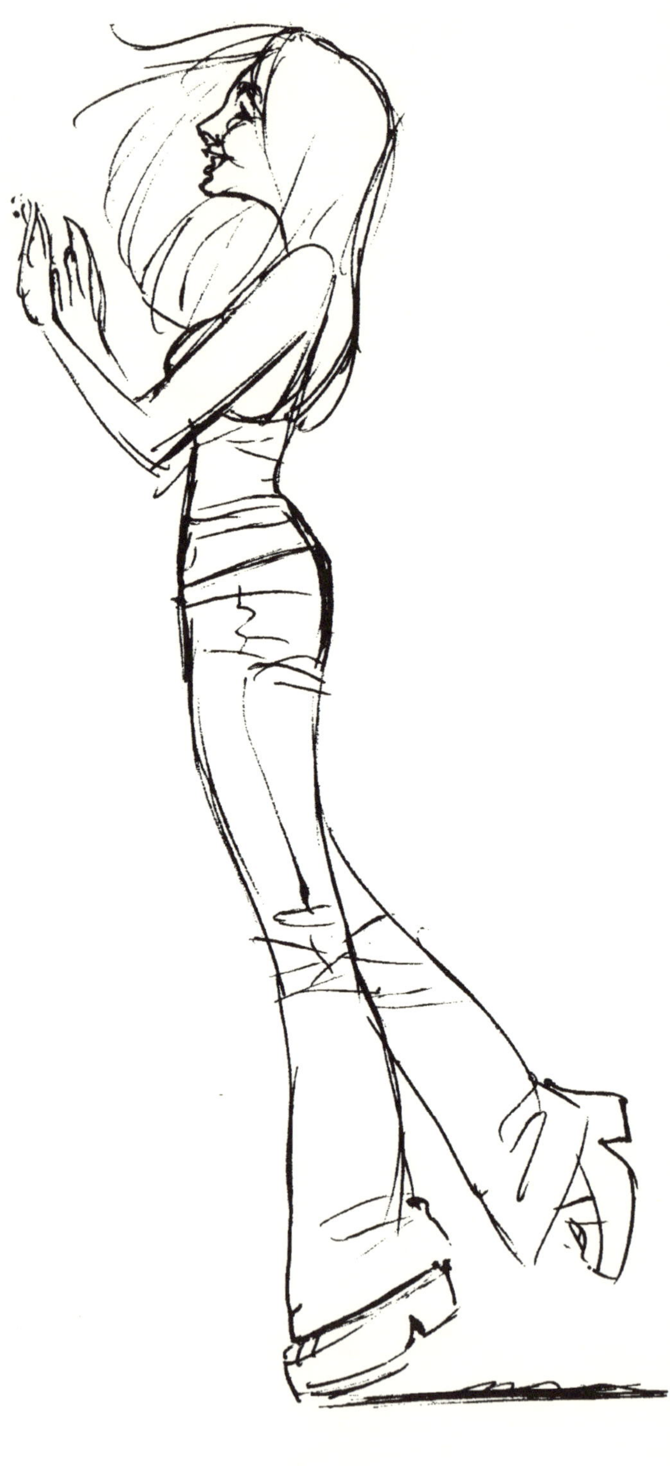

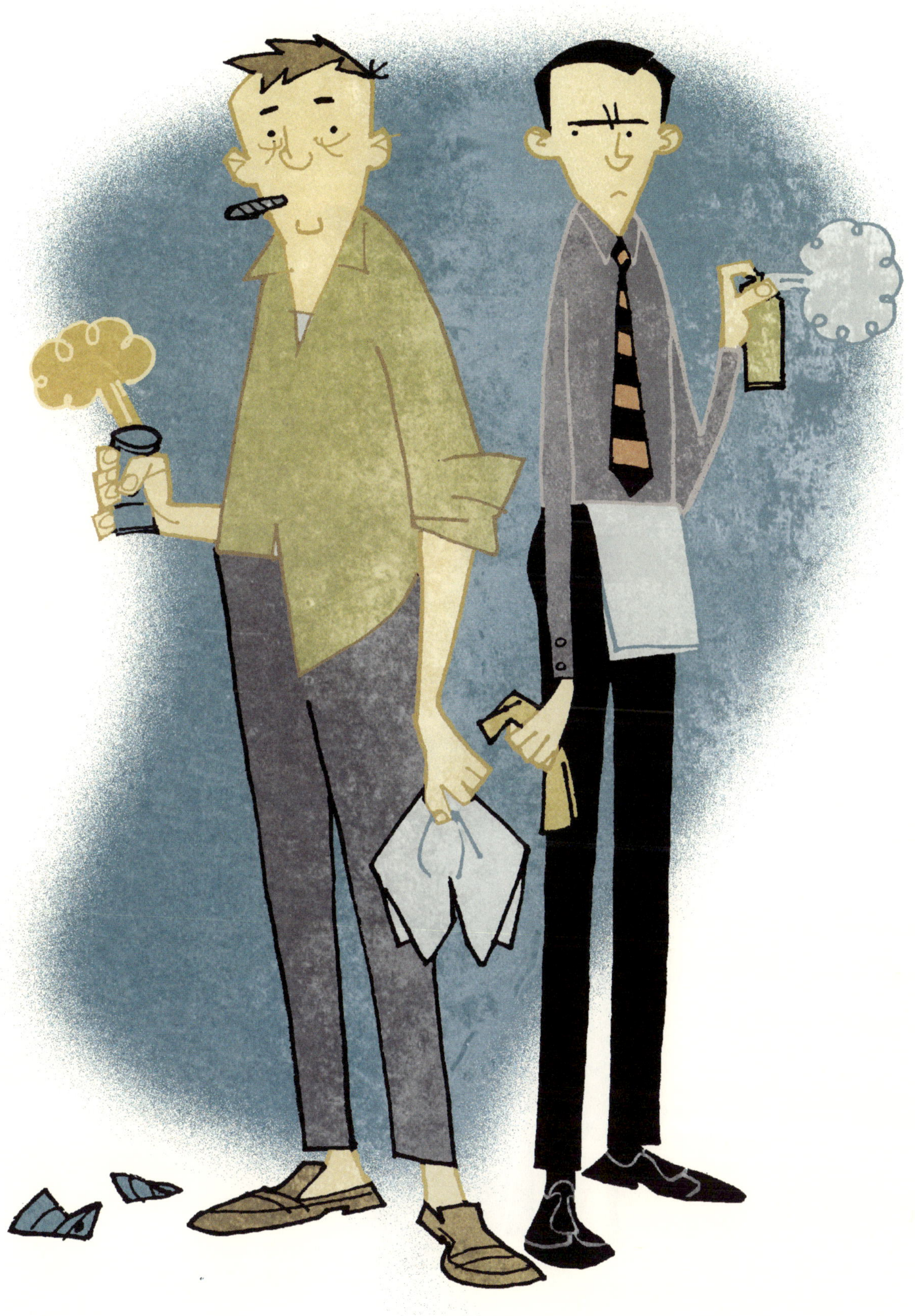

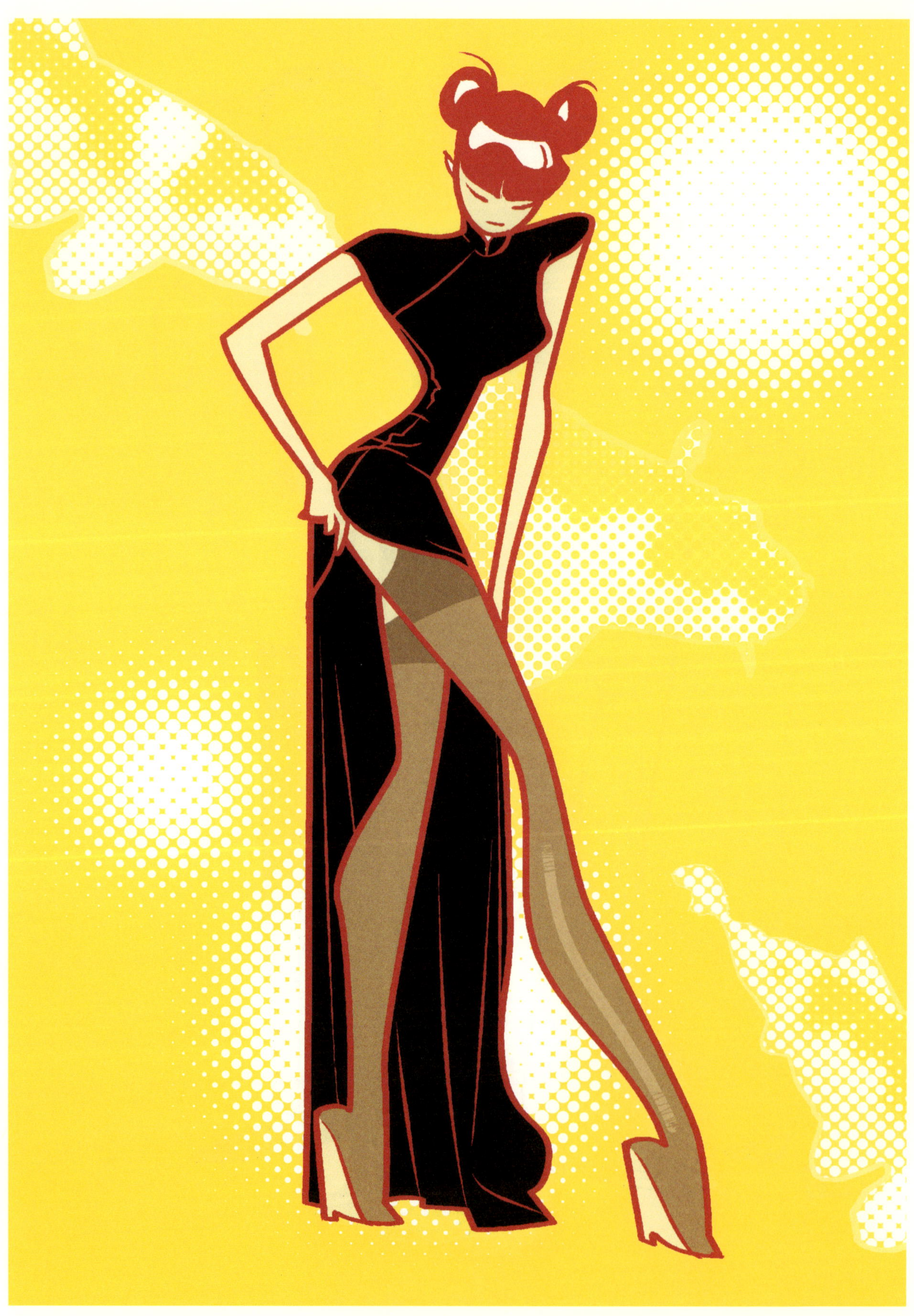

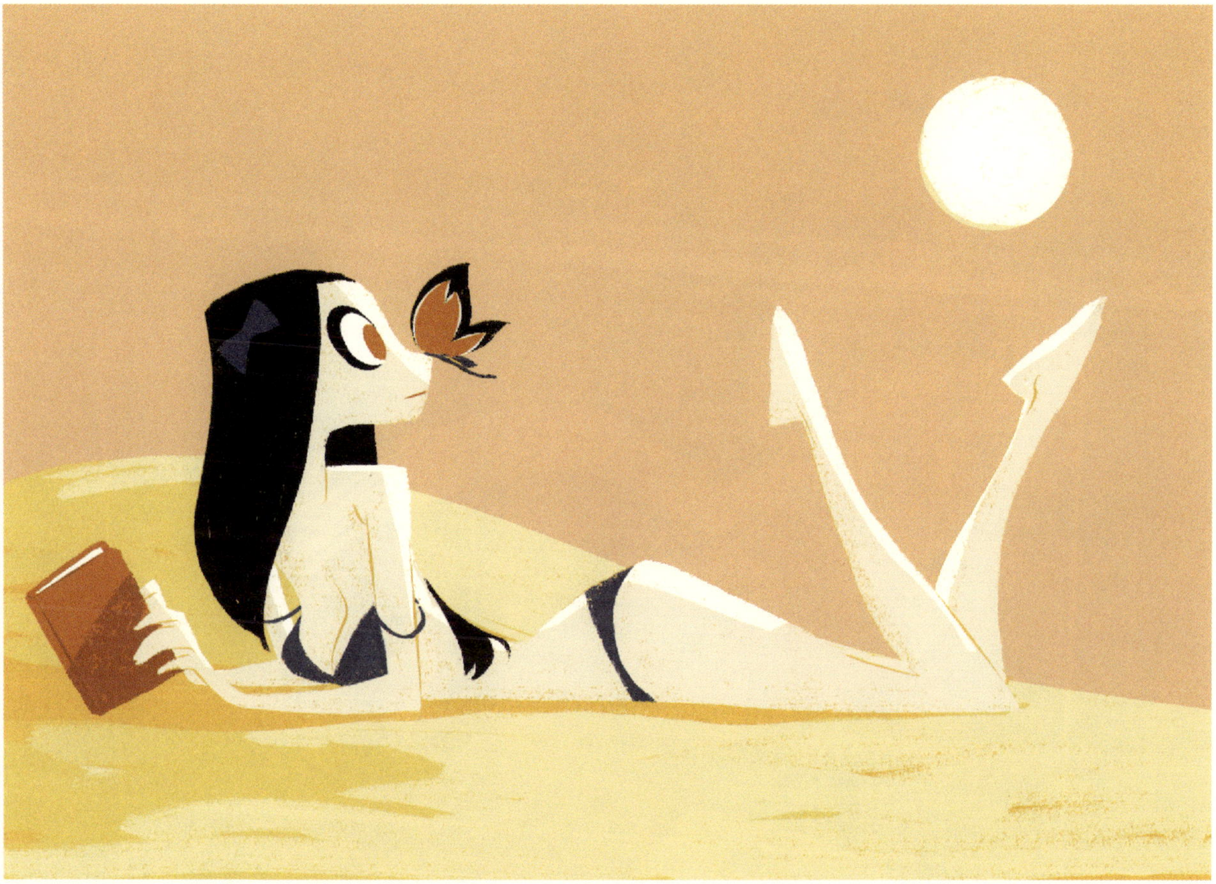

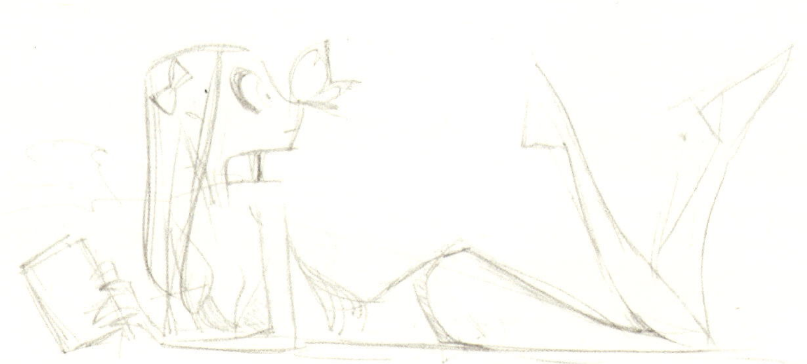

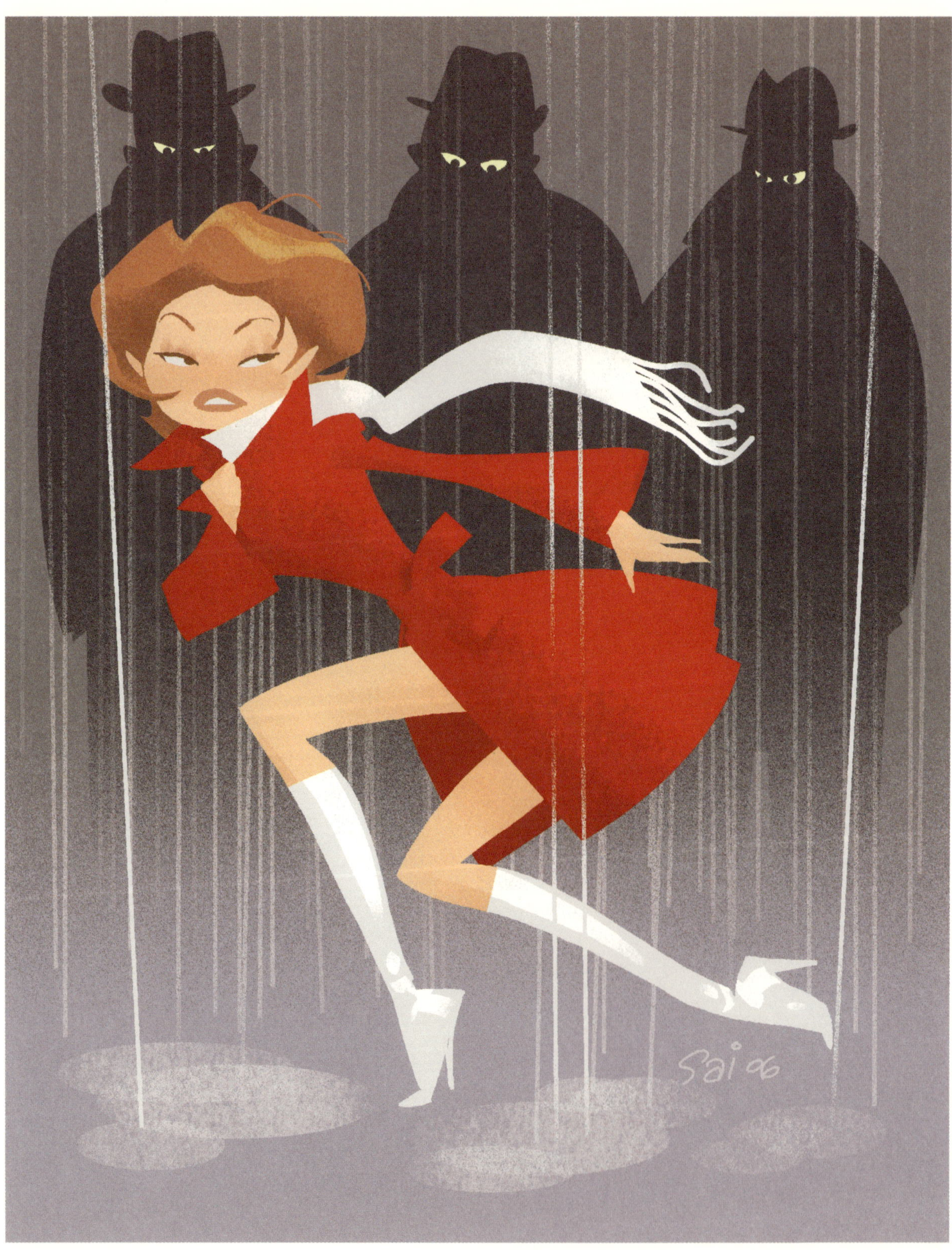
Sai 06

slightly related

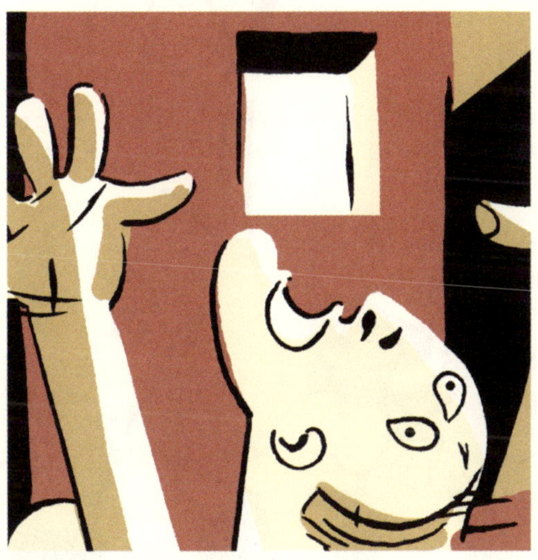

Kathryn & Stuart Immonen

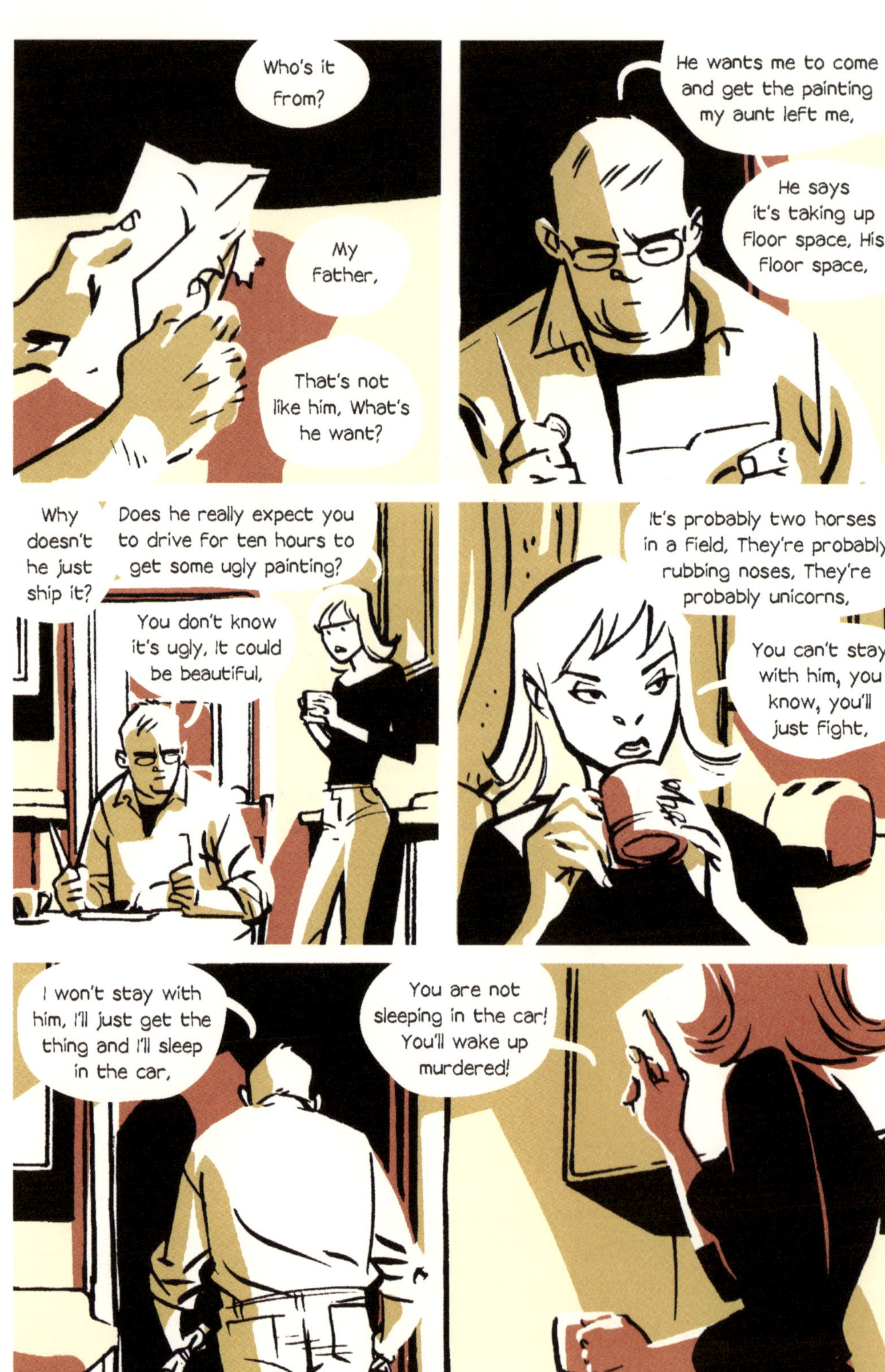
Who's it from?
My Father,
That's not like him, What's he want?
He wants me to come and get the painting my aunt left me,
He says it's taking up Floor space, His Floor space,
Why doesn't he just ship it?
Does he really expect you to drive for ten hours to get some ugly painting?
You don't know it's ugly, It could be beautiful,
It's probably two horses in a Field, They're probably rubbing noses, They're probably unicorns,
You can't stay with him, you know, you'll just Fight,
I won't stay with him, I'll just get the thing and I'll sleep in the car,
You are not sleeping in the car! You'll wake up murdered!

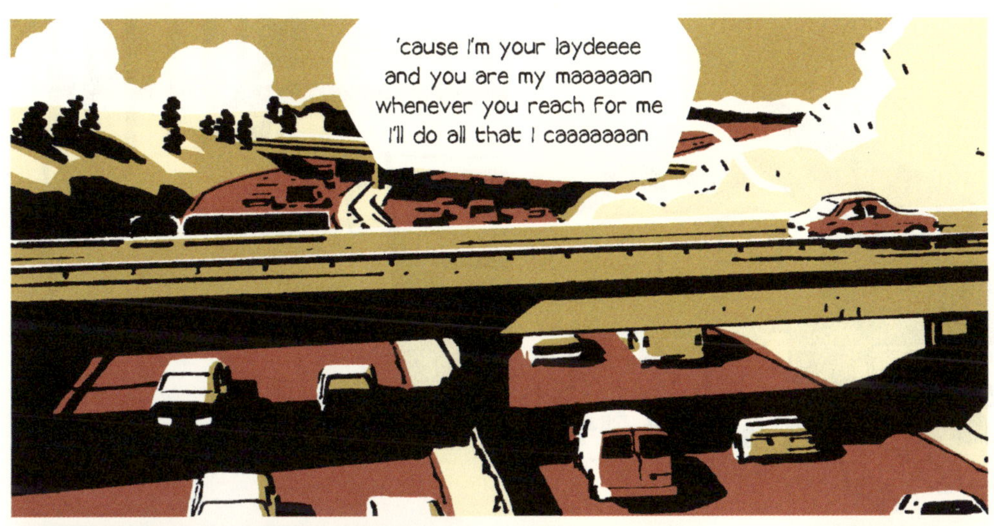
'cause I'm your laydeeee
and you are my maaaaaan
whenever you reach for me
I'll do all that I caaaaaaan

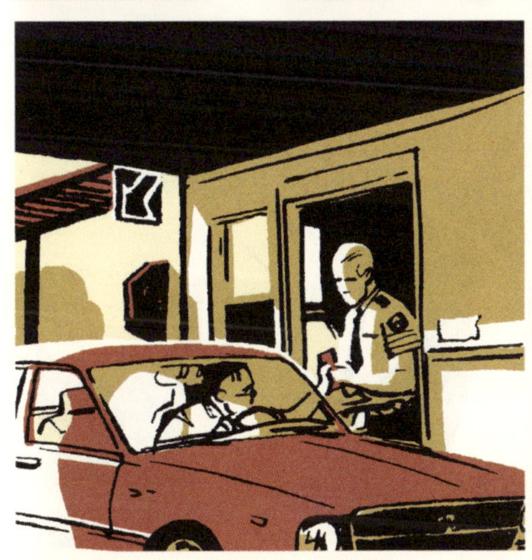

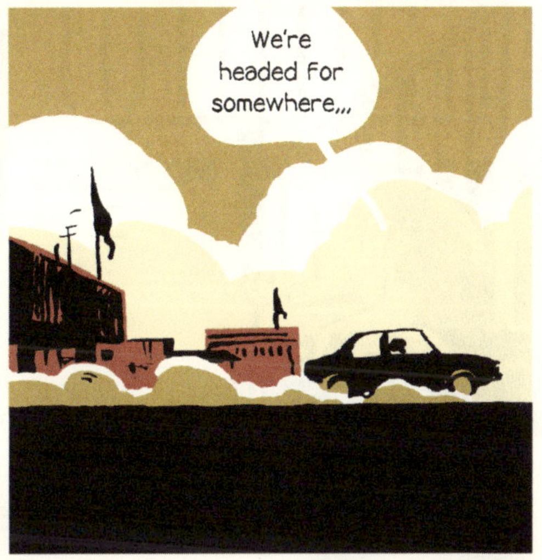
We're headed for somewhere,,,

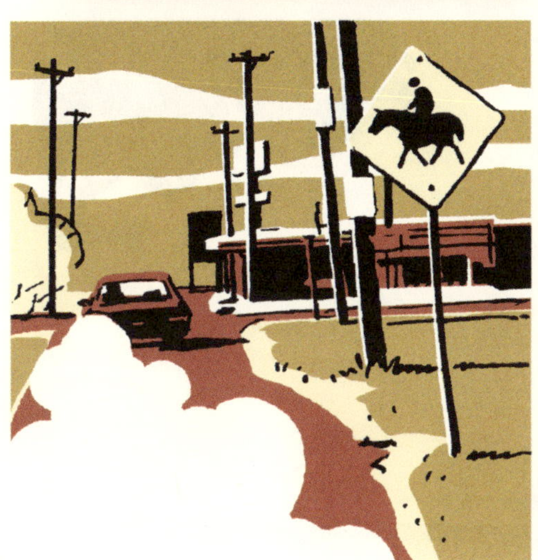

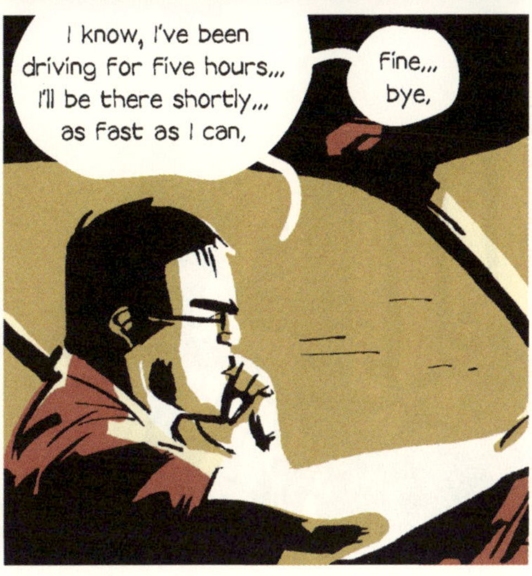
I know, I've been driving for five hours,,, I'll be there shortly,,, as fast as I can,
Fine,,, bye,

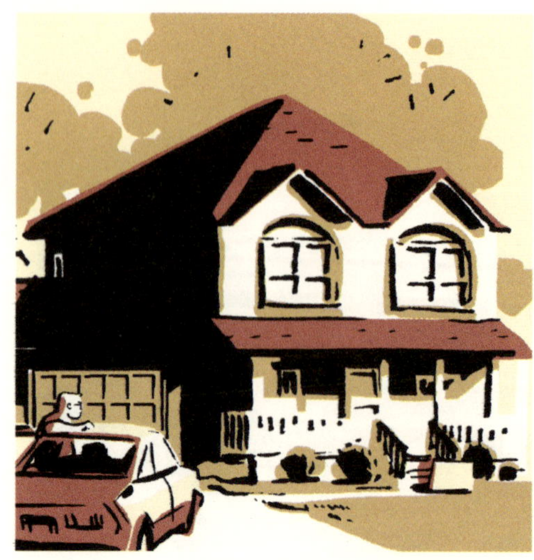

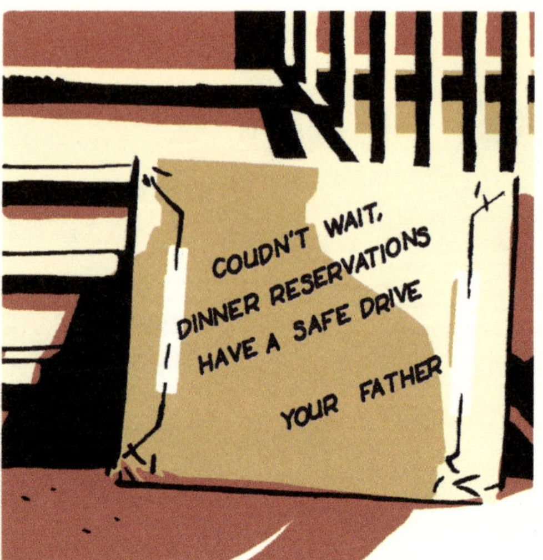
COUDN'T WAIT.
DINNER RESERVATIONS
HAVE A SAFE DRIVE
YOUR FATHER

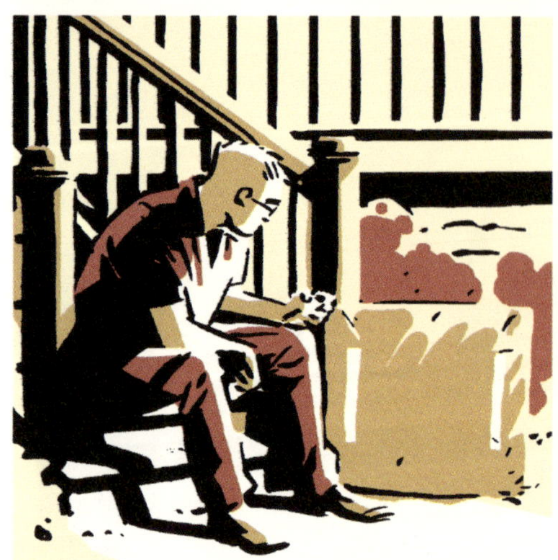

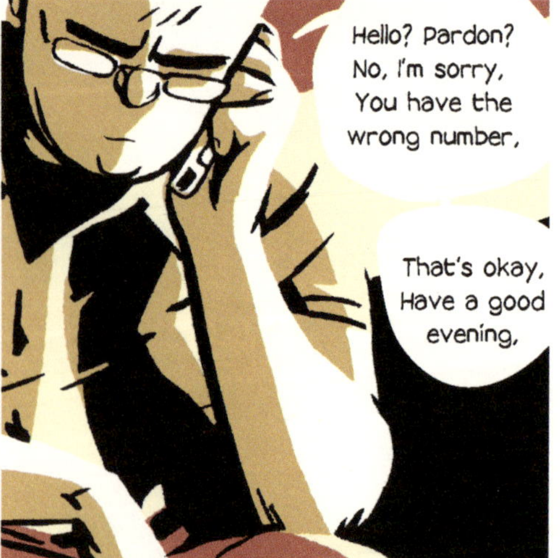
Hello? Pardon? No, I'm sorry, You have the wrong number,
That's okay, Have a good evening,

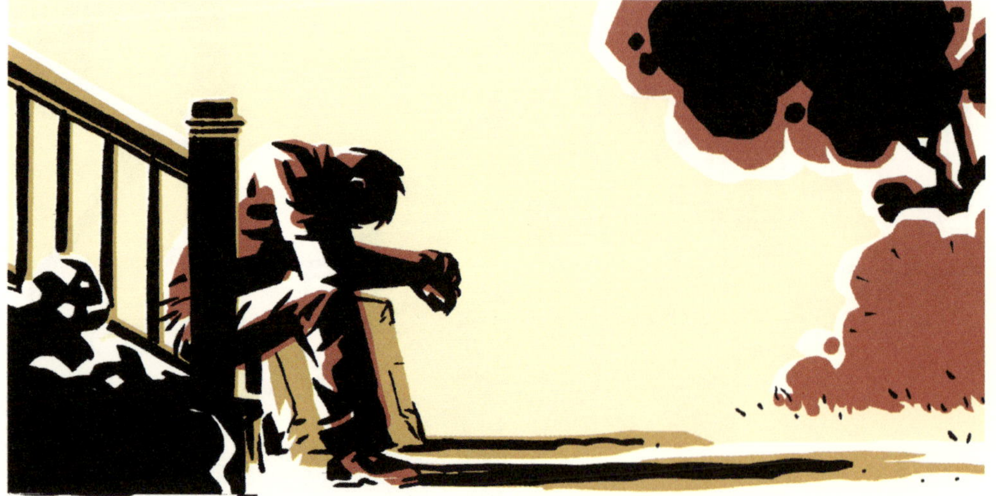

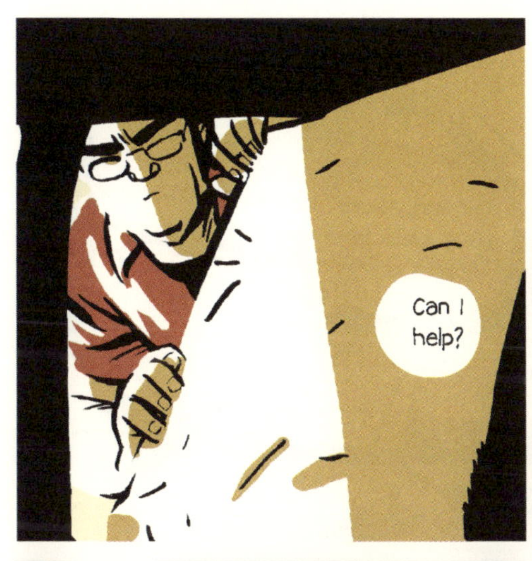
Can I
help?

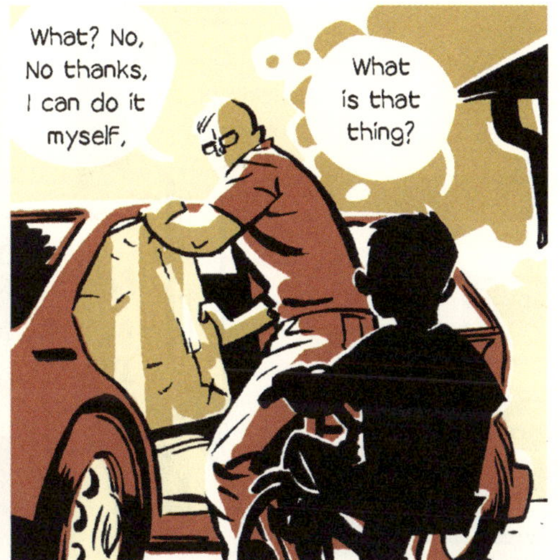
What? No,
No thanks,
I can do it
myself,
What
is that
thing?

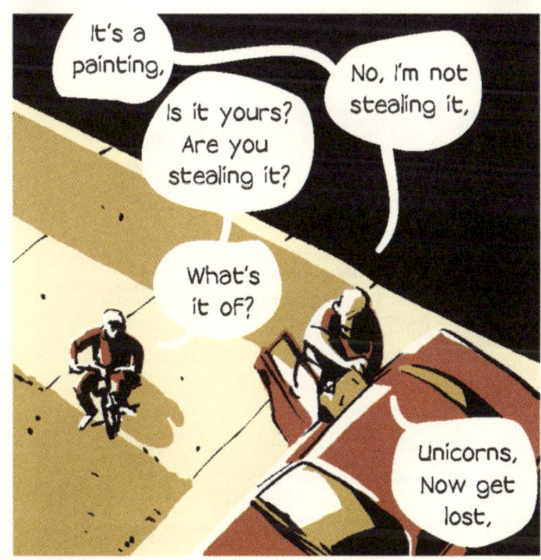
It's a
painting,
Is it yours?
Are you
stealing it?
No, I'm not
stealing it,
What's
it of?
Unicorns,
Now get
lost,

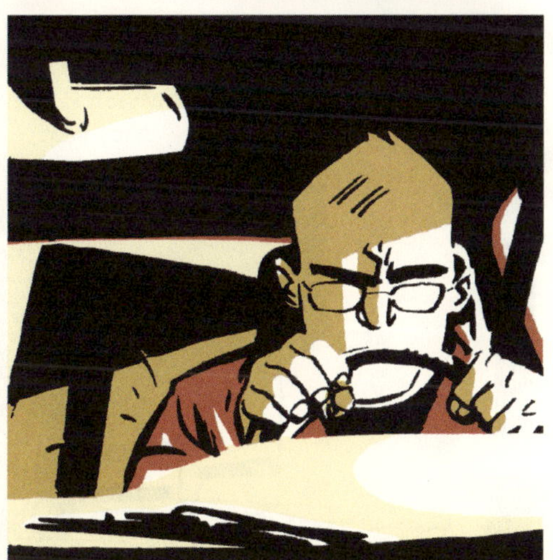

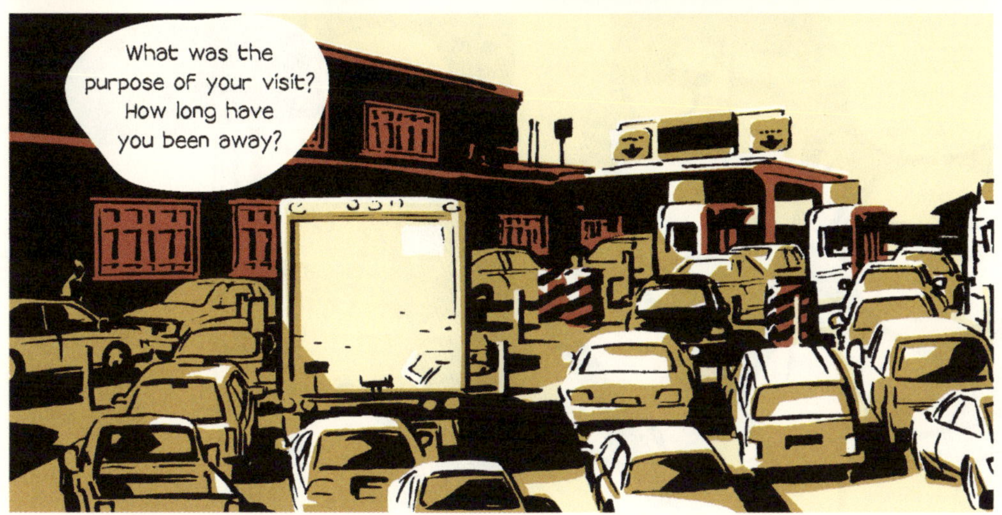
What was the
purpose of your visit?
How long have
you been away?

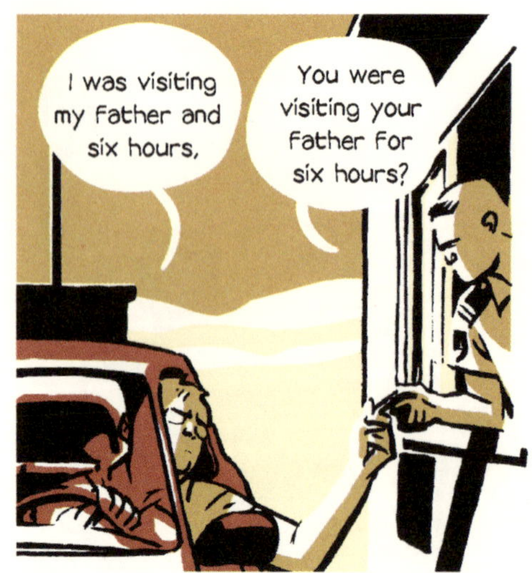
I was visiting my father and six hours,
You were visiting your father for six hours?

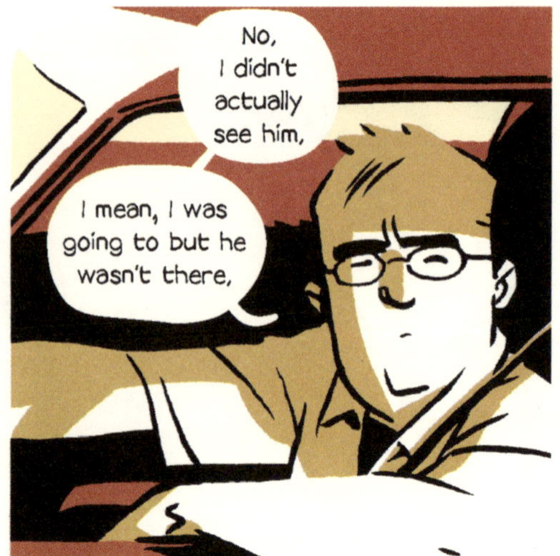
No, I didn't actually see him,
I mean, I was going to but he wasn't there,

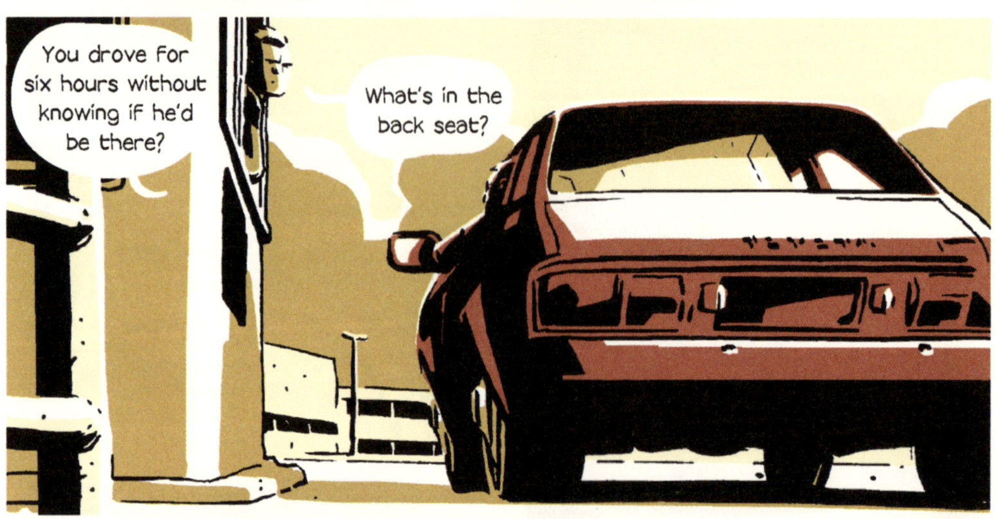
You drove for six hours without knowing if he'd be there?
What's in the back seat?

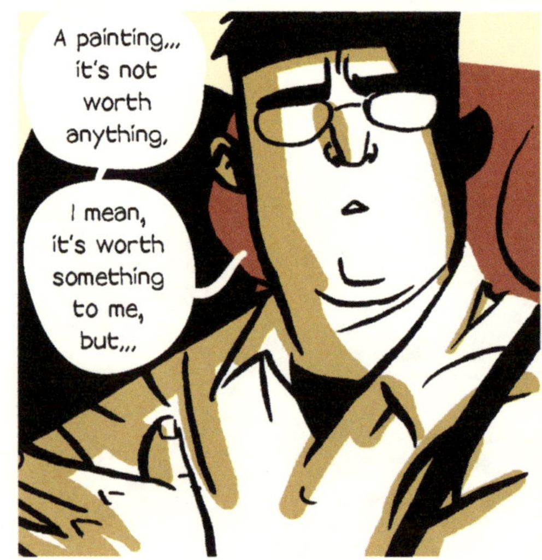
A painting,,, it's not worth anything,
I mean, it's worth something to me, but,,,

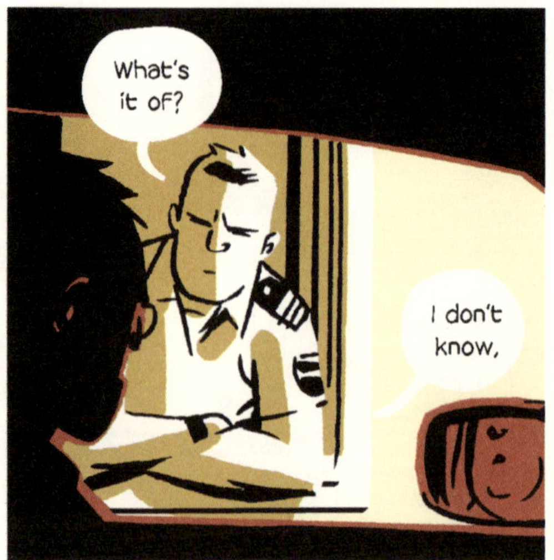
What's it of?
I don't know,

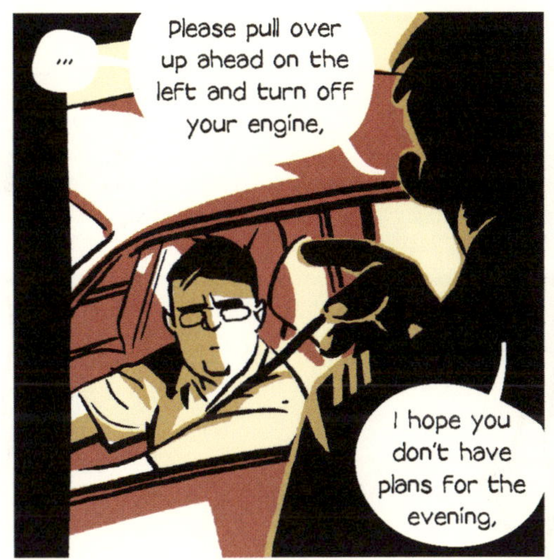
...
Please pull over up ahead on the left and turn off your engine,
I hope you don't have plans for the evening,

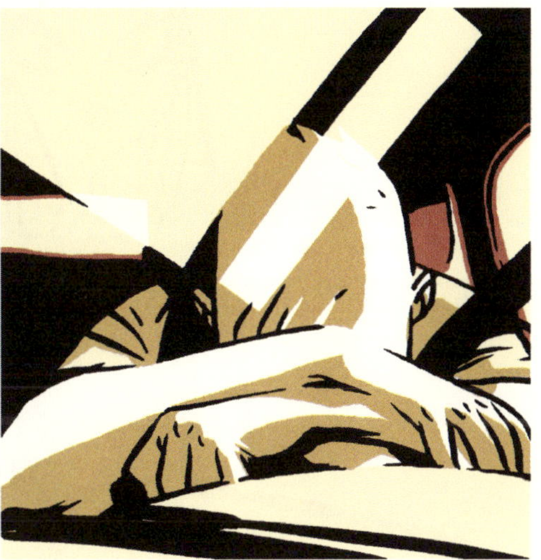

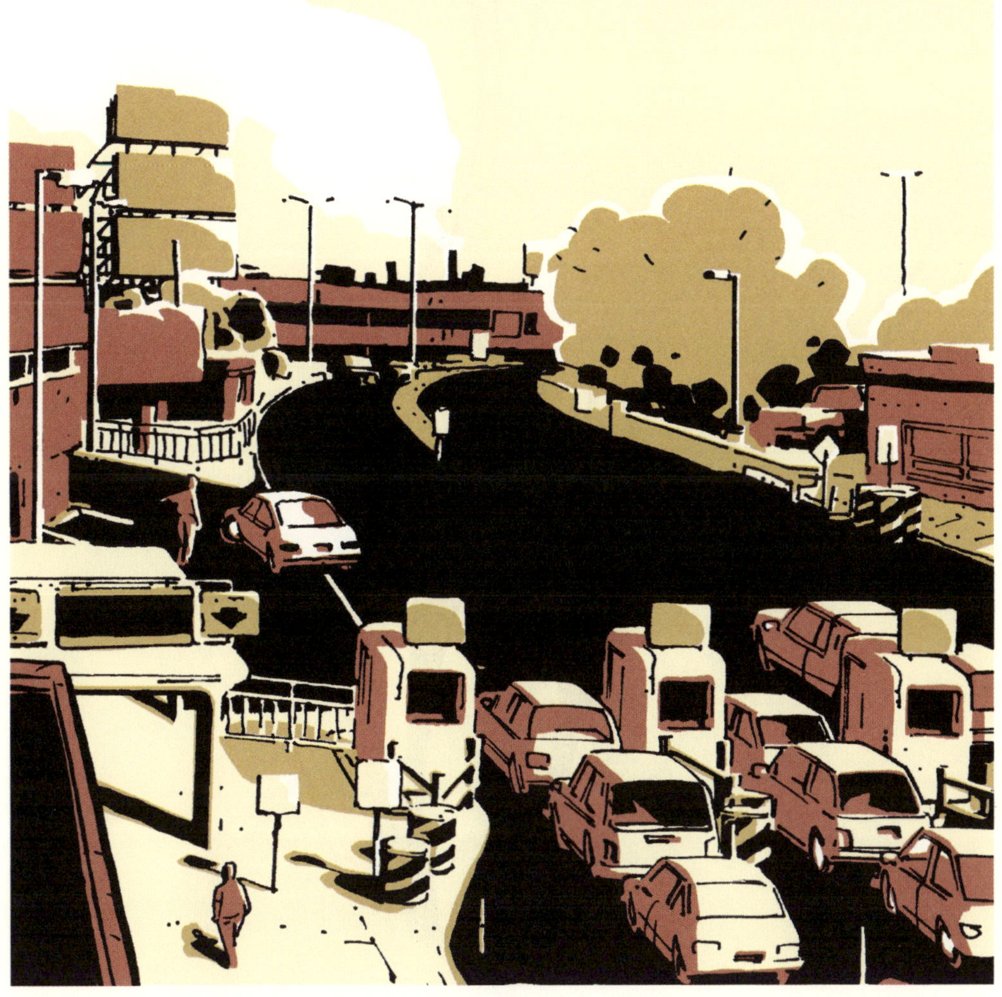

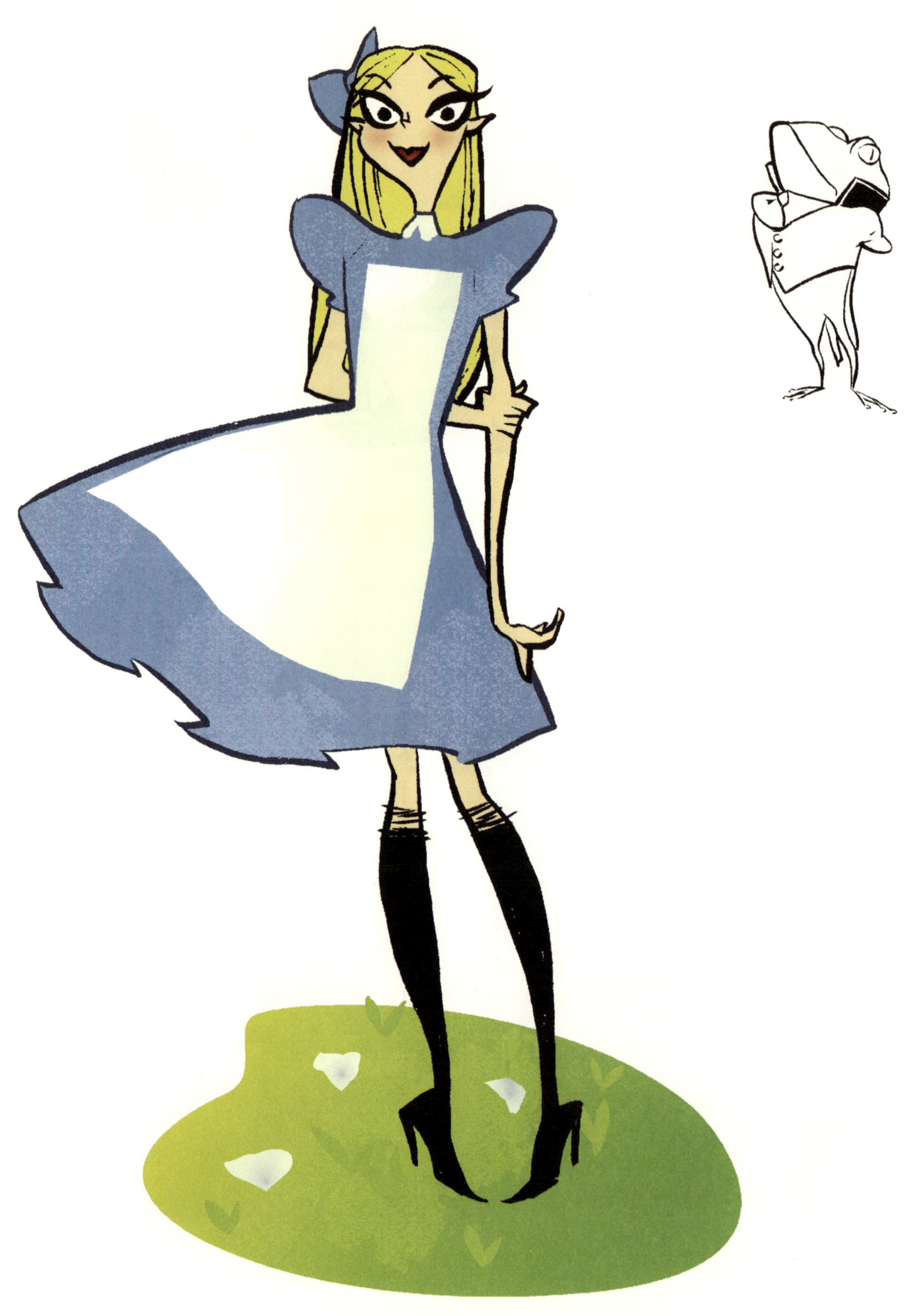

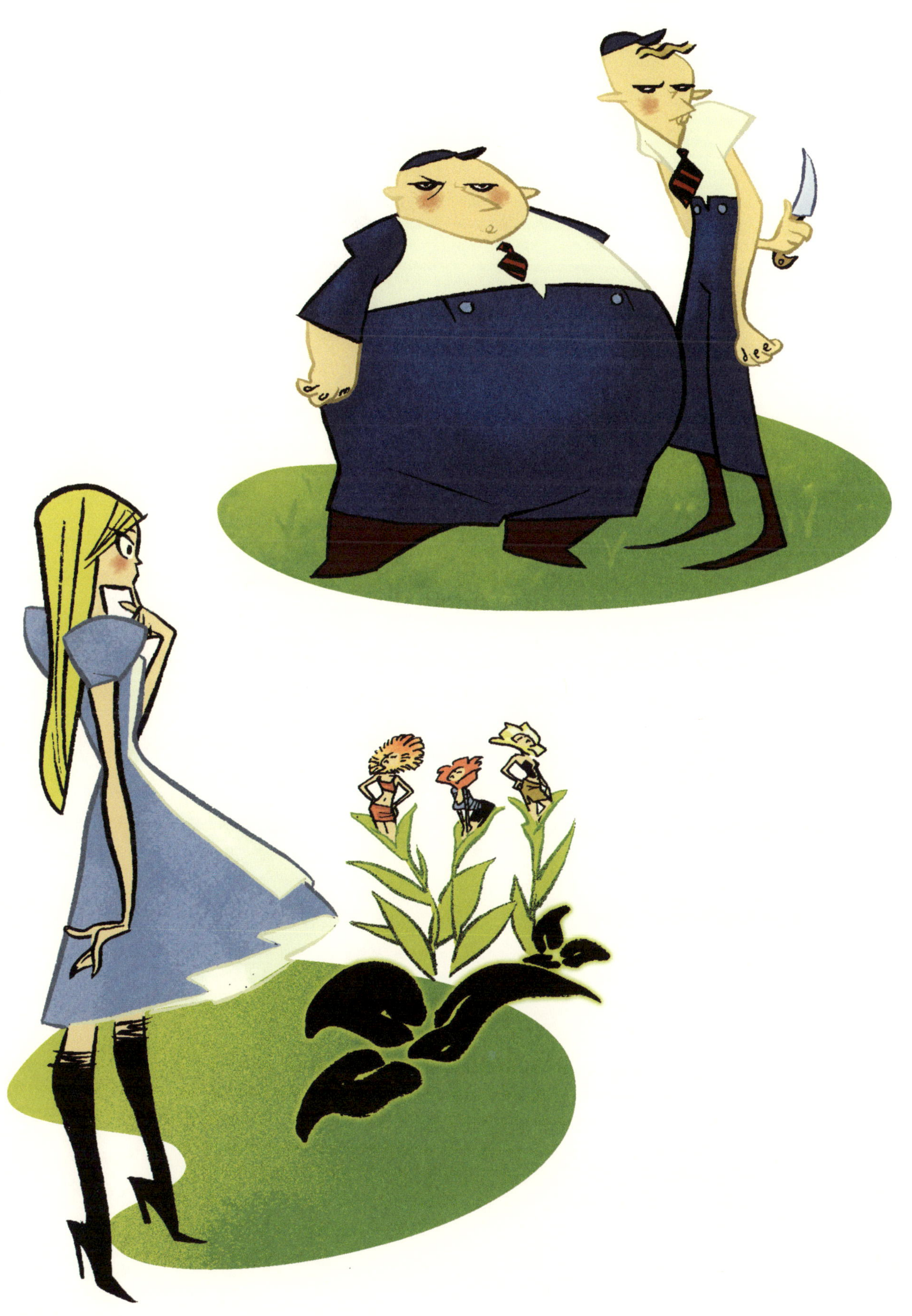
dum
dee

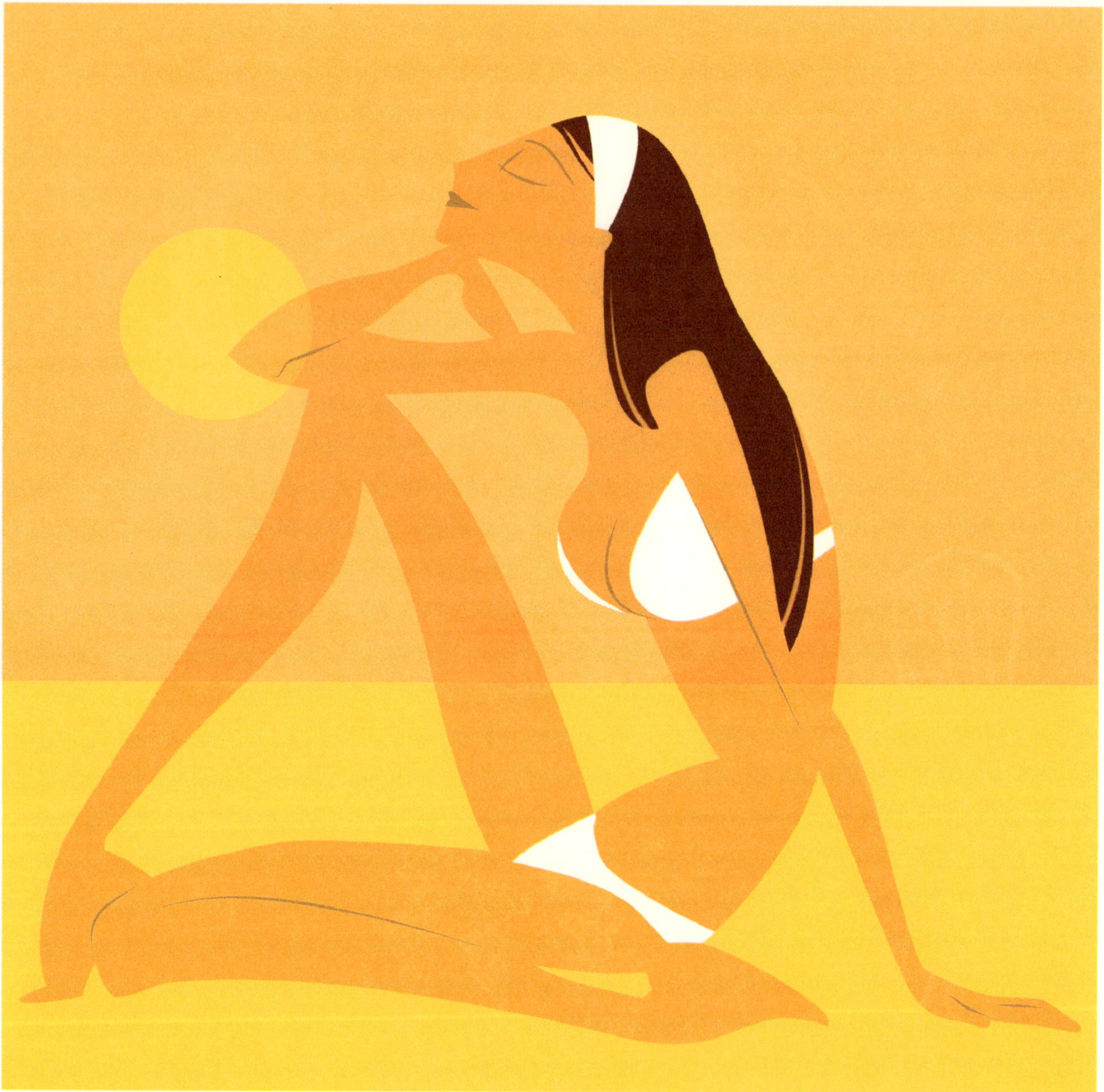

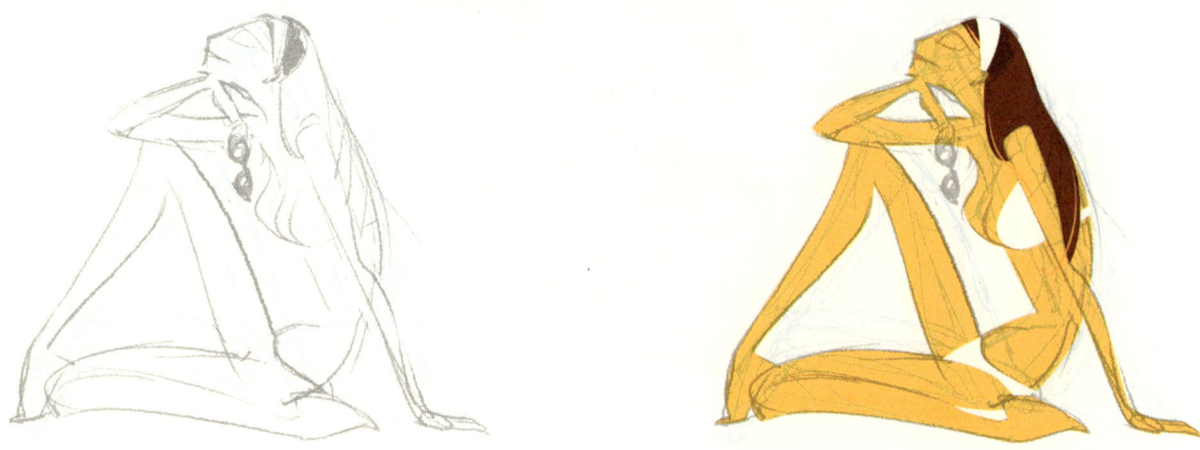

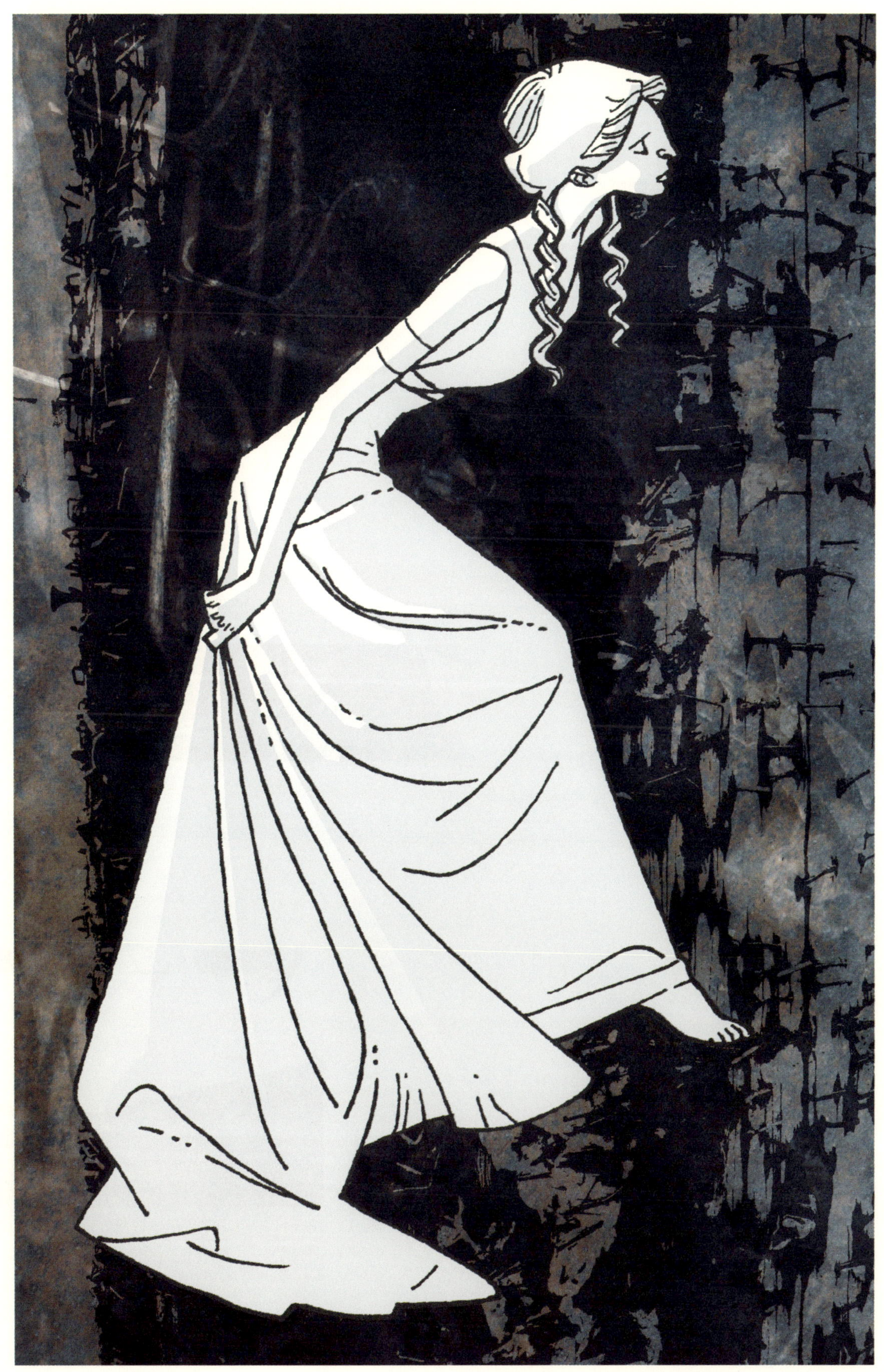

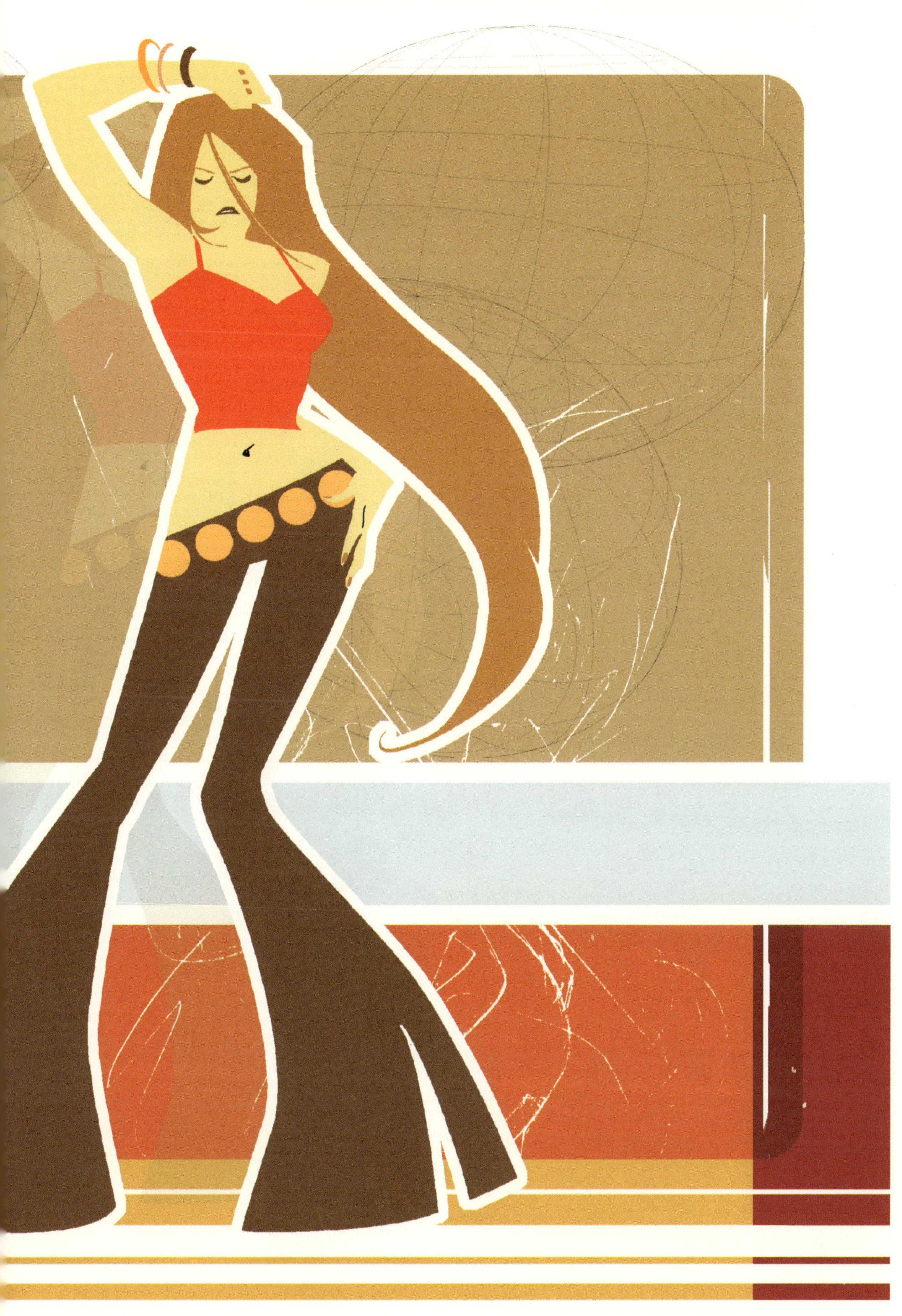

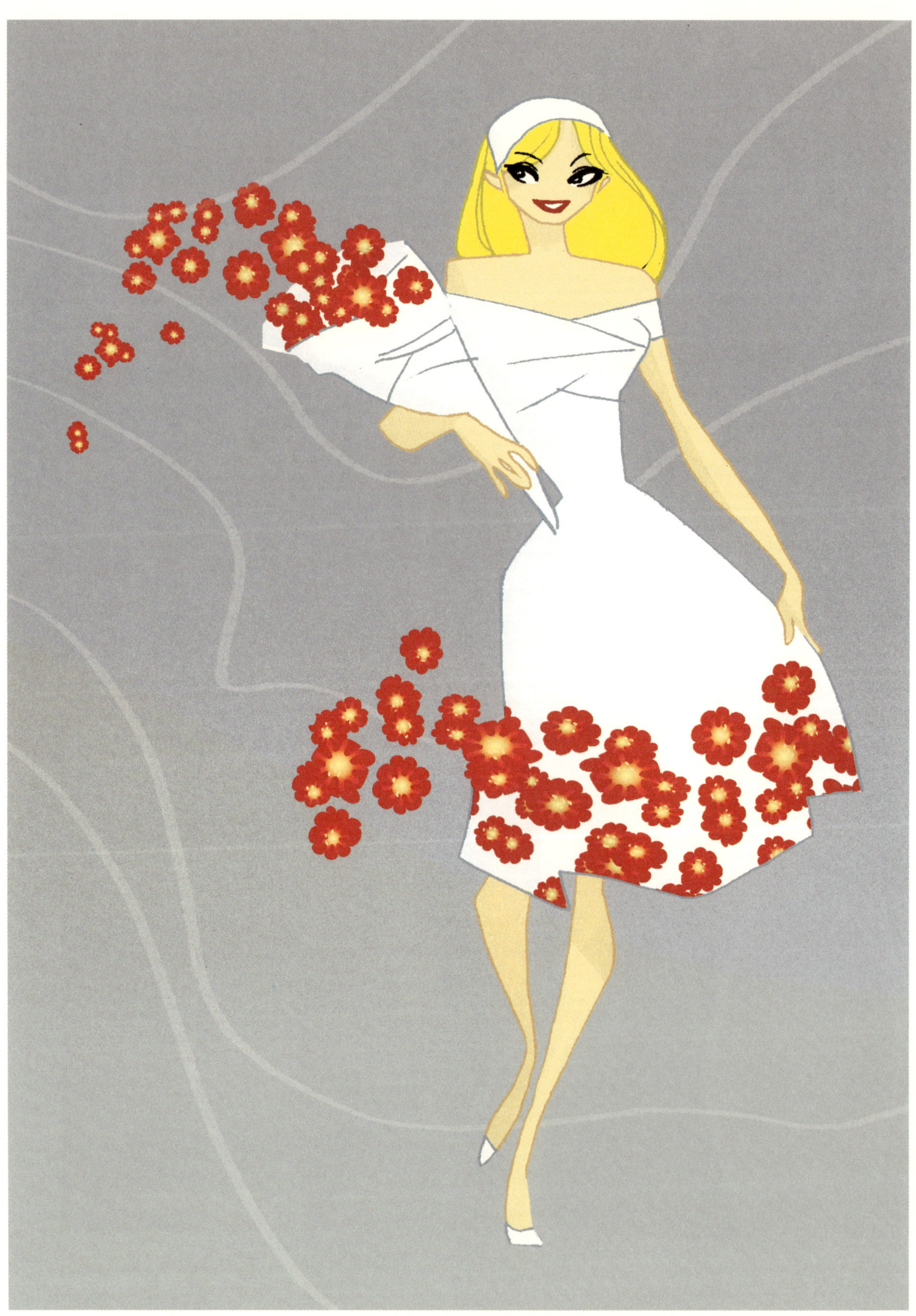

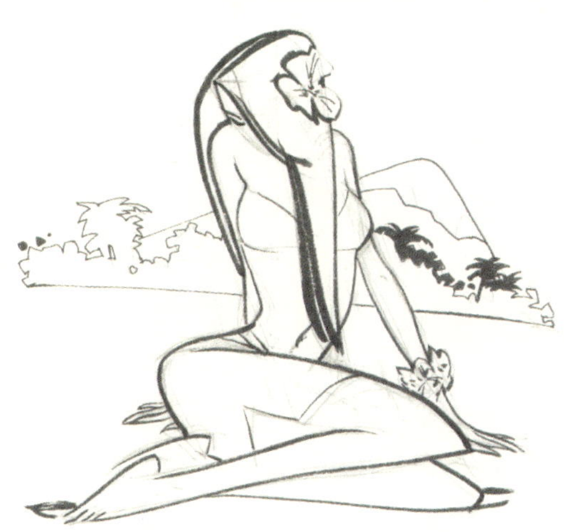

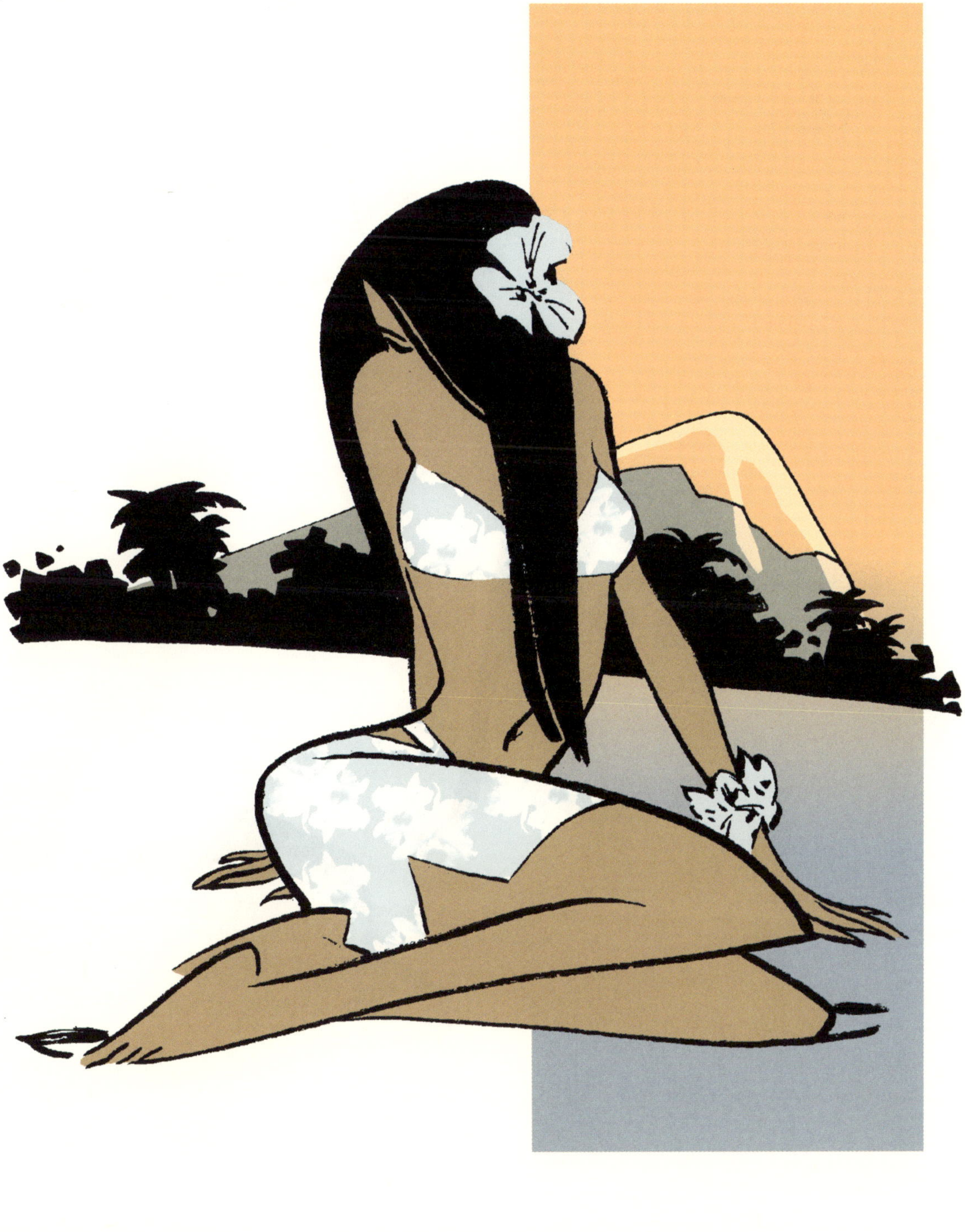

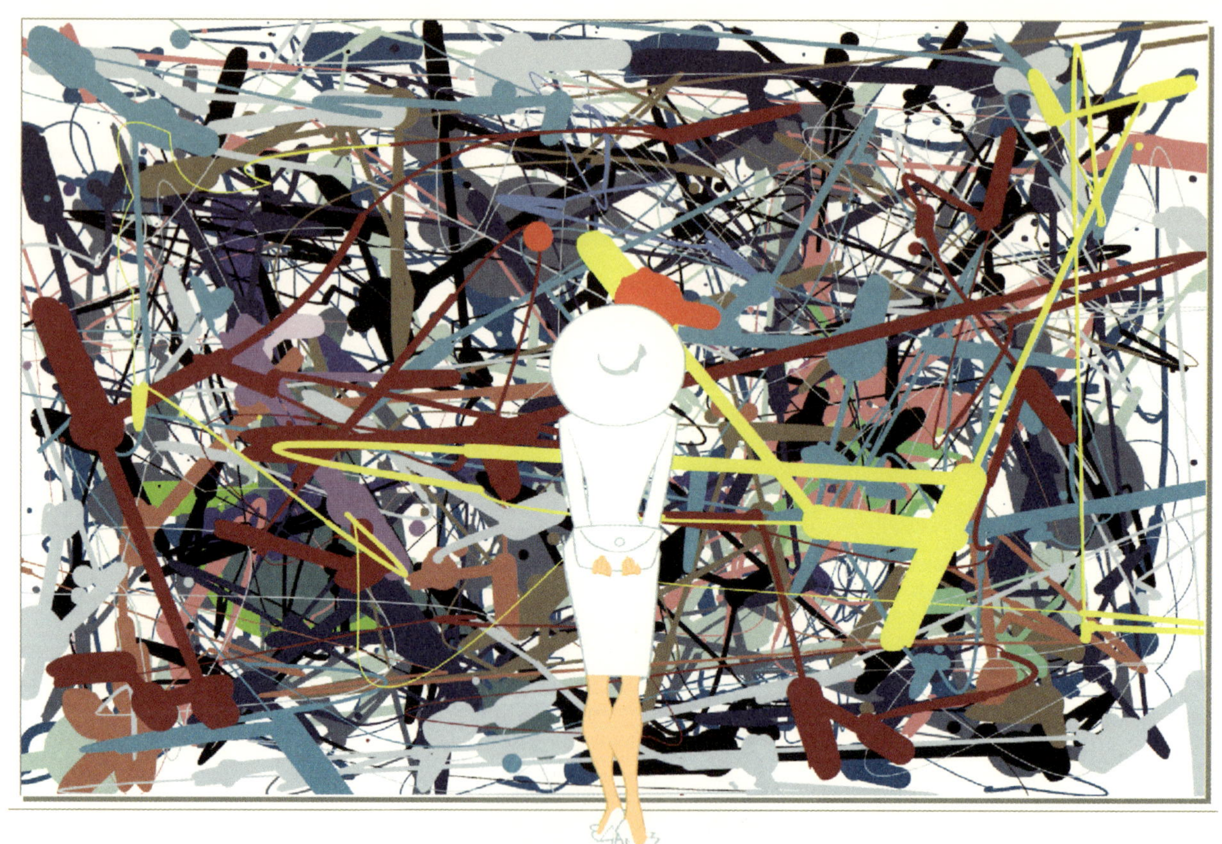

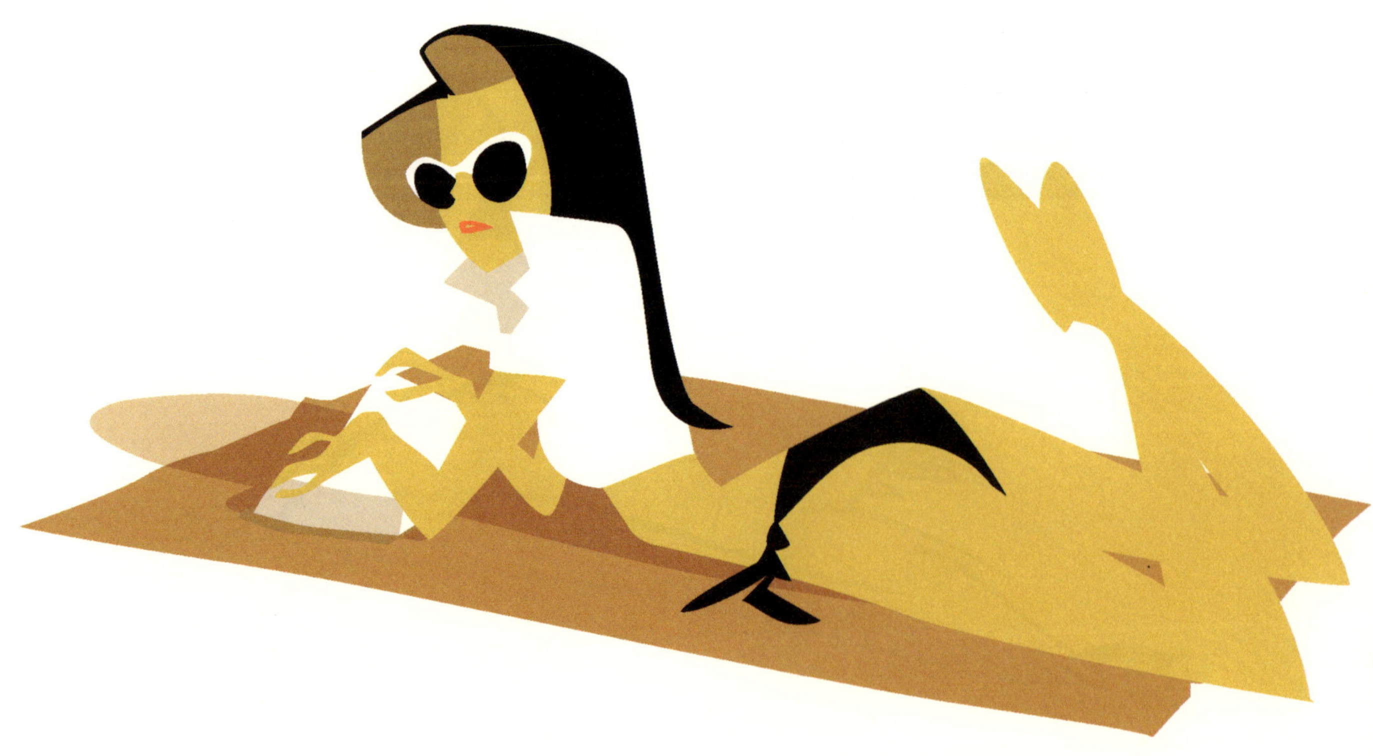

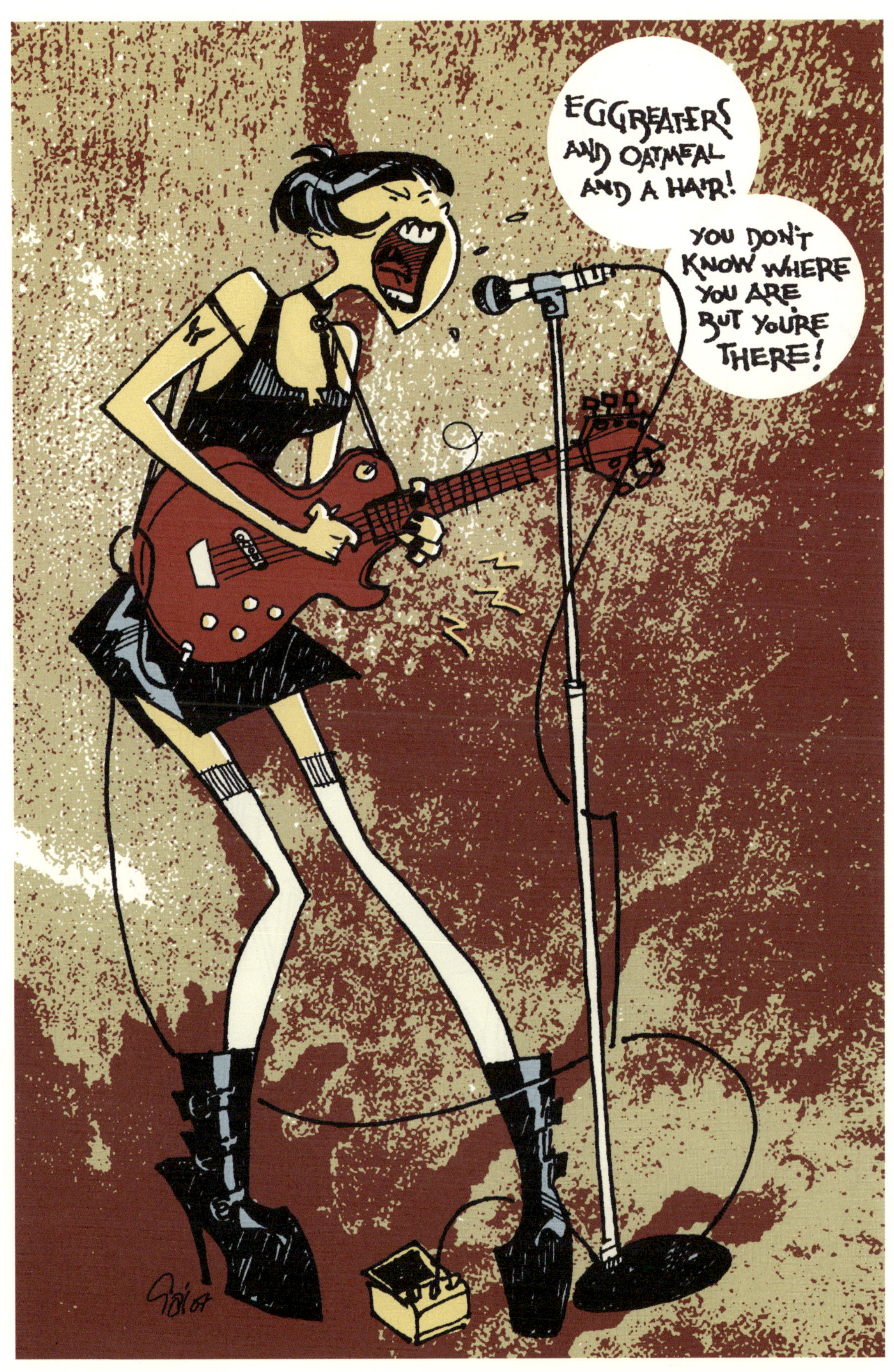
EGGREATERS AND OATMEAL AND A HAIR!
YOU DON'T KNOW WHERE YOU ARE BUT YOU'RE THERE!

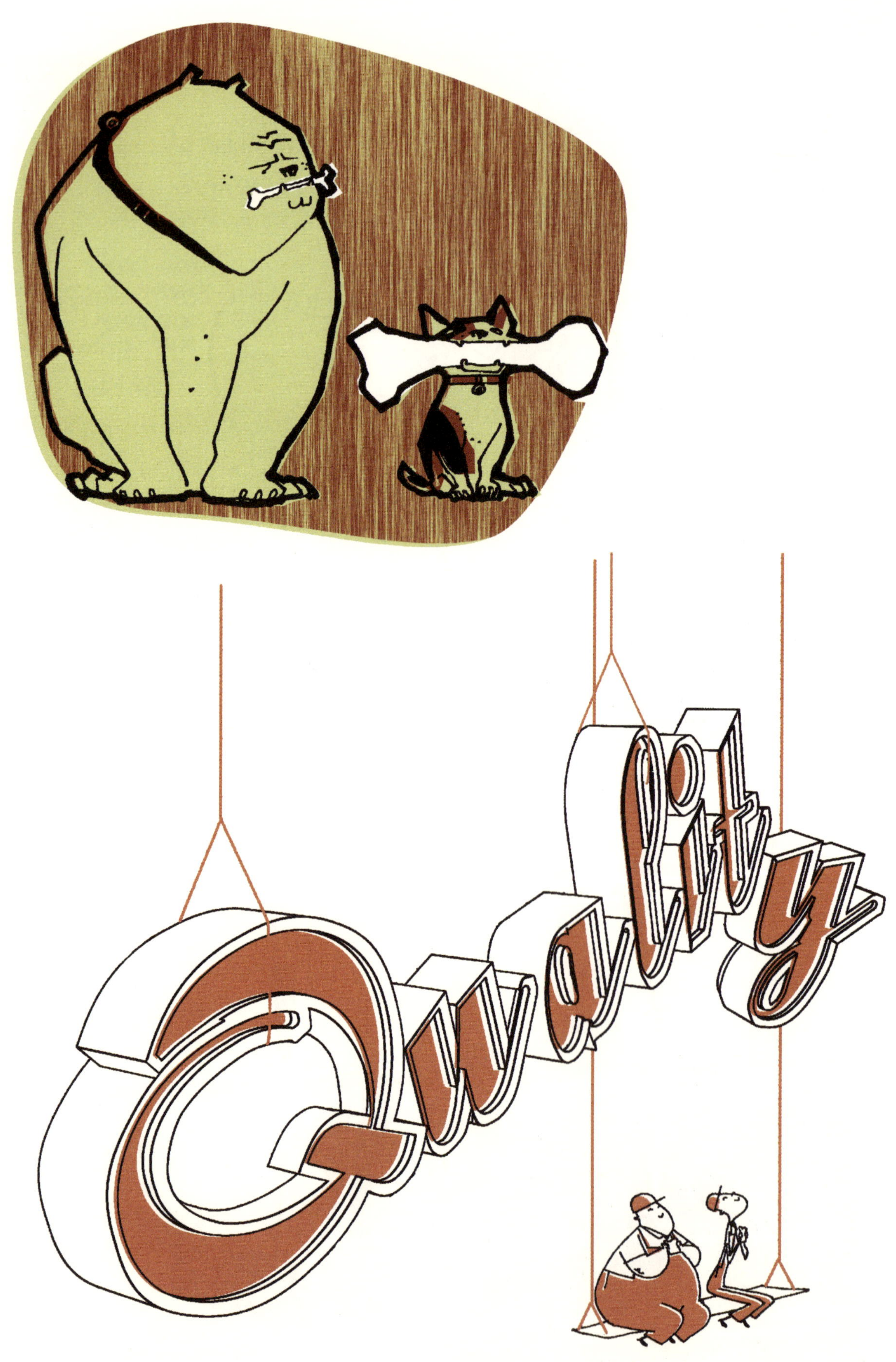
Quality

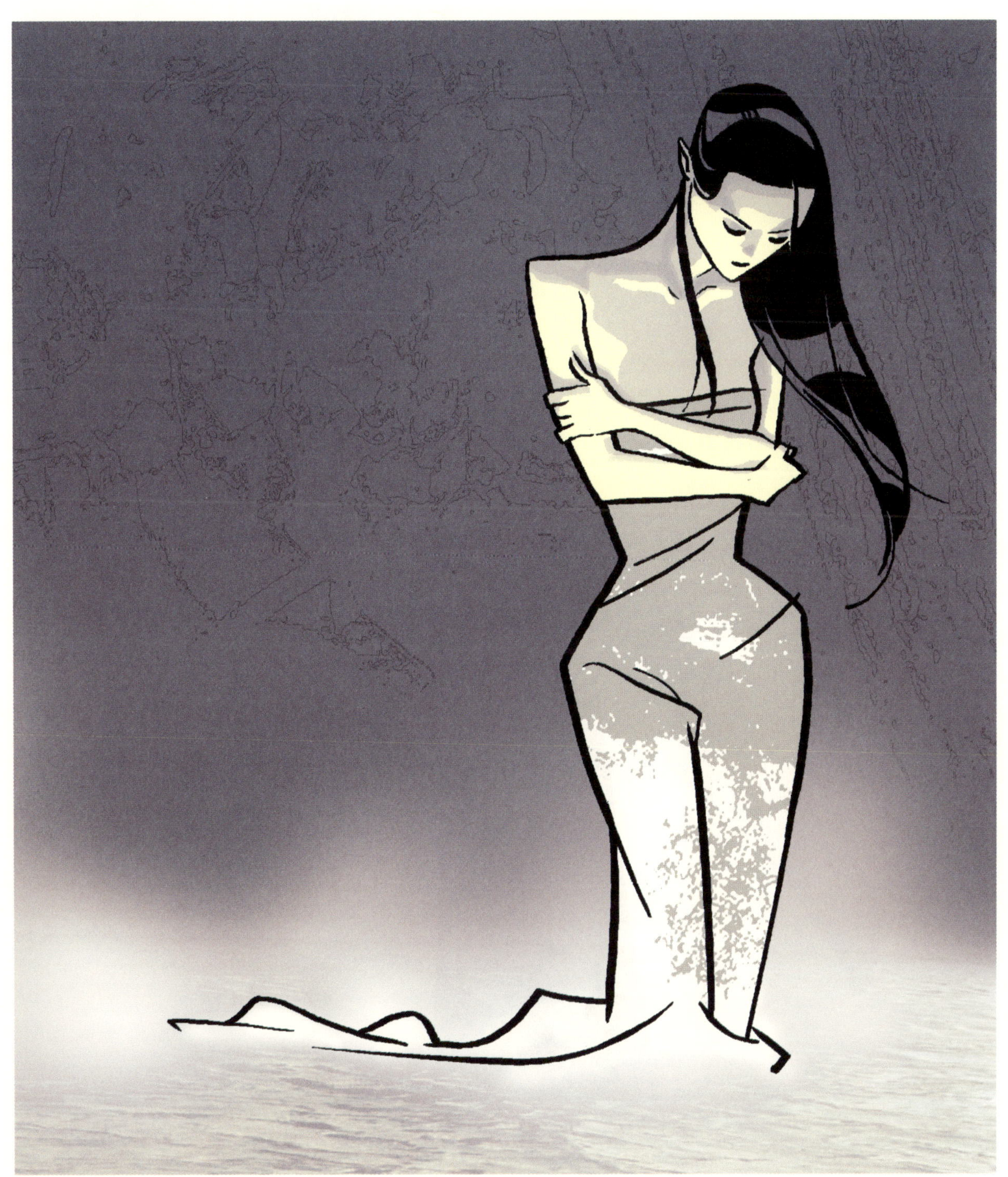

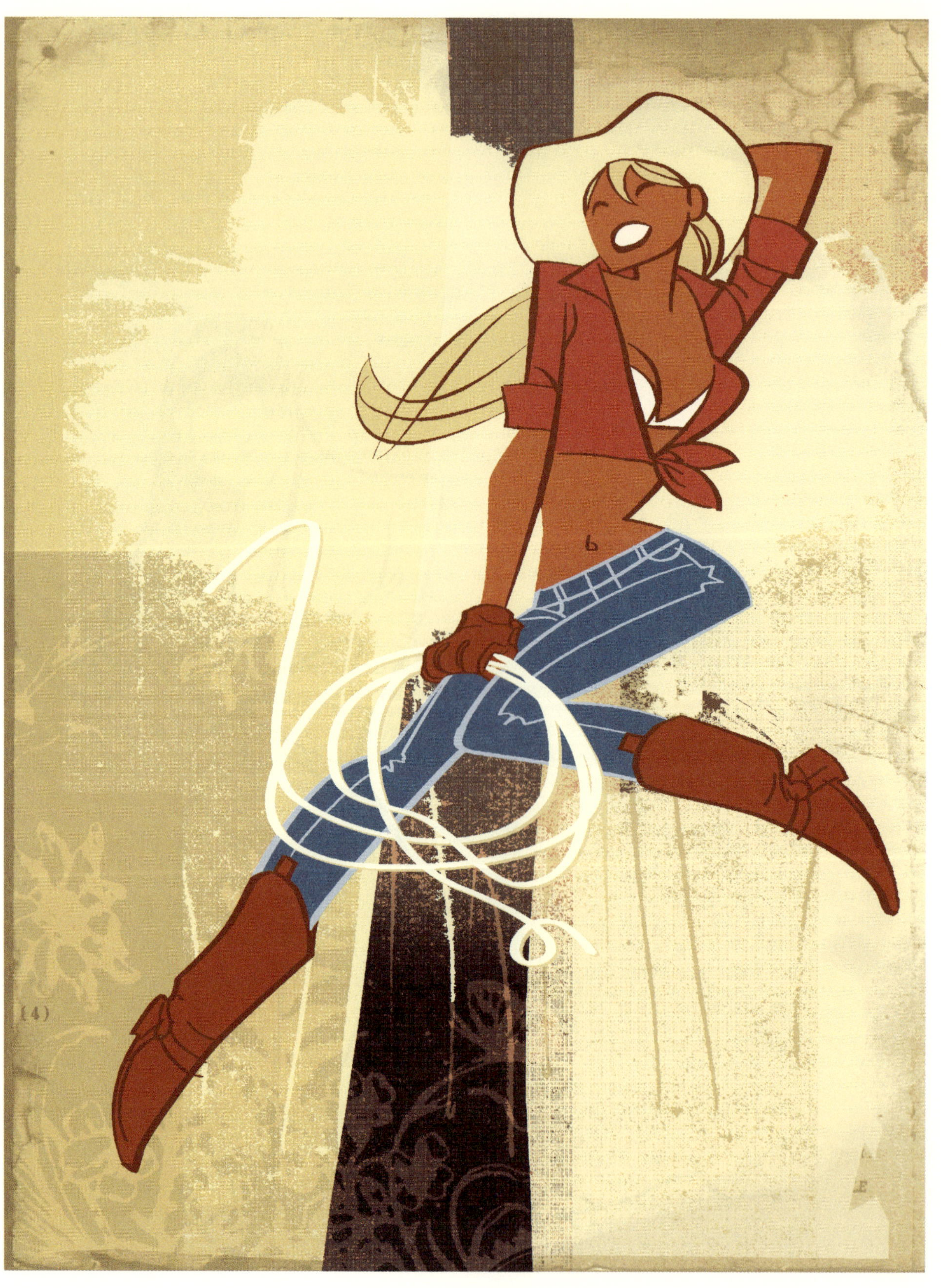

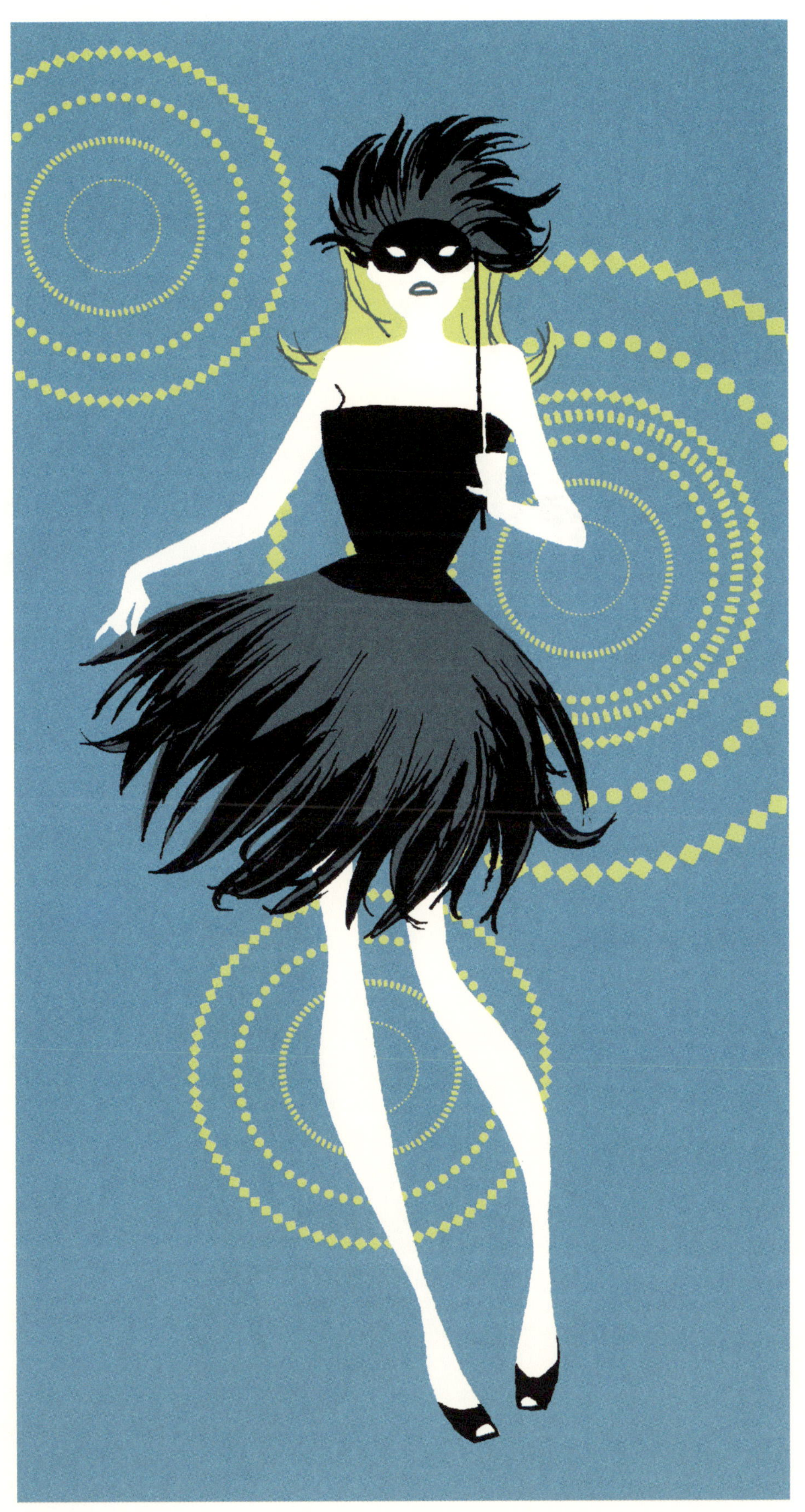

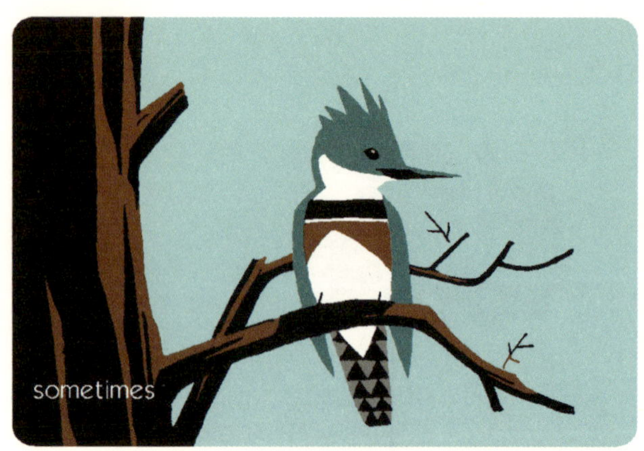
sometimes

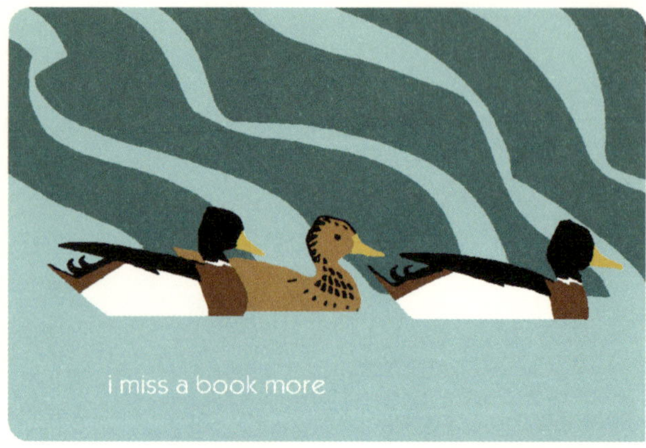
i miss a book more

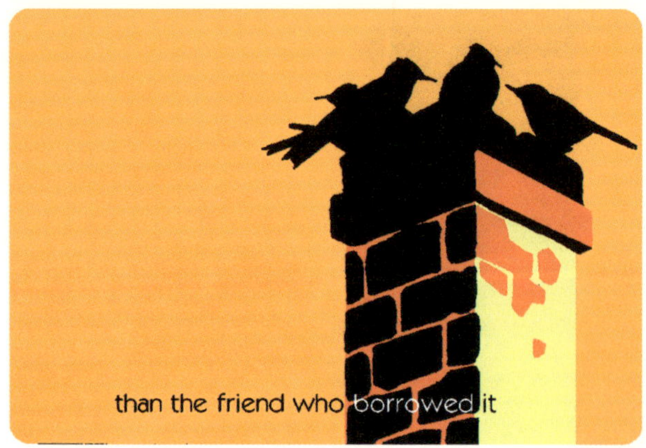
than the friend who borrowed it

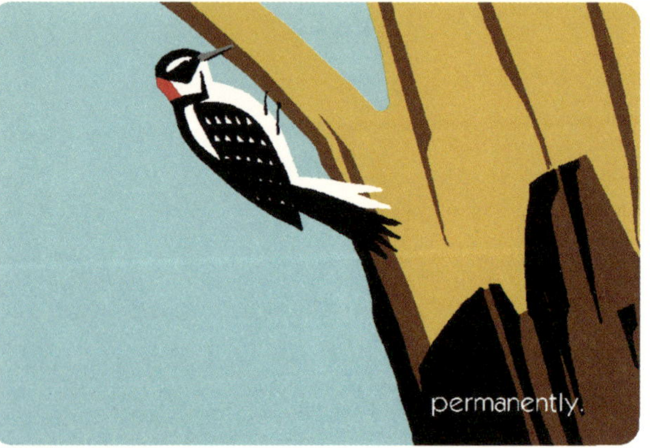
permanently.

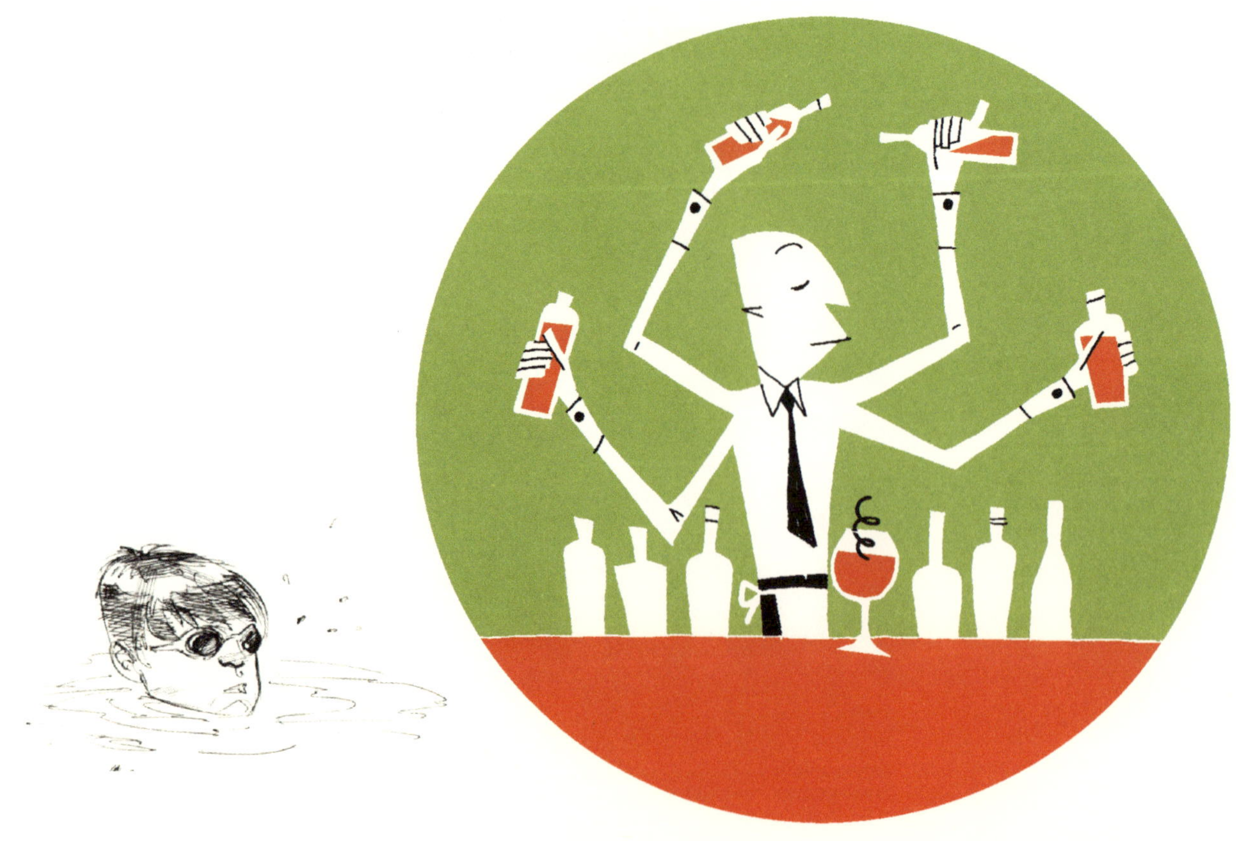

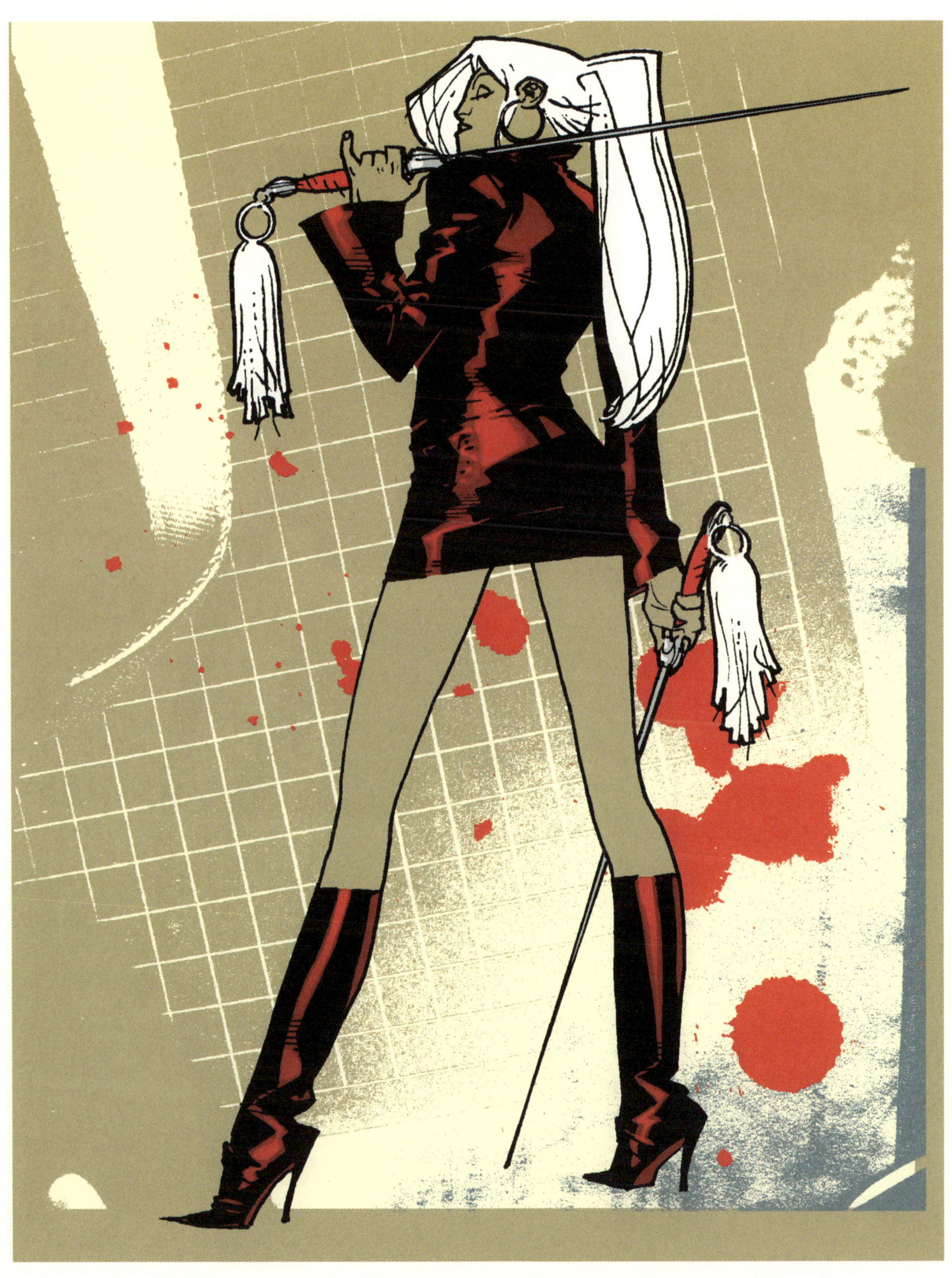

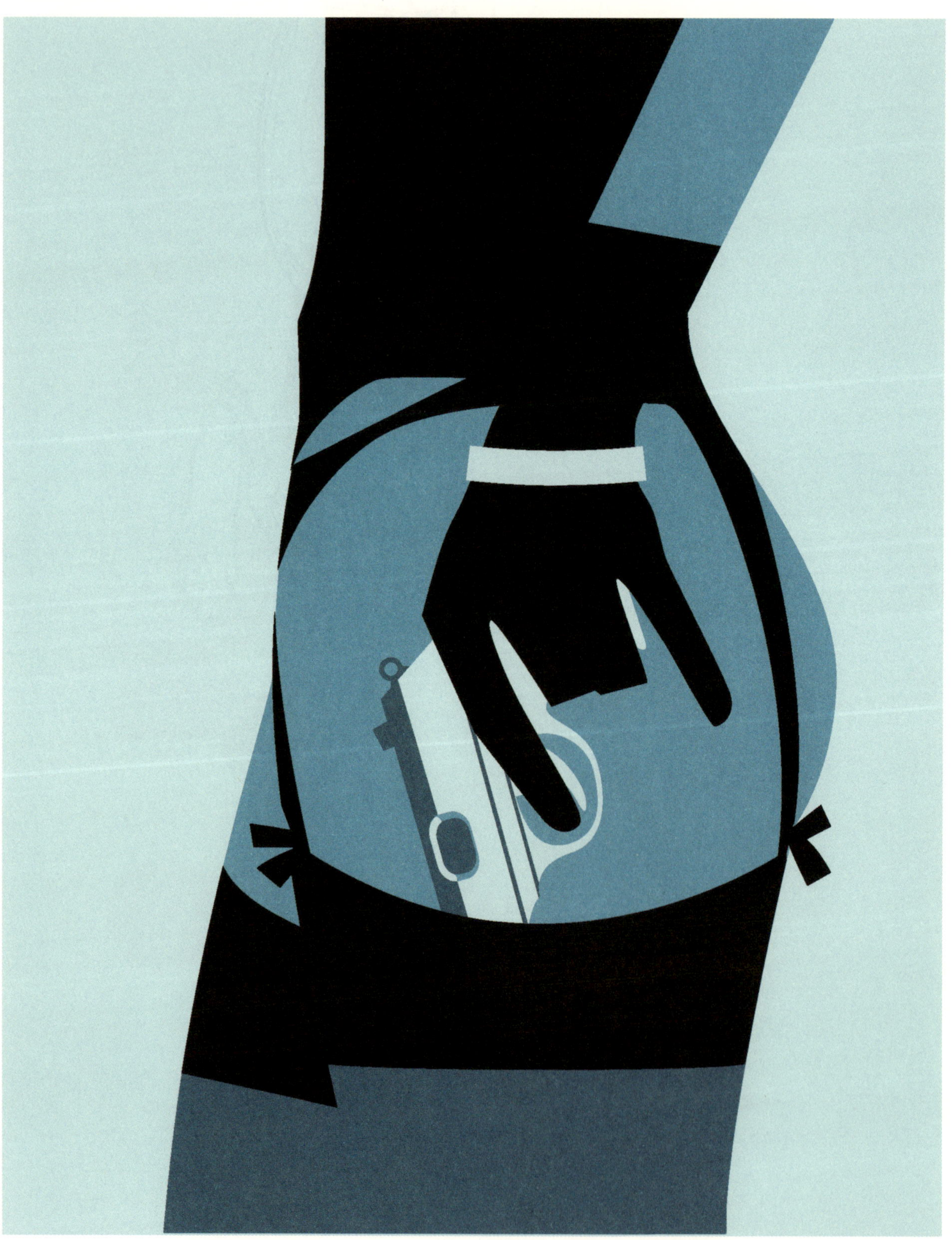

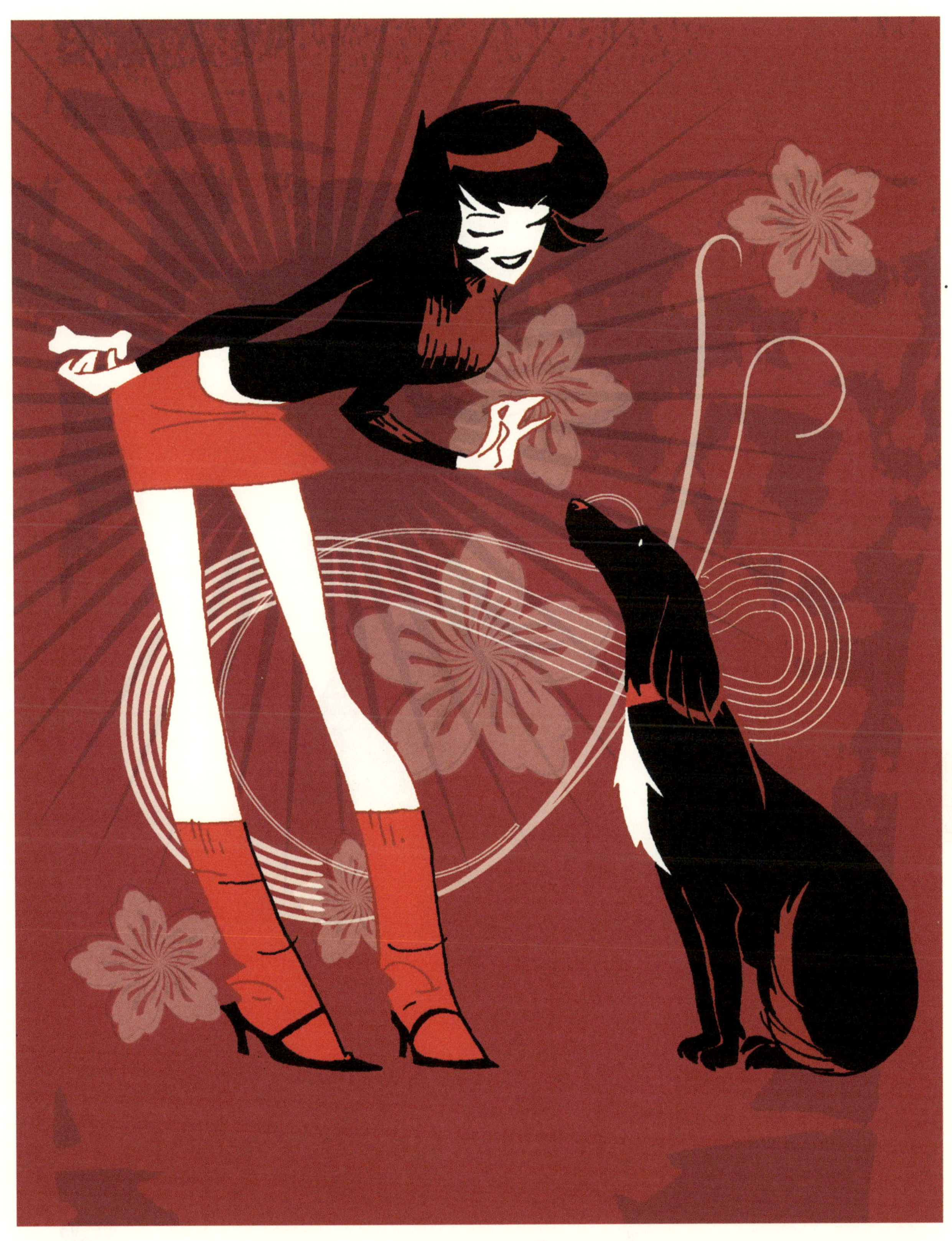

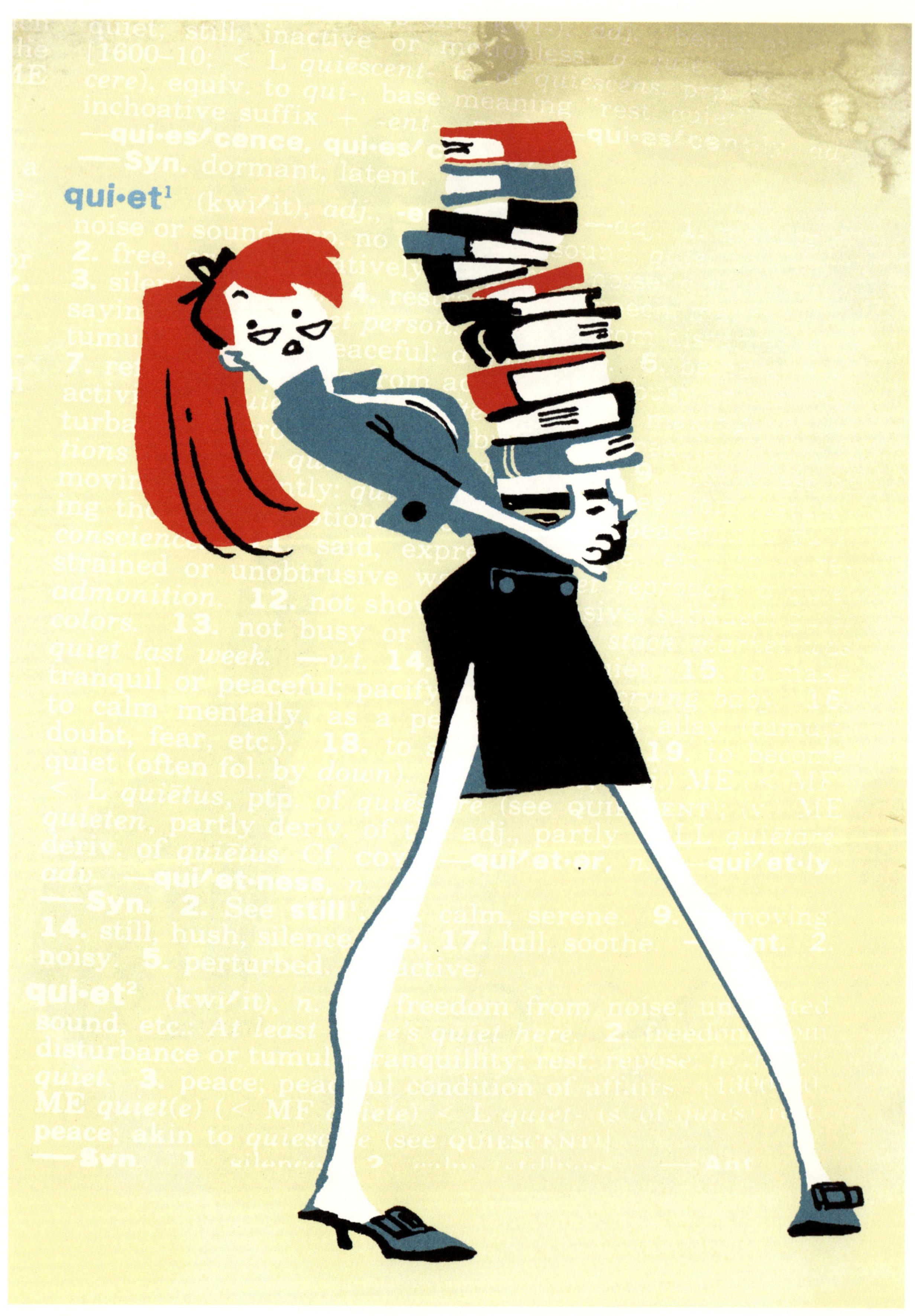
qui•et¹

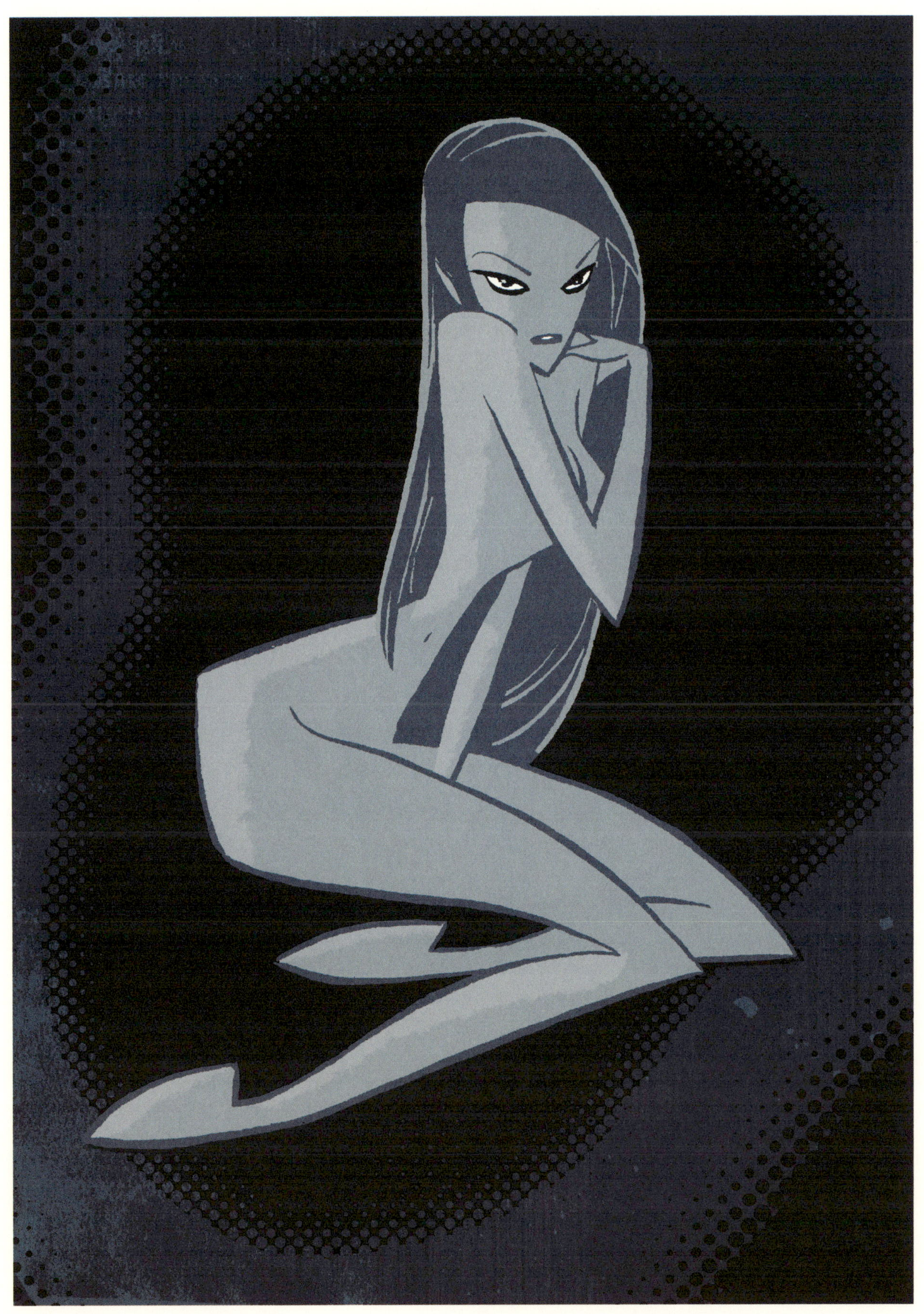

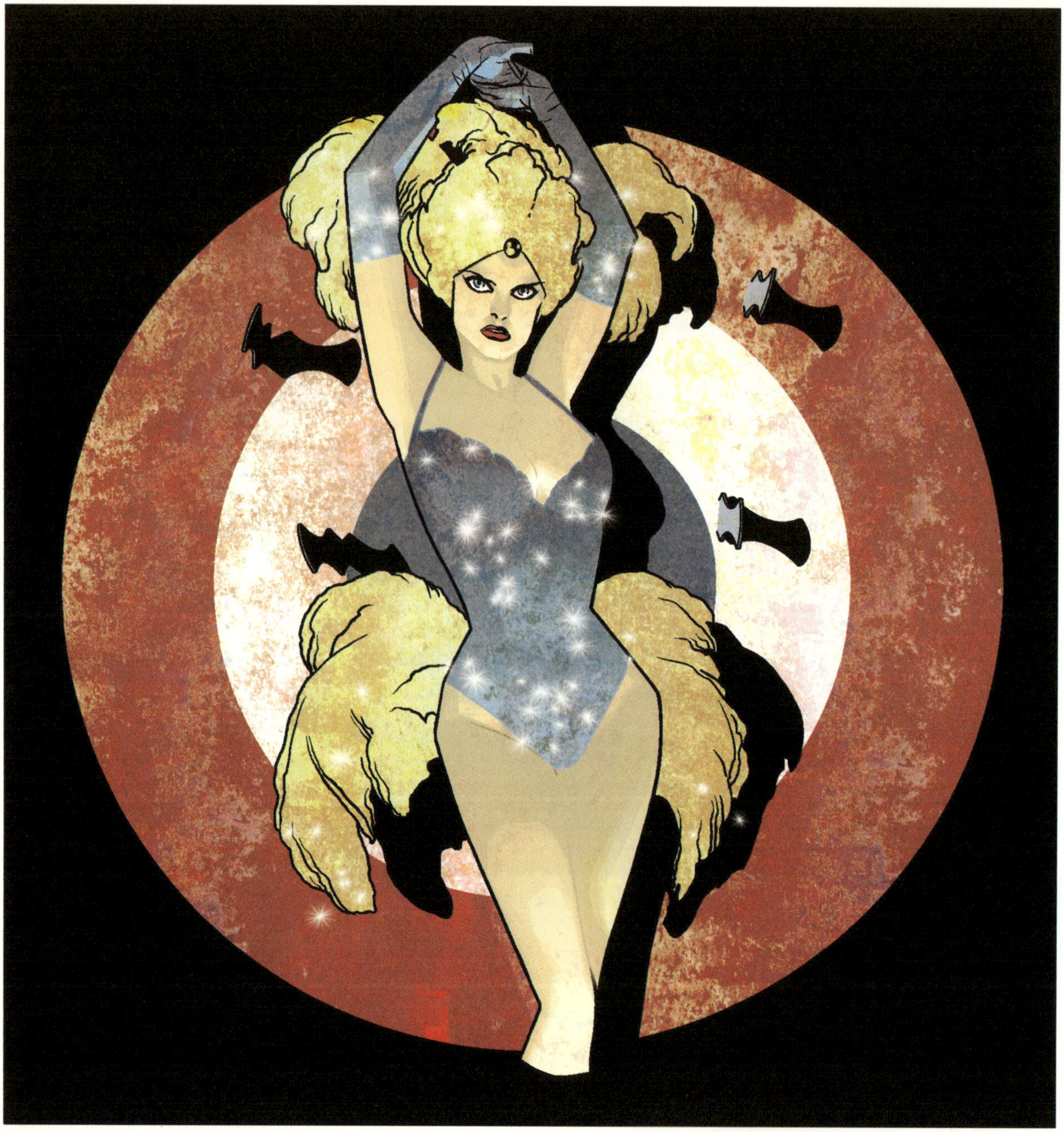

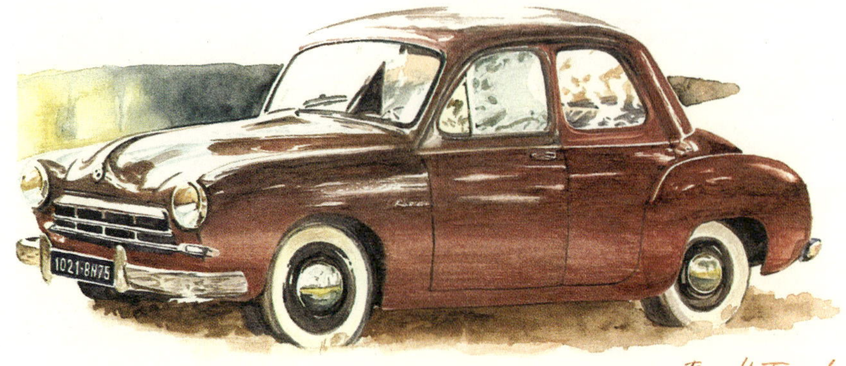
Renault Frégate

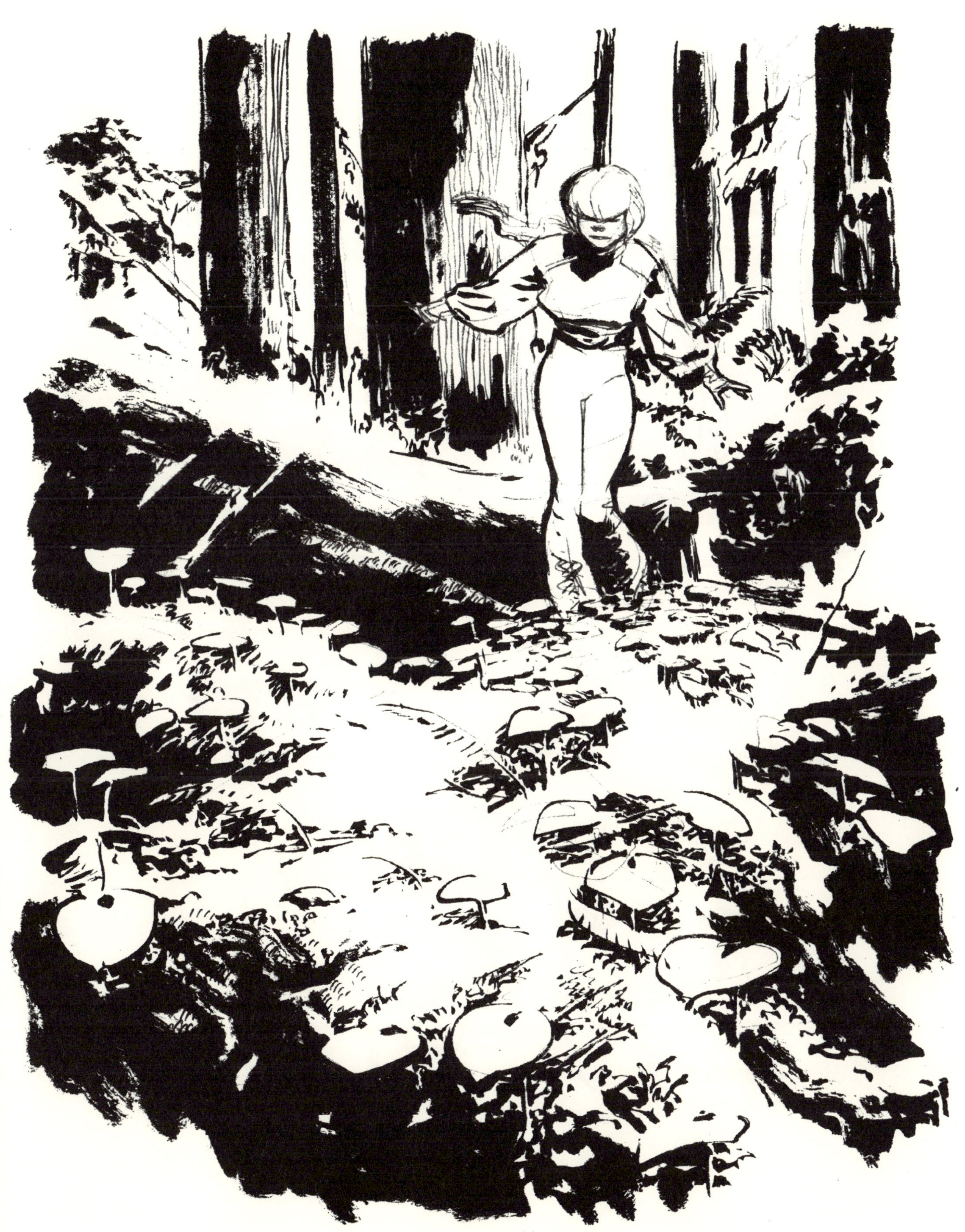

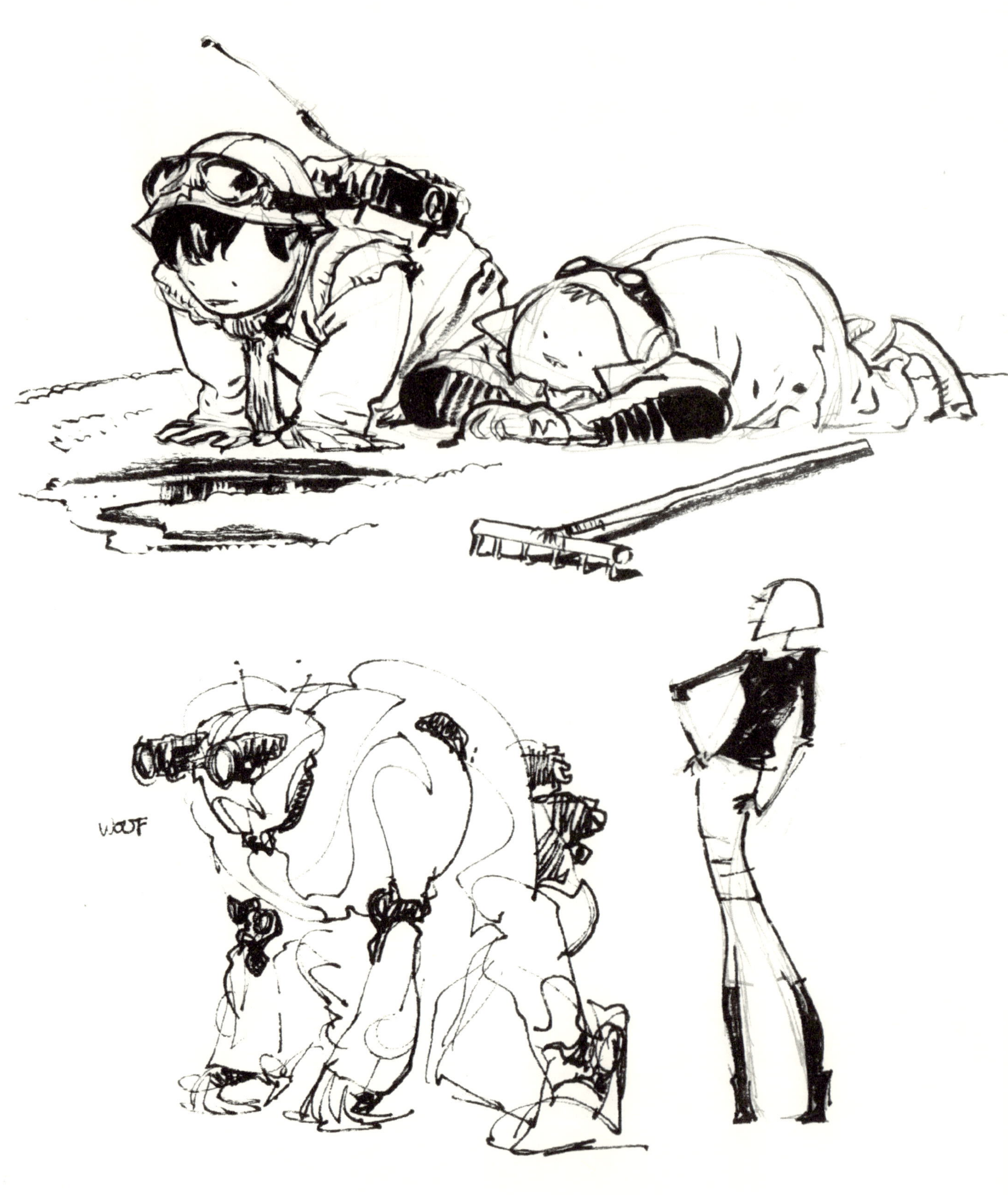
WOUF

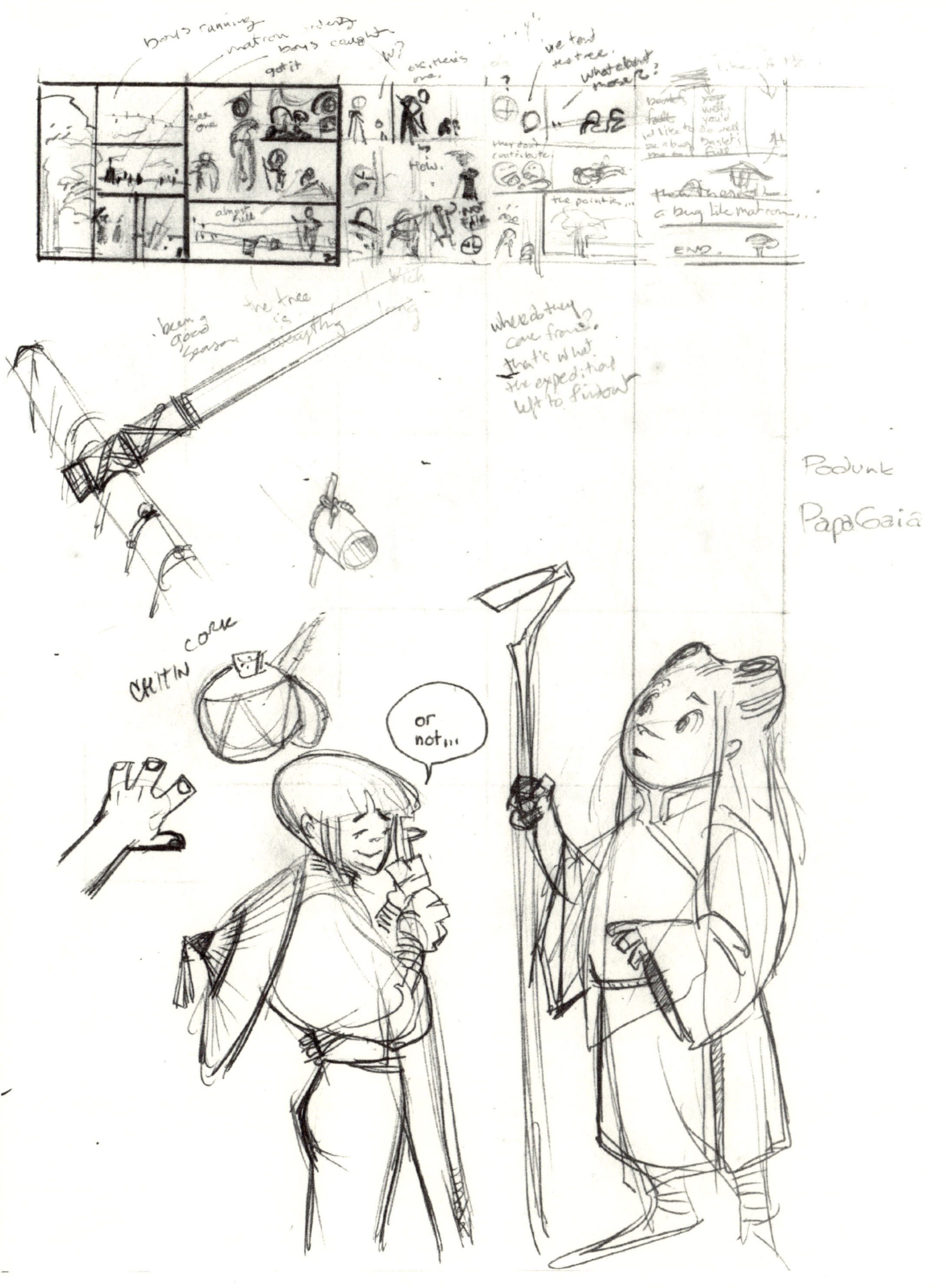
boys running
boys caught
got it
END.
where do they come from?
that's what the expedition left to find out
Podunk
PapaGaia
CHITIN CORK
or not...

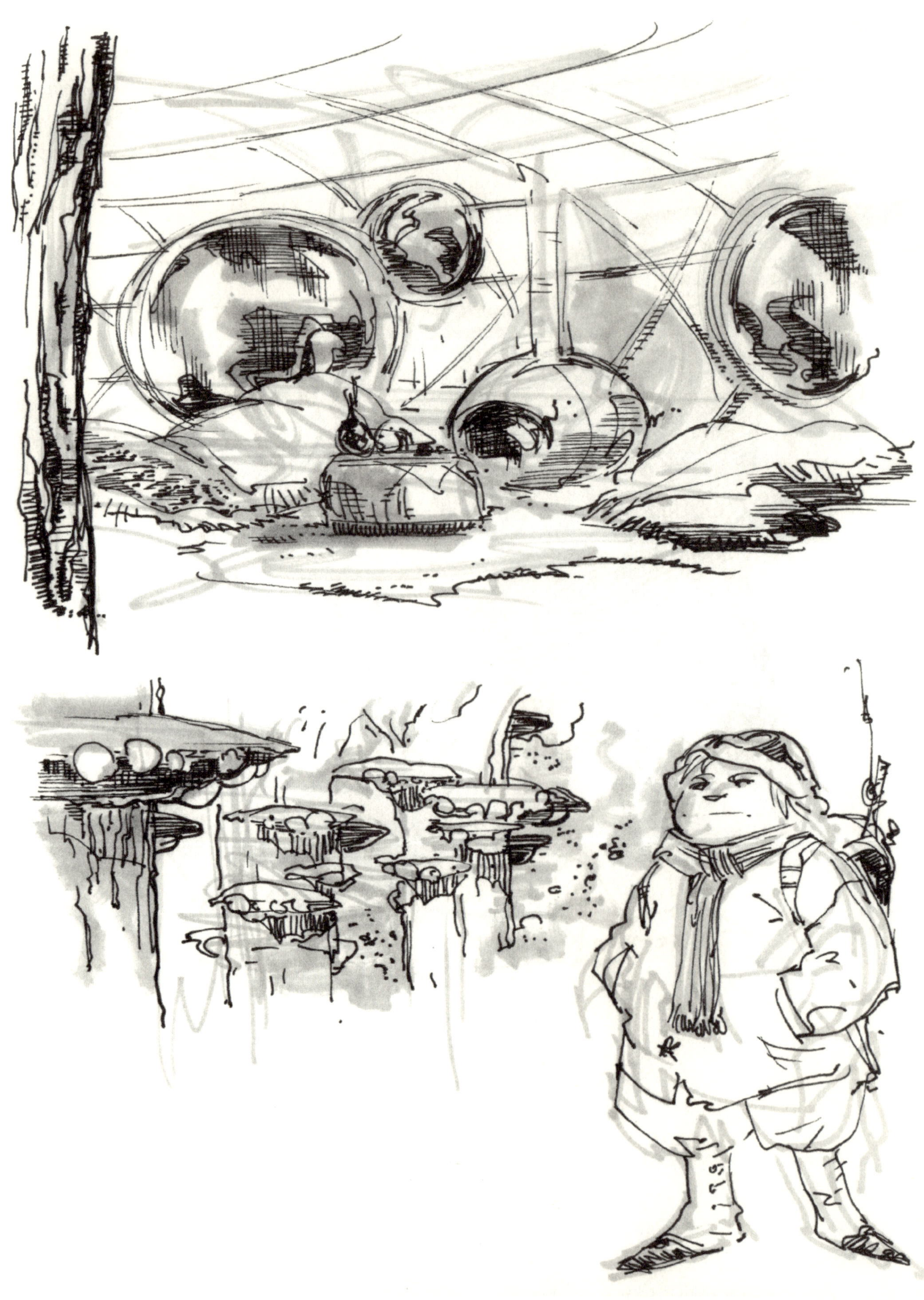

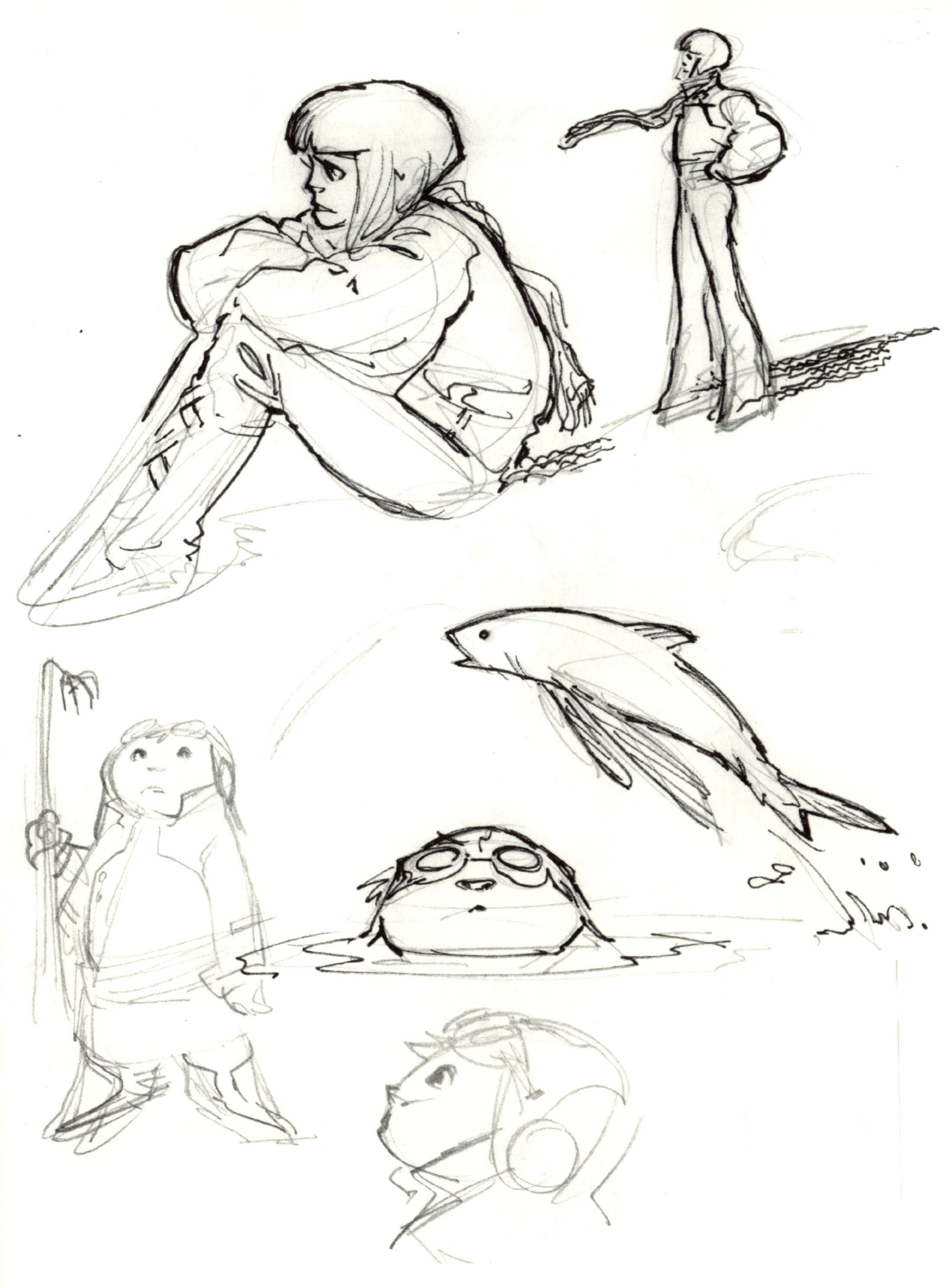

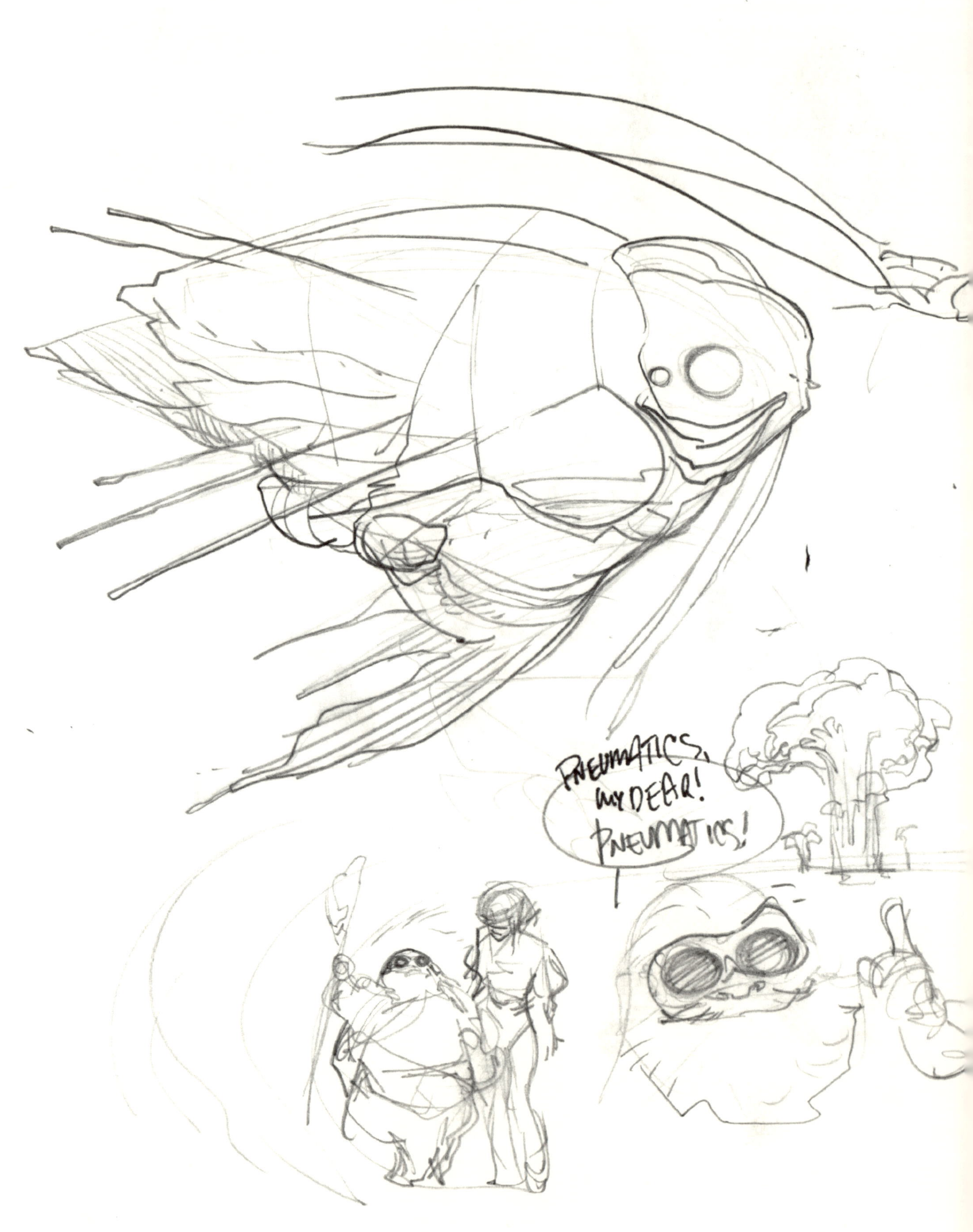
PNEUMATICS, MY DEAR! PNEUMATICS!

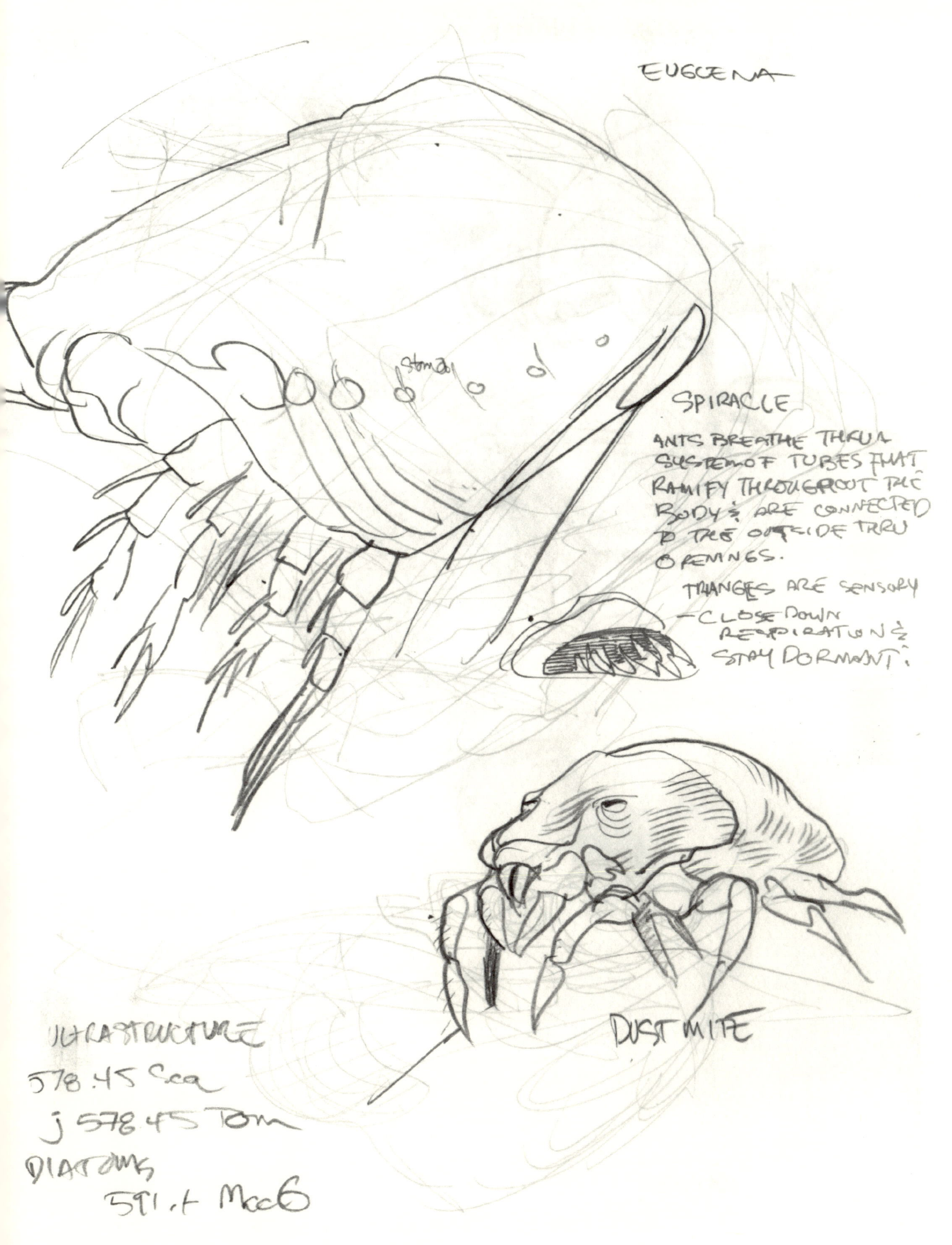
EUGLENA
SPIRACLE
ANTS BREATHE THRU A SYSTEM OF TUBES THAT RAMIFY THROUGHOUT THE BODY & ARE CONNECTED TO THE OUTSIDE THRU OPENINGS.
TRIANGLES ARE SENSORY
– CLOSE DOWN RESPIRATION & STAY DORMANT.
DUST MITE
ULTRASTRUCTURE
578.45 Sea
j 578.45 Tom
DIATOMS
591.4 Mac6

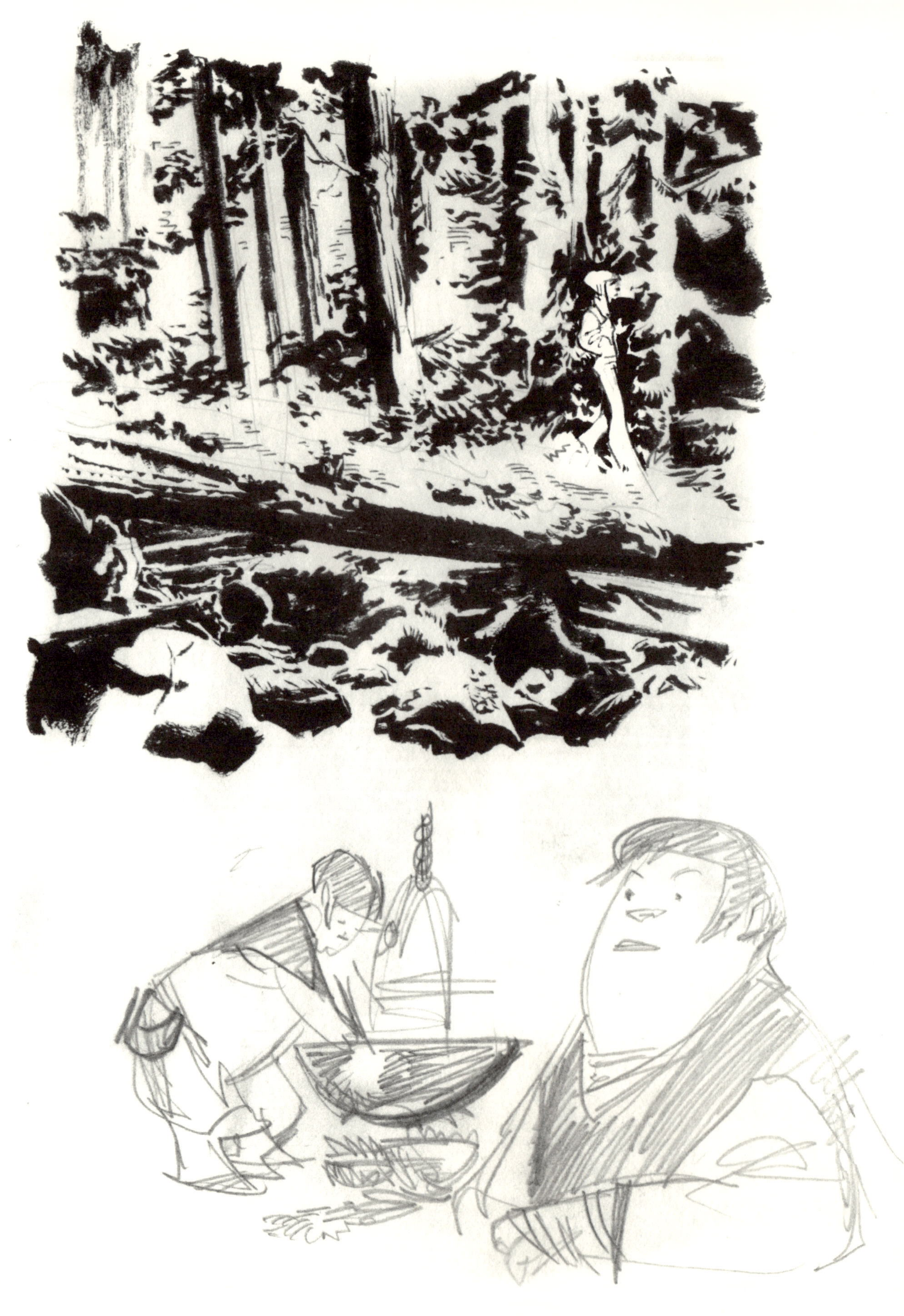

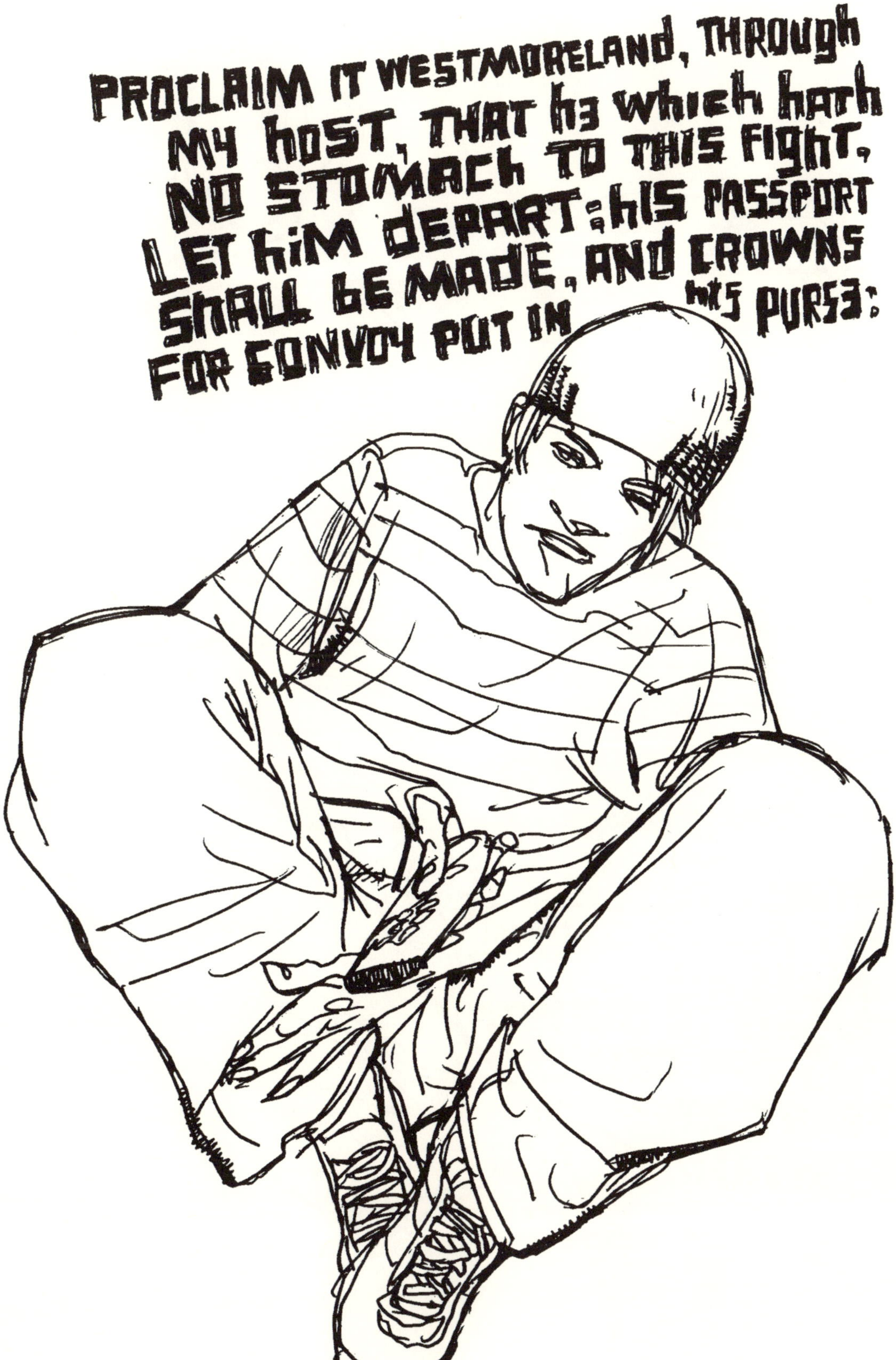

PROCLAIM IT WESTMORELAND, THROUGH
MY HOST, THAT HE WHICH HATH
NO STOMACH TO THIS FIGHT,
LET HIM DEPART; HIS PASSPORT
SHALL BE MADE, AND CROWNS
FOR CONVOY PUT IN HIS PURSE;

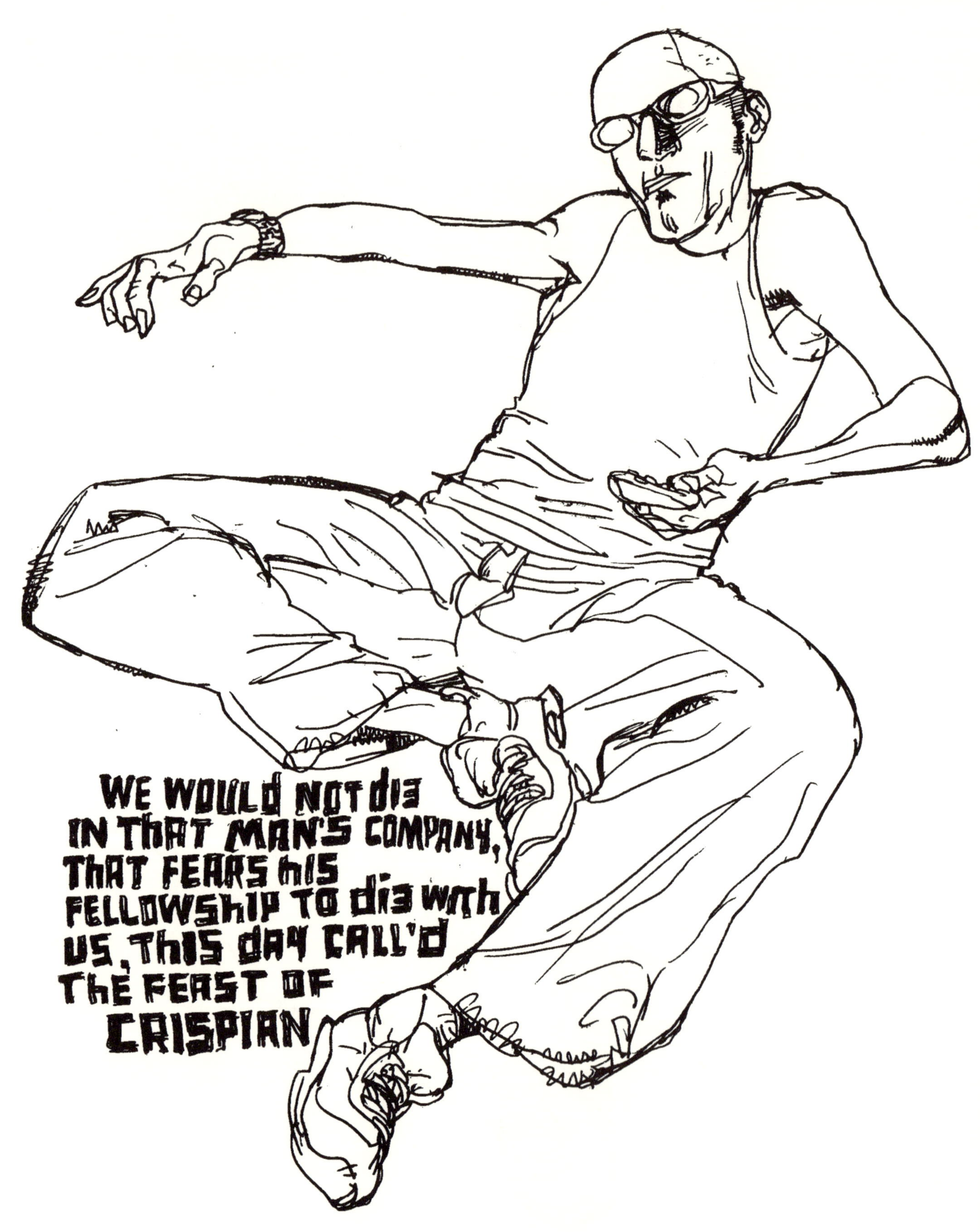
WE WOULD NOT DIE
IN THAT MAN'S COMPANY,
THAT FEARS HIS
FELLOWSHIP TO DIE WITH
US, THIS DAY CALL'D
THE FEAST OF
CRISPIAN

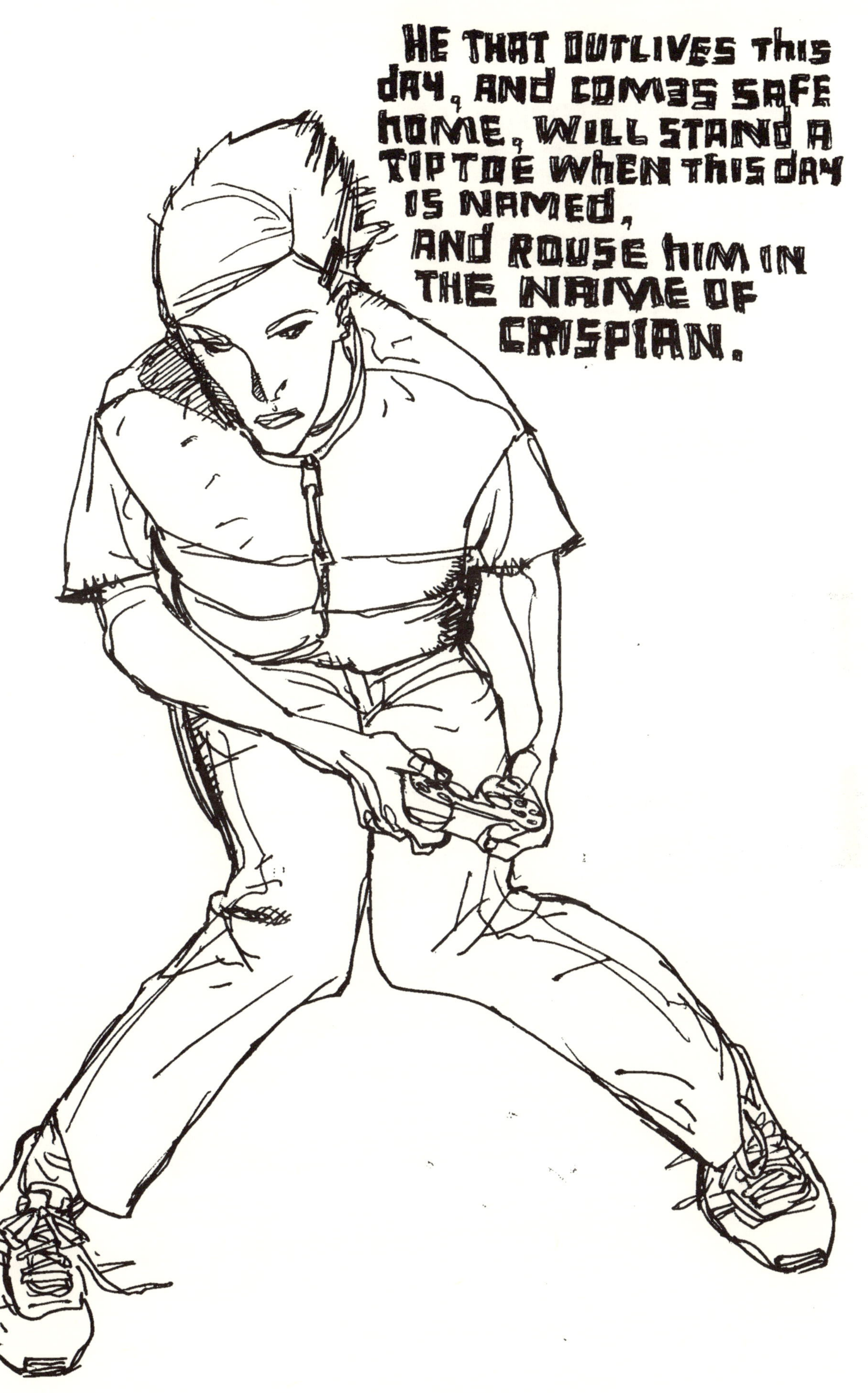
HE THAT OUTLIVES this day, AND COMES SAFE home, WILL STAND A TIPTOE WHEN THIS DAY IS NAMED,
AND ROUSE him IN THE NAME OF CRISPIAN.

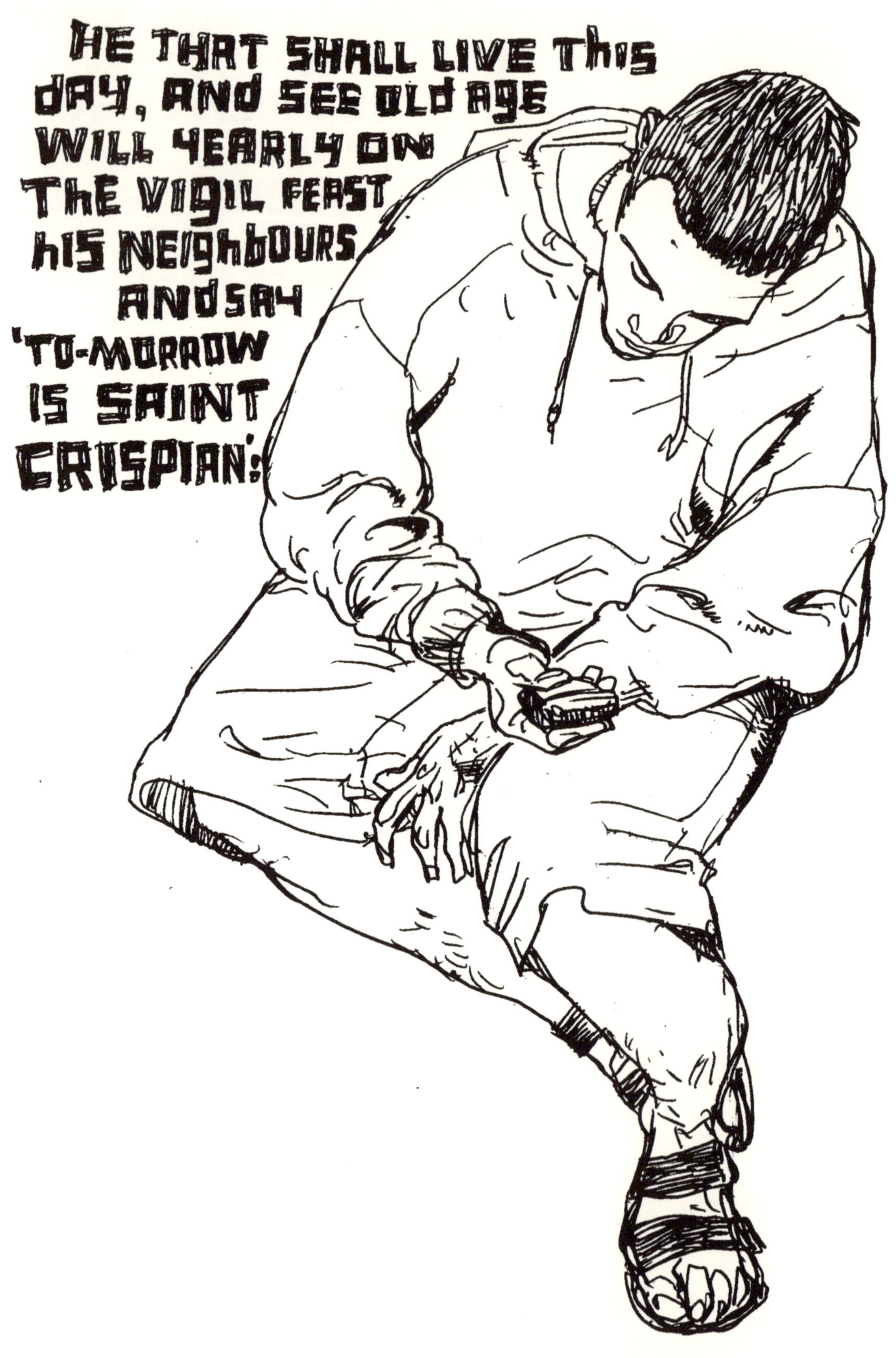
HE THAT SHALL LIVE THIS
DAY, AND SEE OLD AGE
WILL YEARLY ON
THE VIGIL FEAST
HIS NEIGHBOURS
AND SAY
'TO-MORROW
IS SAINT
CRISPIAN':

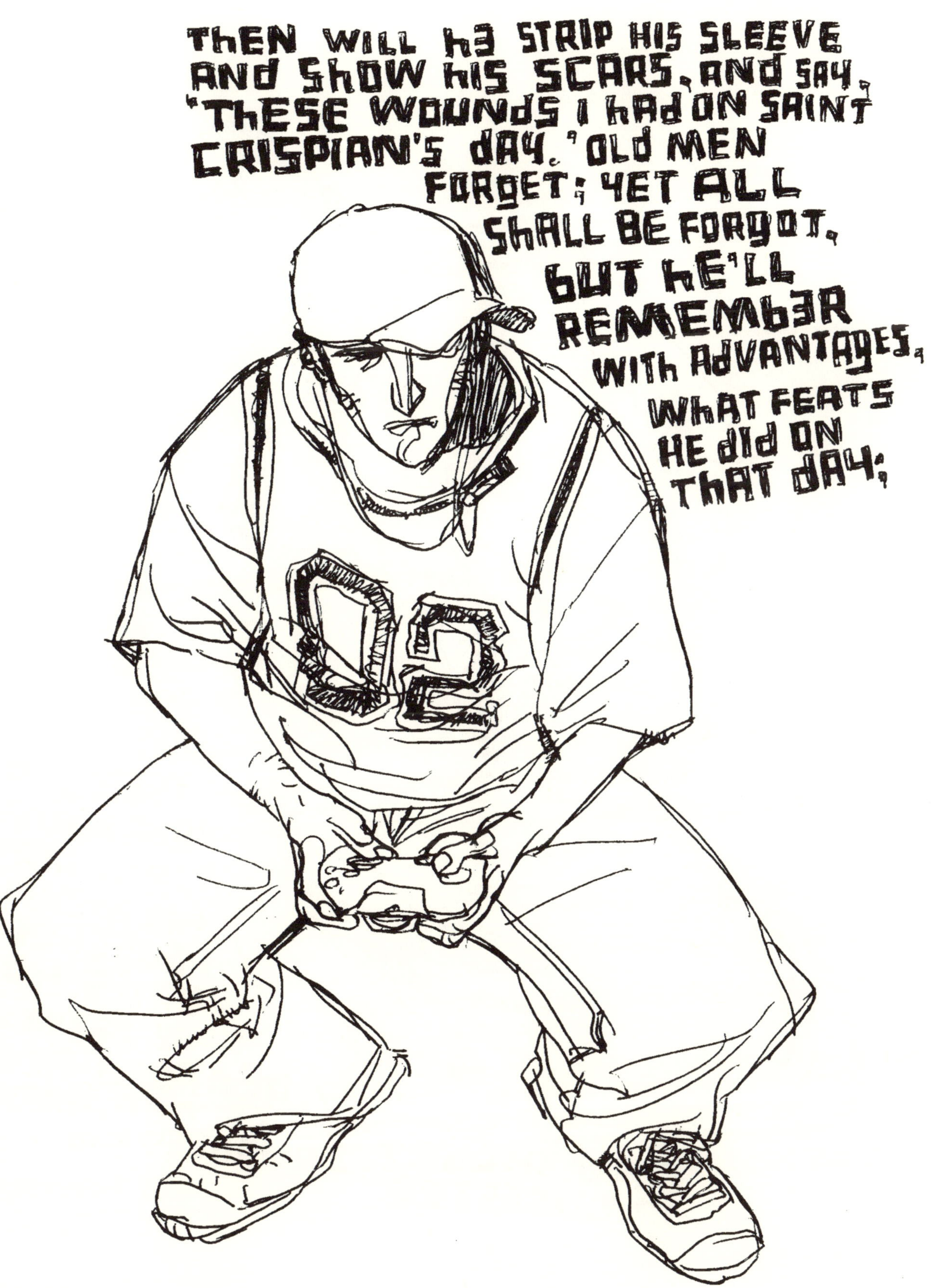
THEN WILL HE STRIP HIS SLEEVE
AND SHOW HIS SCARS, AND SAY,
"THESE WOUNDS I HAD ON SAINT
CRISPIAN'S DAY.' OLD MEN
FORGET; YET ALL
SHALL BE FORGOT,
BUT HE'LL
REMEMBER
WITH ADVANTAGES,
WHAT FEATS
HE DID ON
THAT DAY;

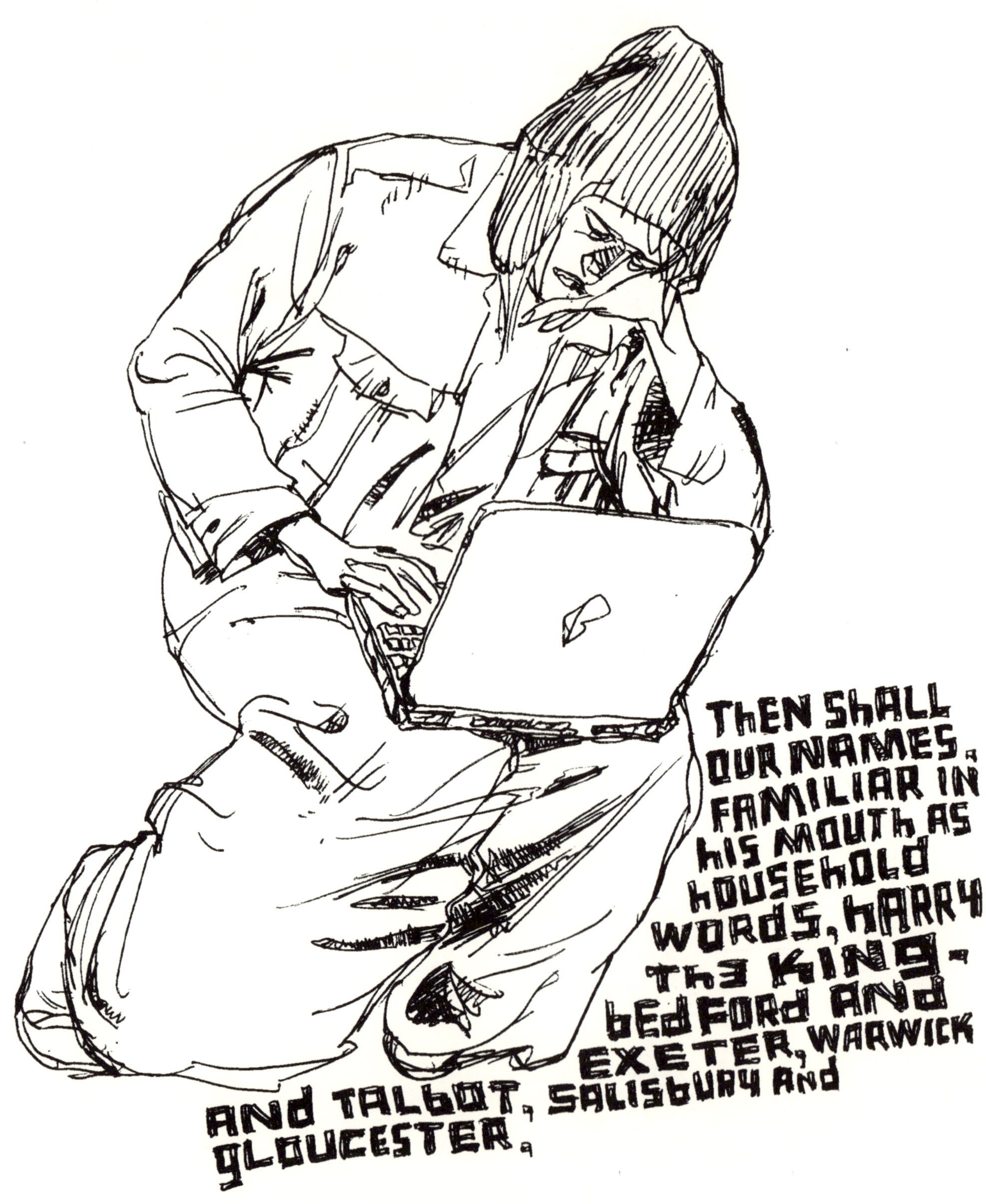
THEN SHALL
OUR NAMES,
FAMILIAR IN
HIS MOUTH AS
HOUSEHOLD
WORDS, HARRY
THE KING-
BEDFORD AND
EXETER, WARWICK
AND TALBOT, SALISBURY AND
GLOUCESTER,

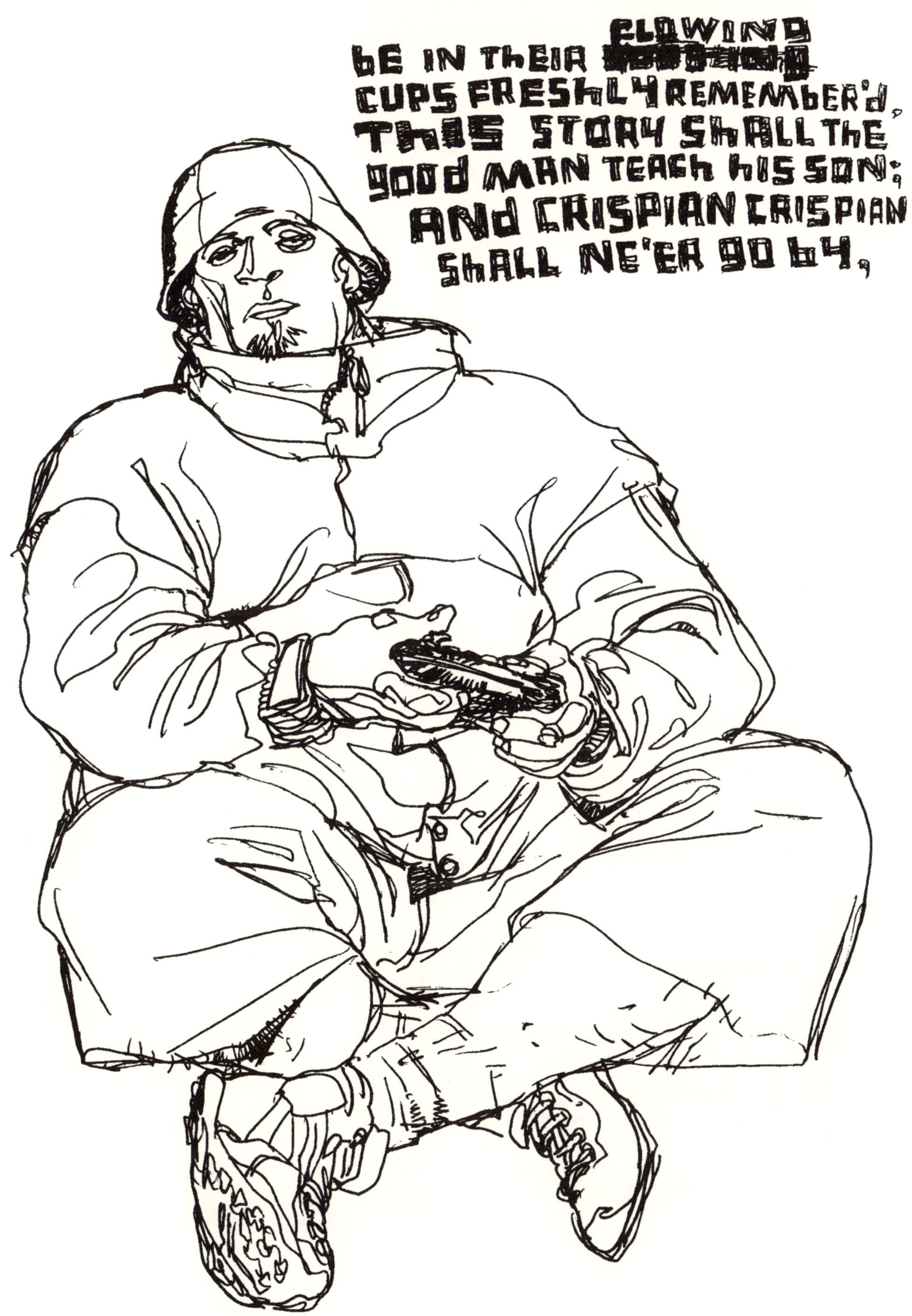
be in their flowing
cups freshly remember'd,
This story shall the
good man teach his son;
And Crispian Crispian
shall ne'er go by,

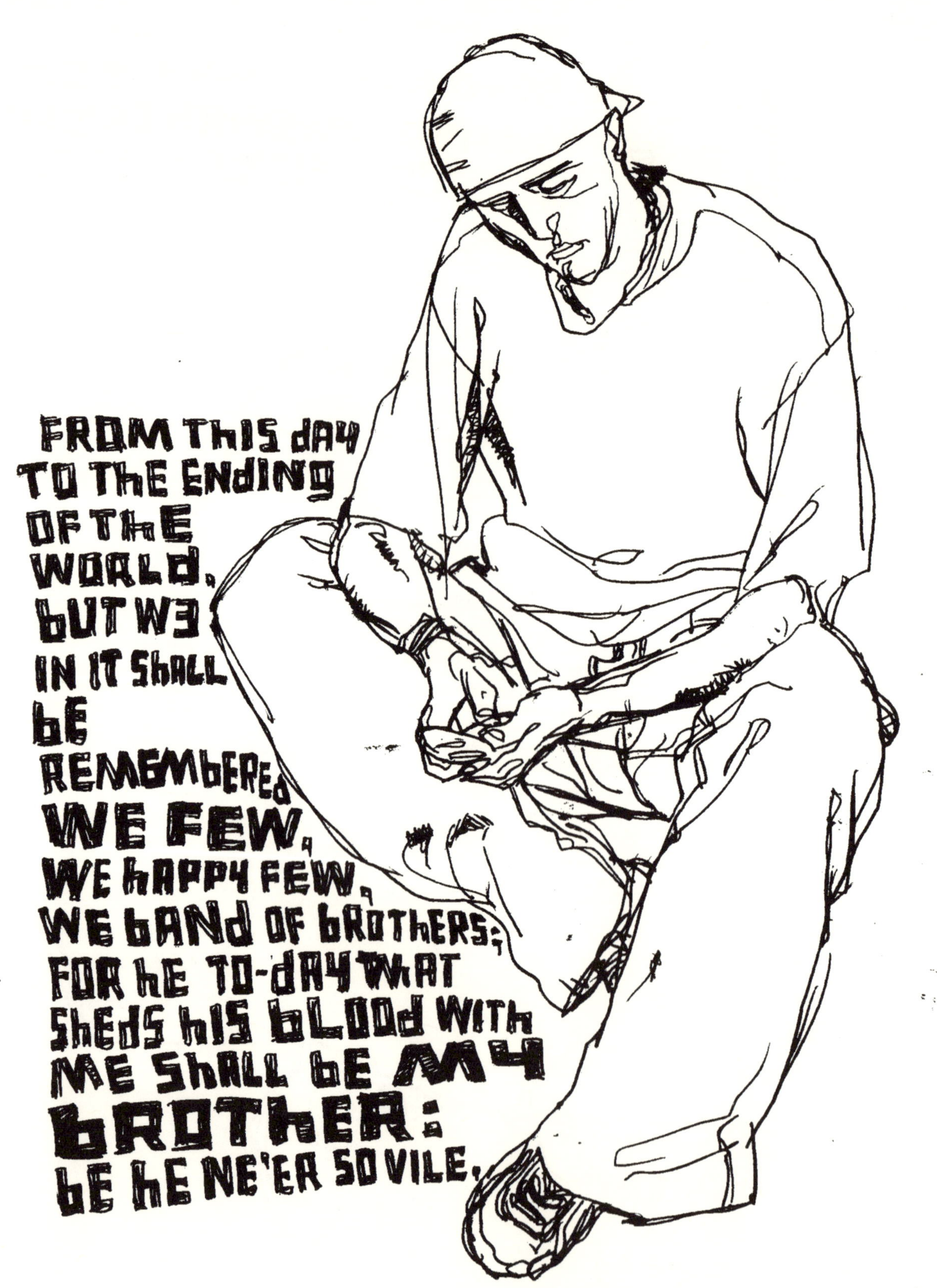
FROM THIS DAY
TO THE ENDING
OF THE
WORLD,
BUT WE
IN IT SHALL
BE
REMEMBERED
WE FEW,
WE HAPPY FEW,
WE BAND OF BROTHERS;
FOR HE TO-DAY THAT
SHEDS HIS BLOOD WITH
ME SHALL BE MY
BROTHER;
BE HE NE'ER SO VILE,

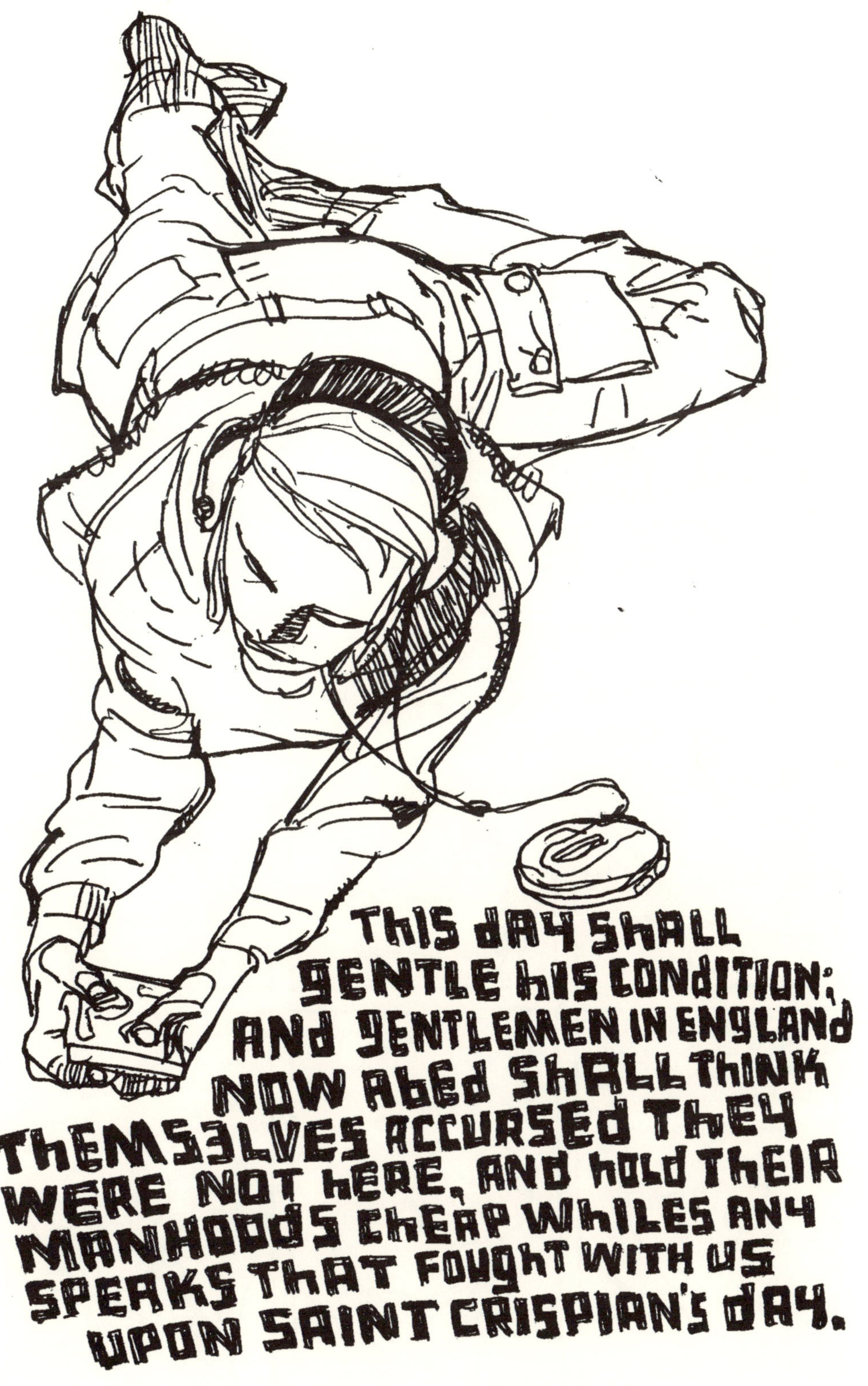
THIS DAY SHALL
GENTLE HIS CONDITION;
AND GENTLEMEN IN ENGLAND
NOW ABED SHALL THINK
THEMSELVES ACCURSED THEY
WERE NOT HERE, AND HOLD THEIR
MANHOODS CHEAP WHILES ANY
SPEAKS THAT FOUGHT WITH US
UPON SAINT CRISPIAN'S DAY.

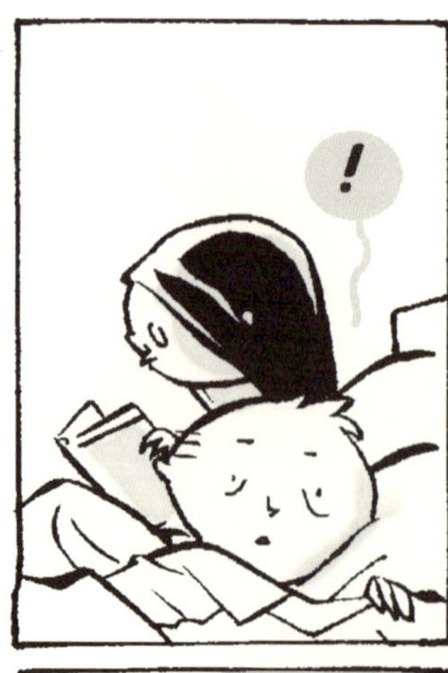
!
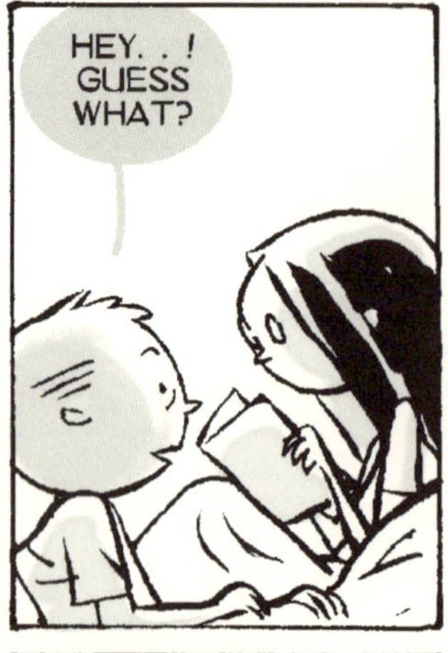
HEY. . ! GUESS WHAT?
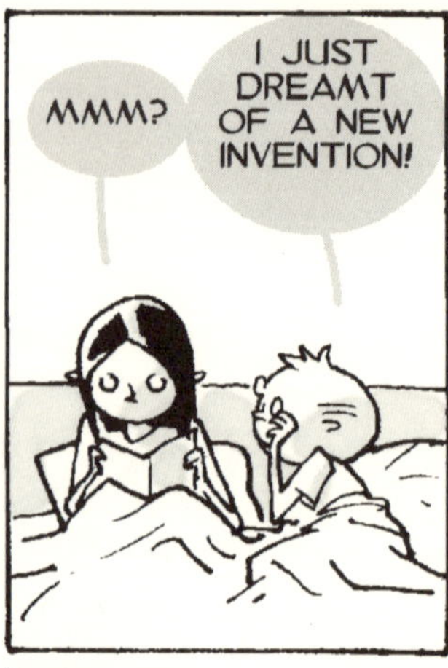
MMM?
I JUST DREAMT OF A NEW INVENTION!
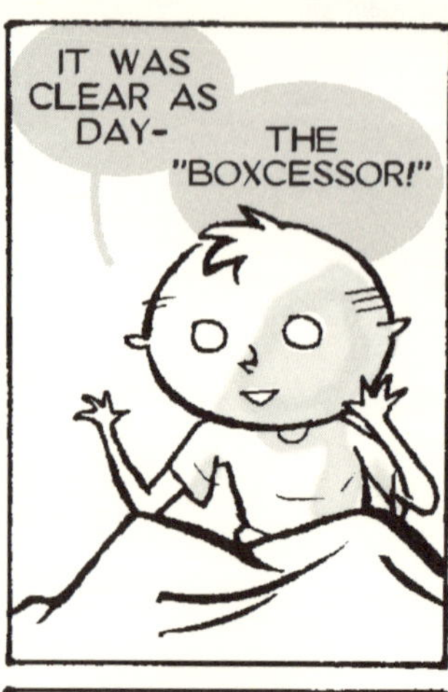
IT WAS CLEAR AS DAY-
THE "BOXCESSOR!"
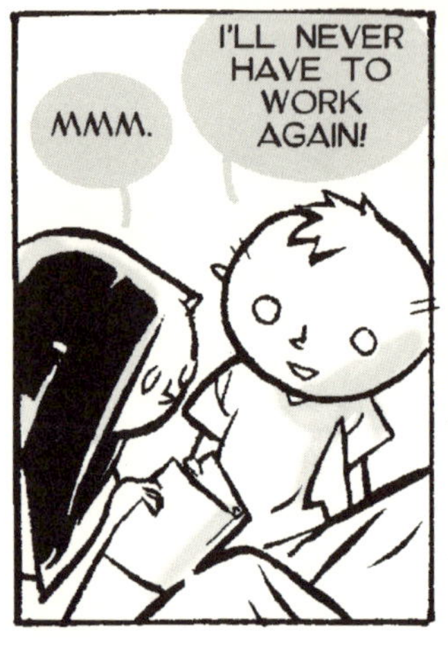
MMM.
I'LL NEVER HAVE TO WORK AGAIN!
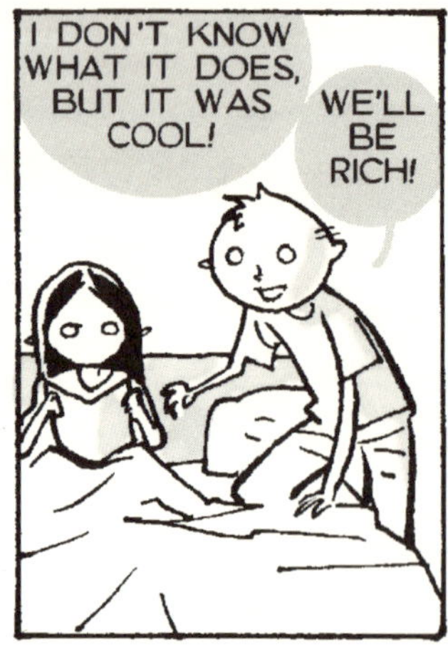
I DON'T KNOW WHAT IT DOES, BUT IT WAS COOL!
WE'LL BE RICH!
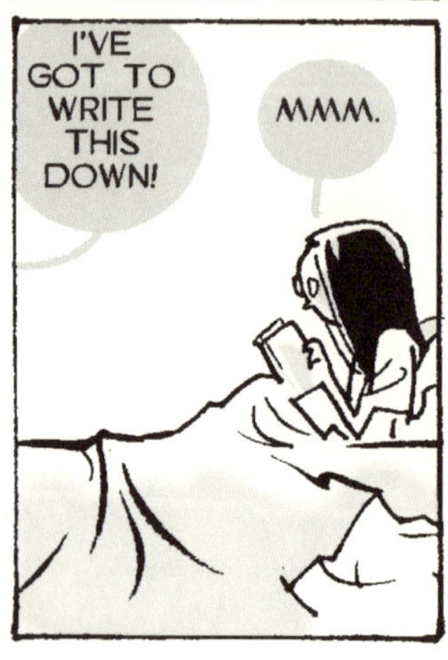
I'VE GOT TO WRITE THIS DOWN!
MMM.
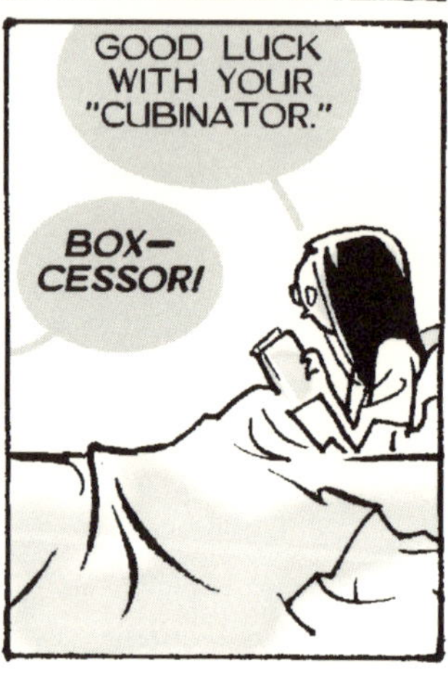
GOOD LUCK WITH YOUR "CUBINATOR."
BOX-CESSOR!
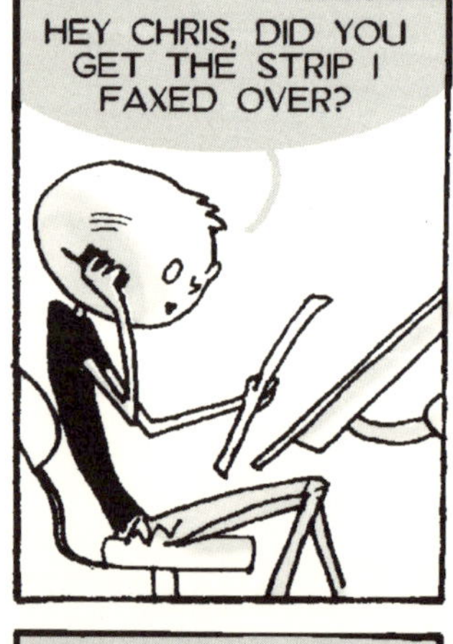
HEY CHRIS, DID YOU GET THE STRIP I FAXED OVER?
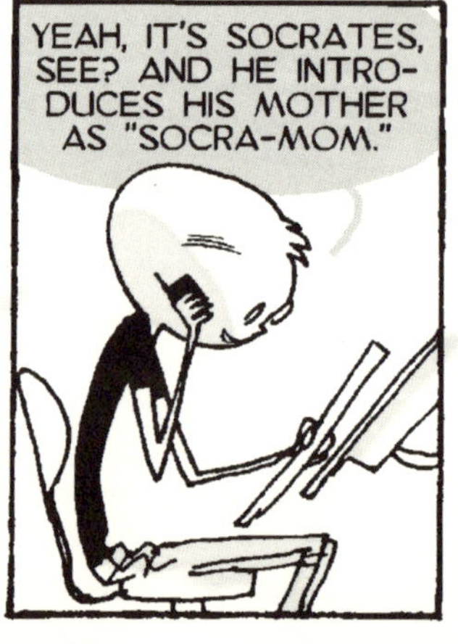
YEAH, IT'S SOCRATES, SEE? AND HE INTRODUCES HIS MOTHER AS "SOCRA-MOM."
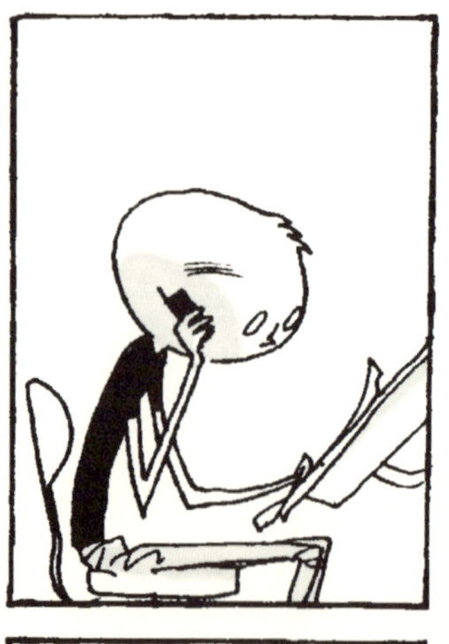
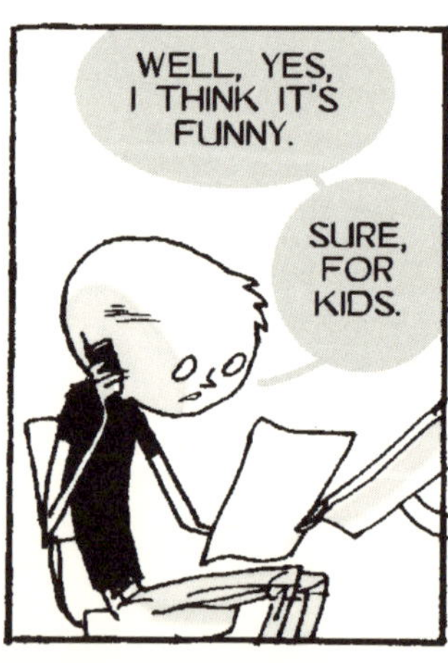
WELL, YES, I THINK IT'S FUNNY.
SURE, FOR KIDS.
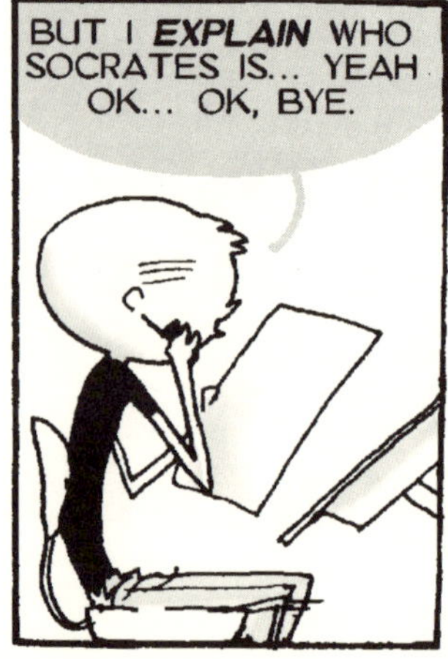
BUT I **EXPLAIN** WHO SOCRATES IS... YEAH OK... OK, BYE.
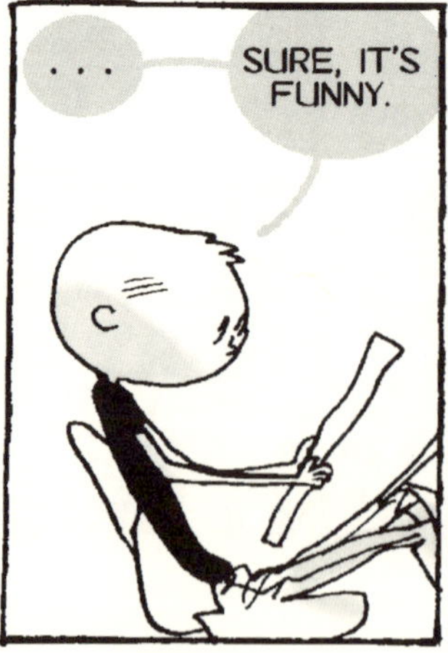
. . .
SURE, IT'S FUNNY.
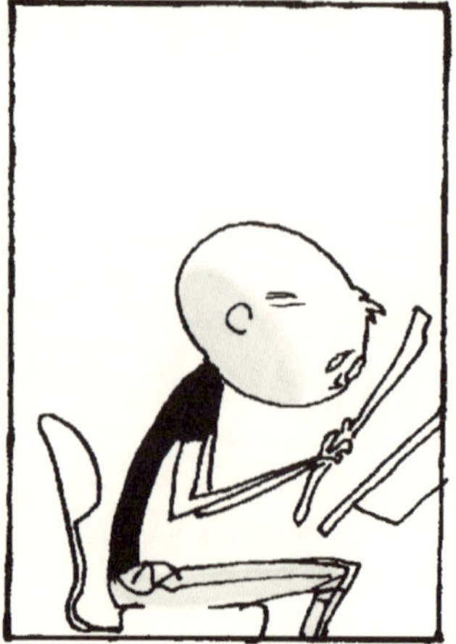
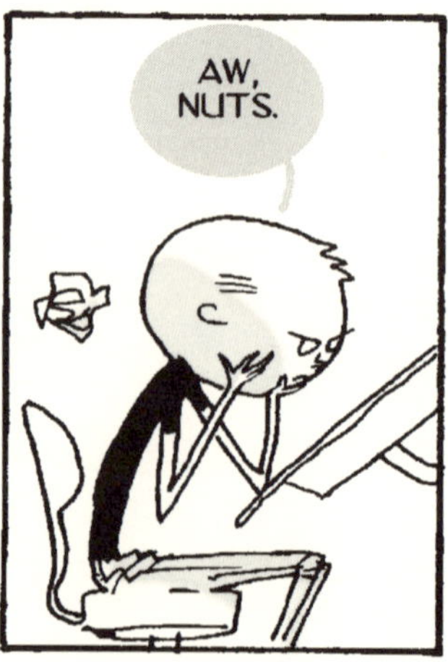
AW, NUTS.

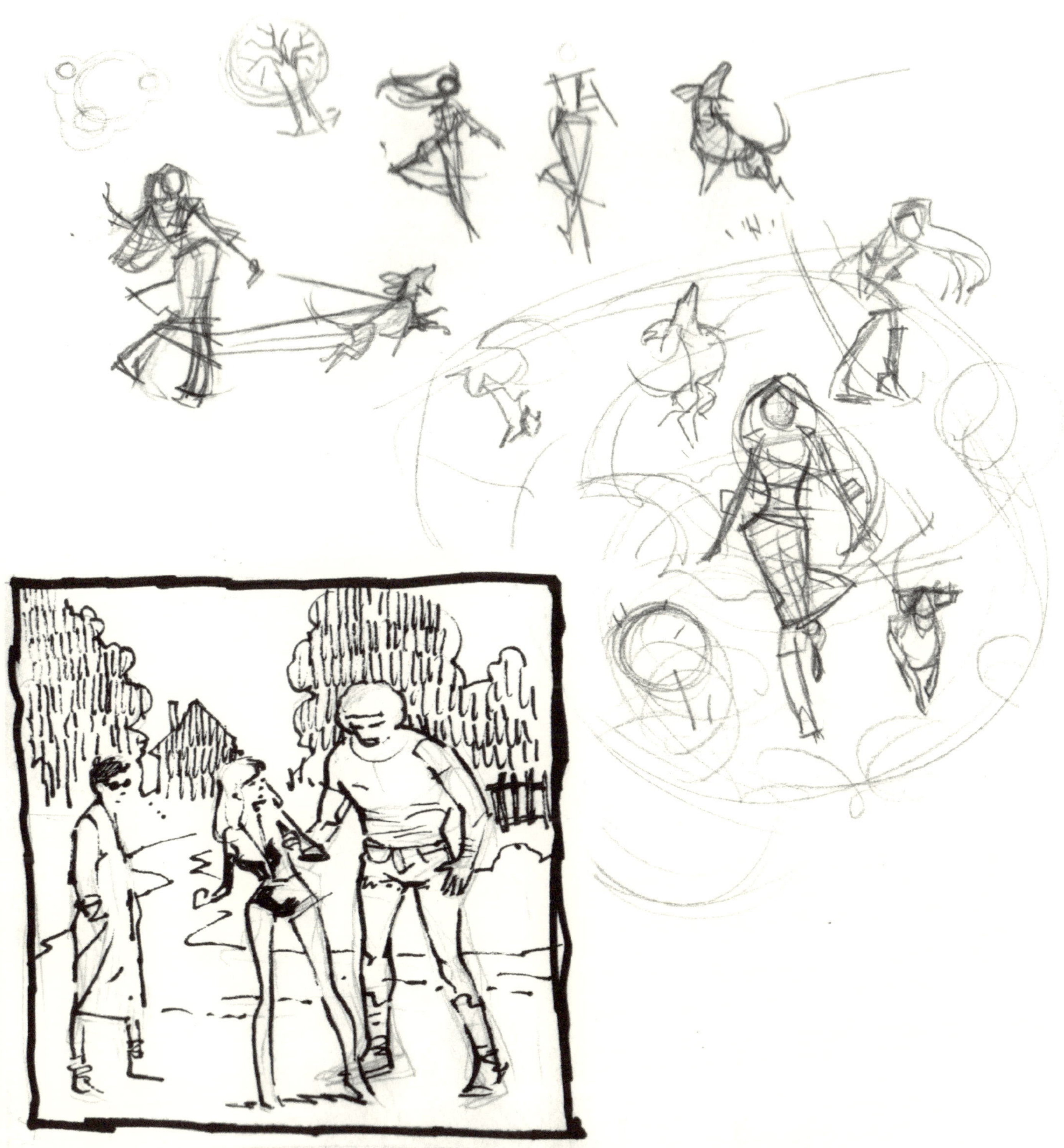

CHARACTERS FROM A DREAM 07/06

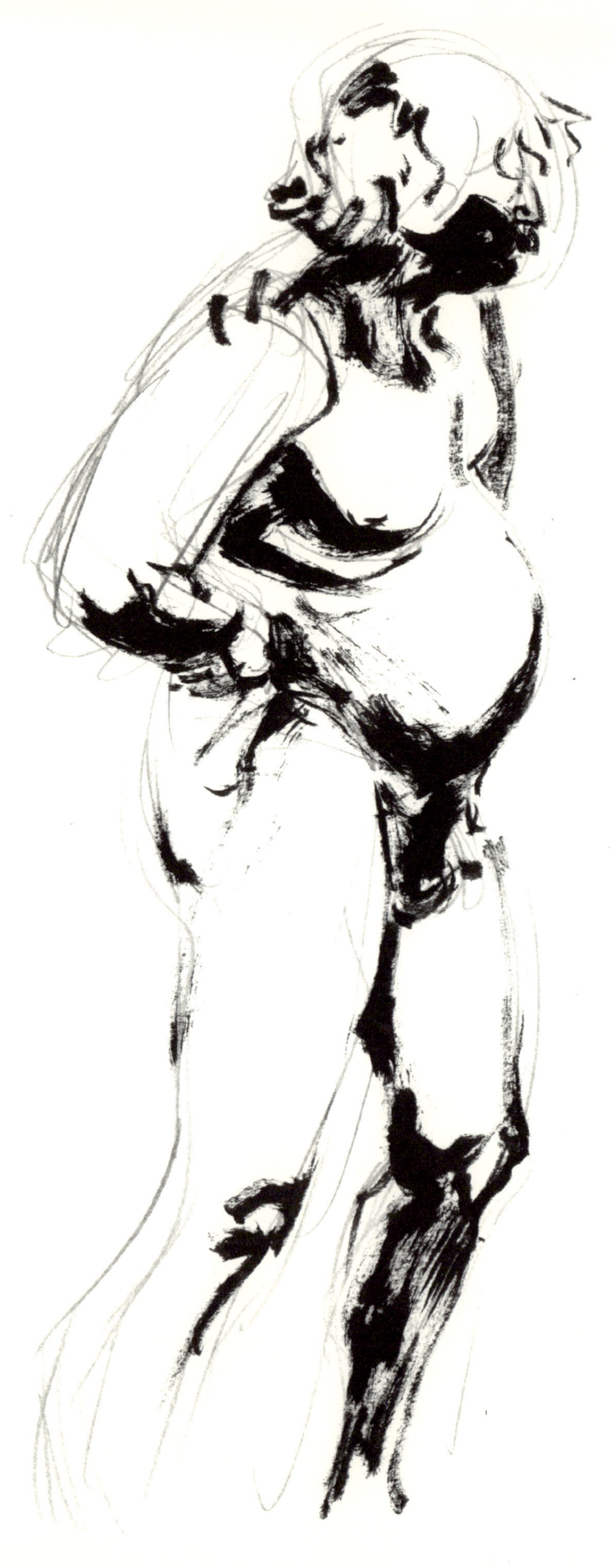

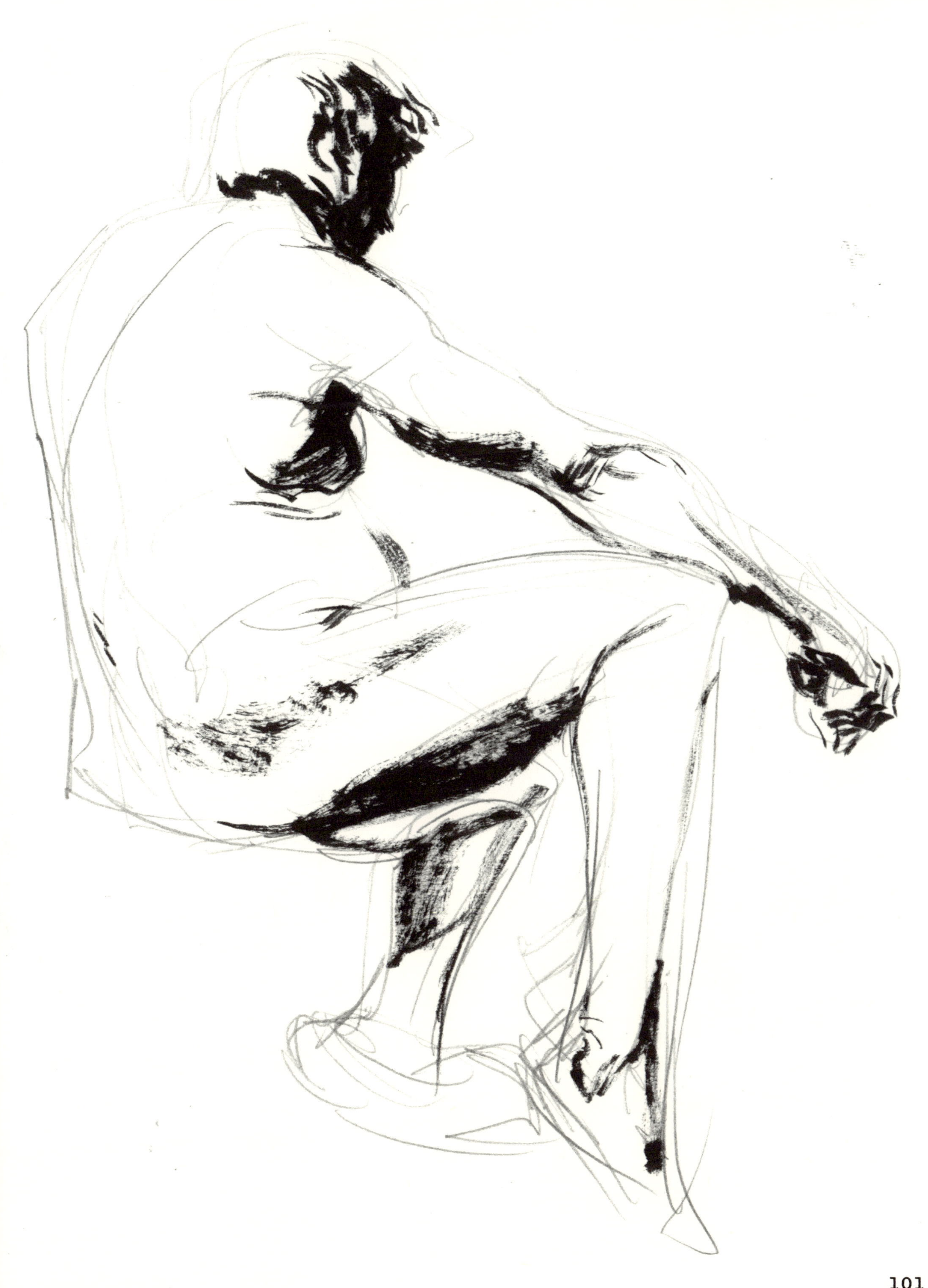

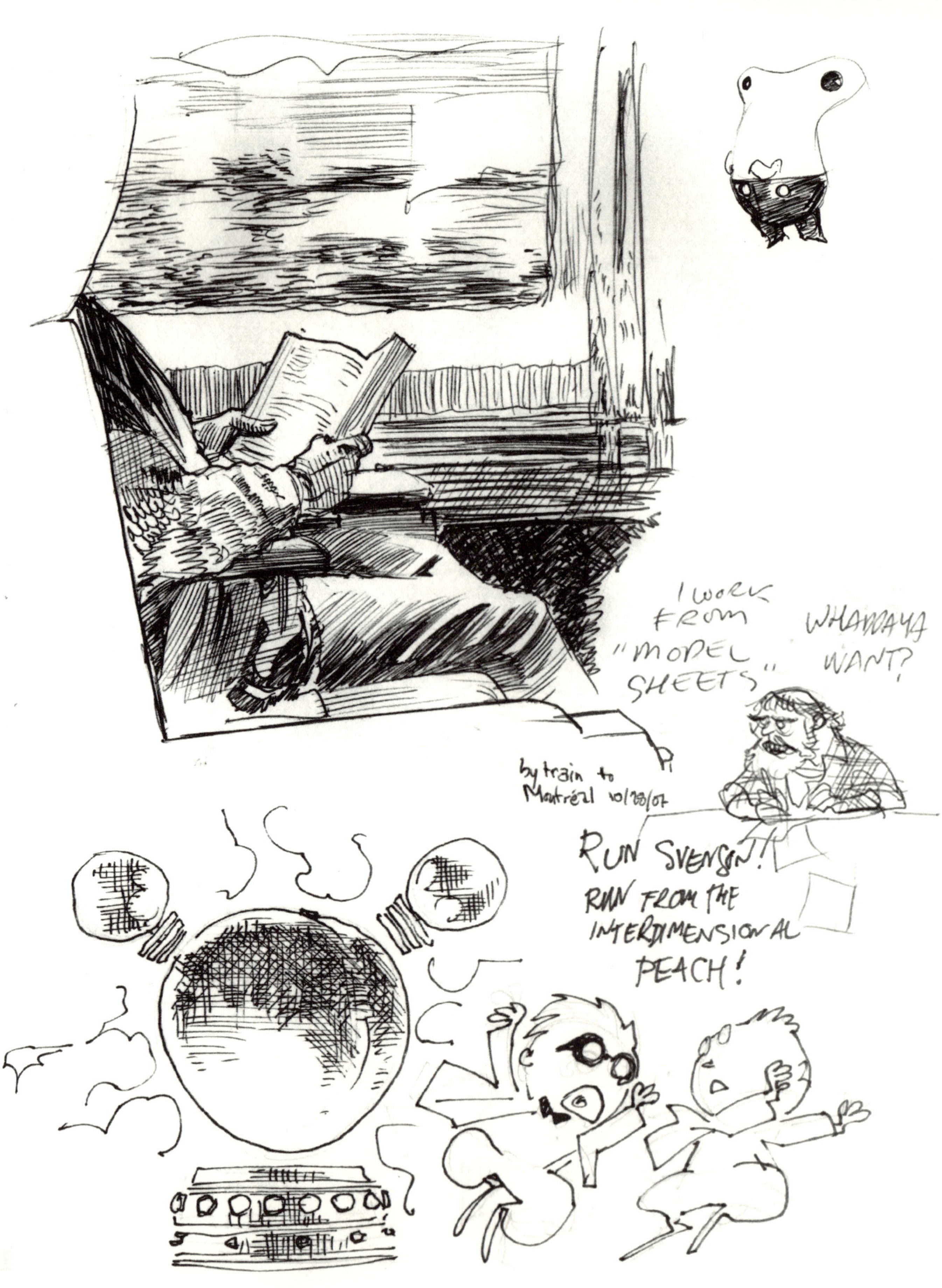
by train to
Montréal 10/28/07
I WORK
FROM
"MODEL
SHEETS"
WHADDAYA
WANT?
RUN SVENSON!
RUN FROM THE
INTERDIMENSIONAL
PEACH!

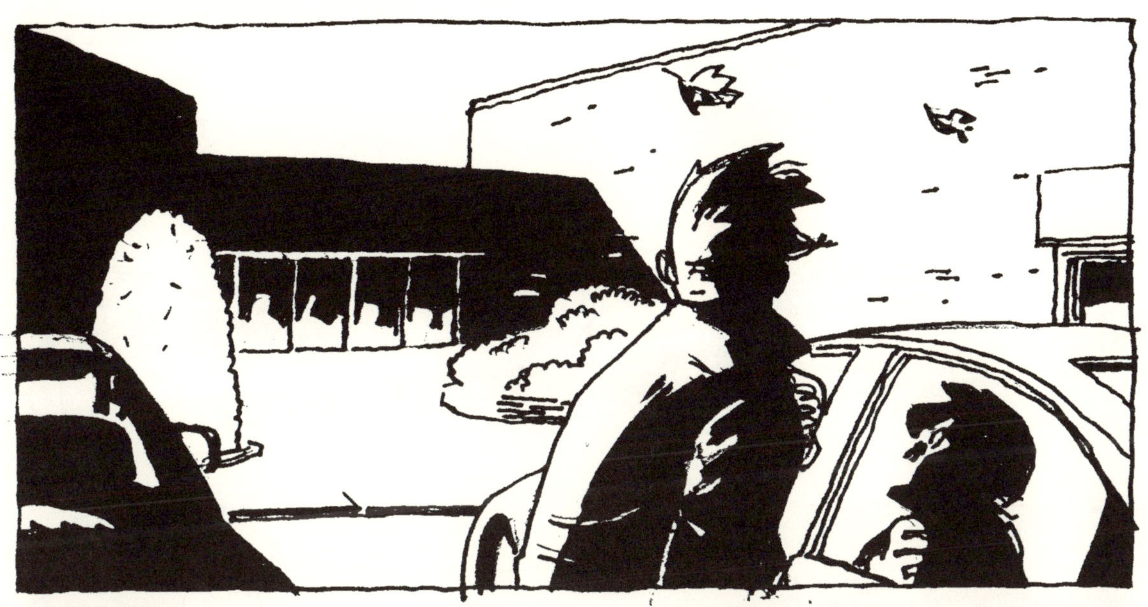

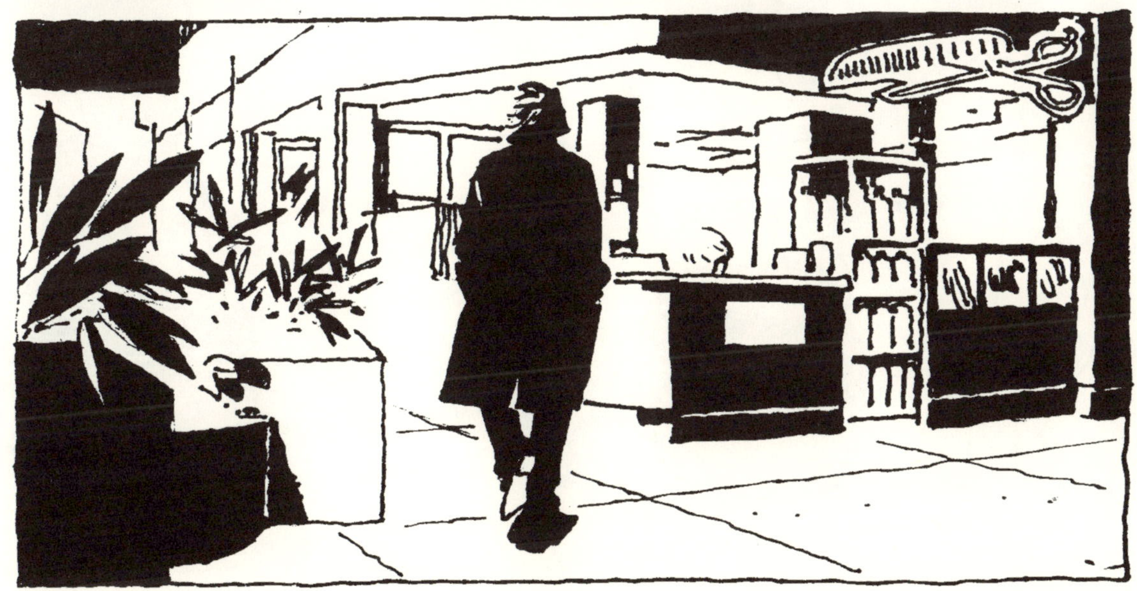

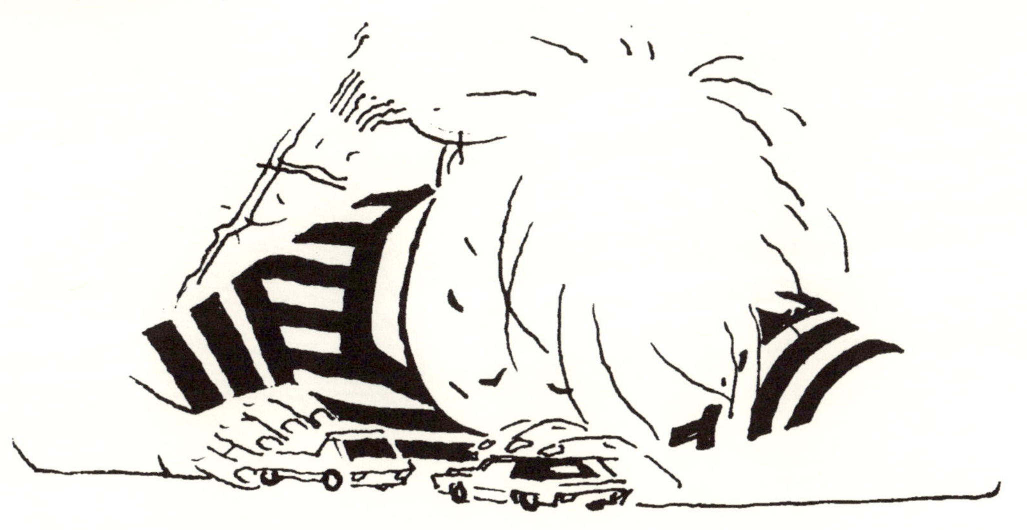

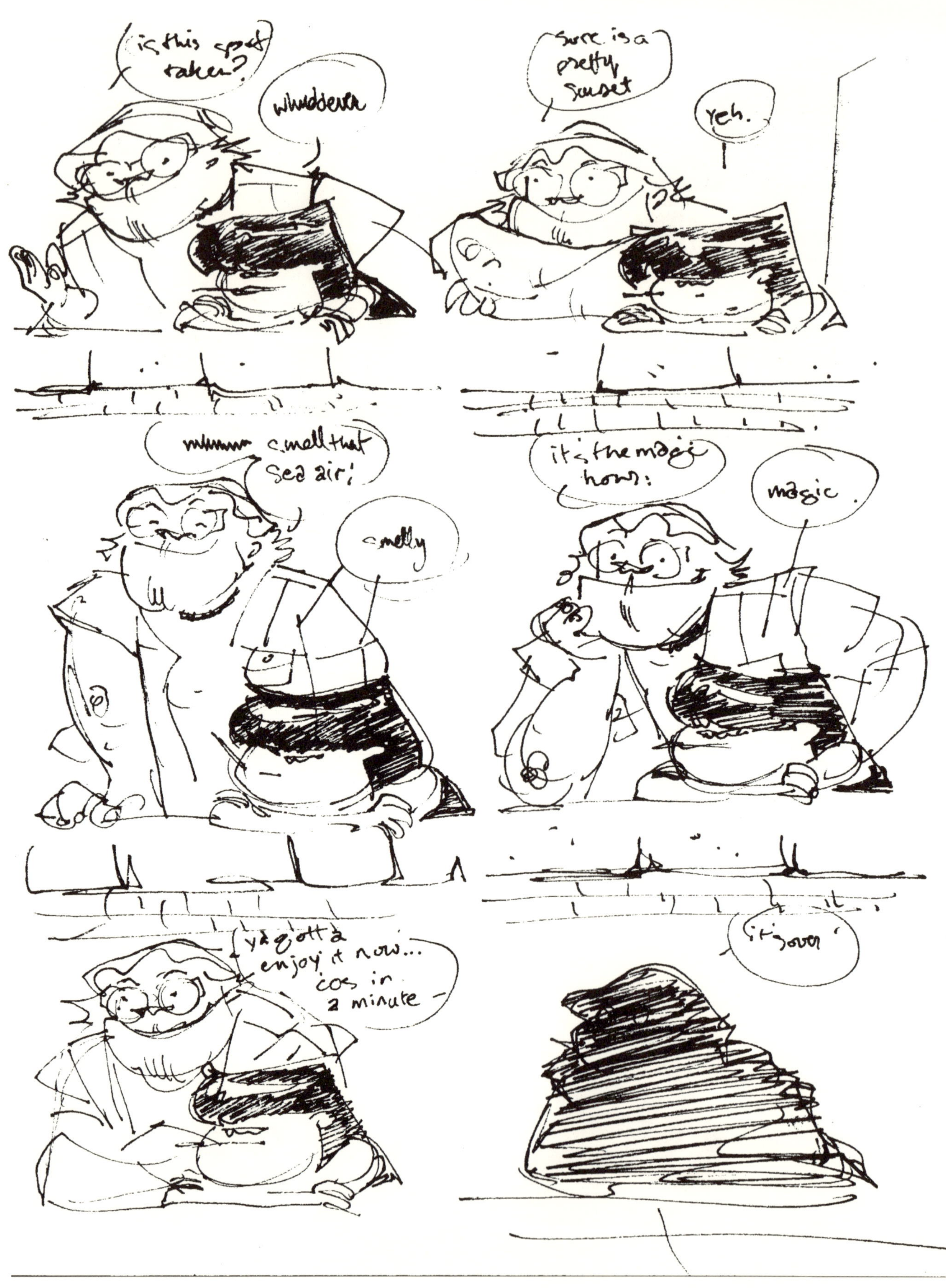
is this spot taken?
whuddever
sure is a pretty sunset
yeh.
mmmm smell that sea air!
smelly
it's the magic hour!
magic.
ya gotta enjoy it now... cos in a minute
it's over

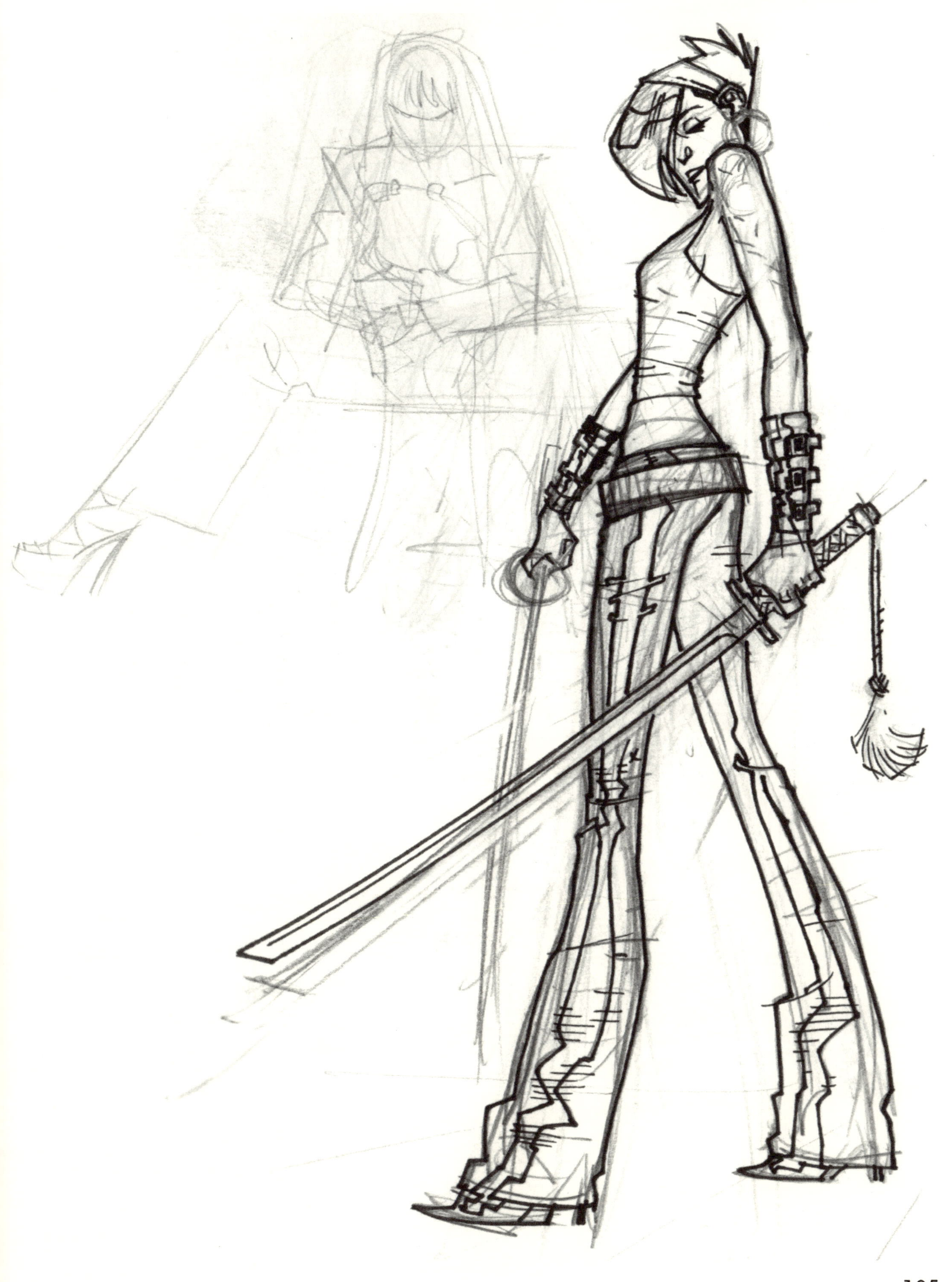

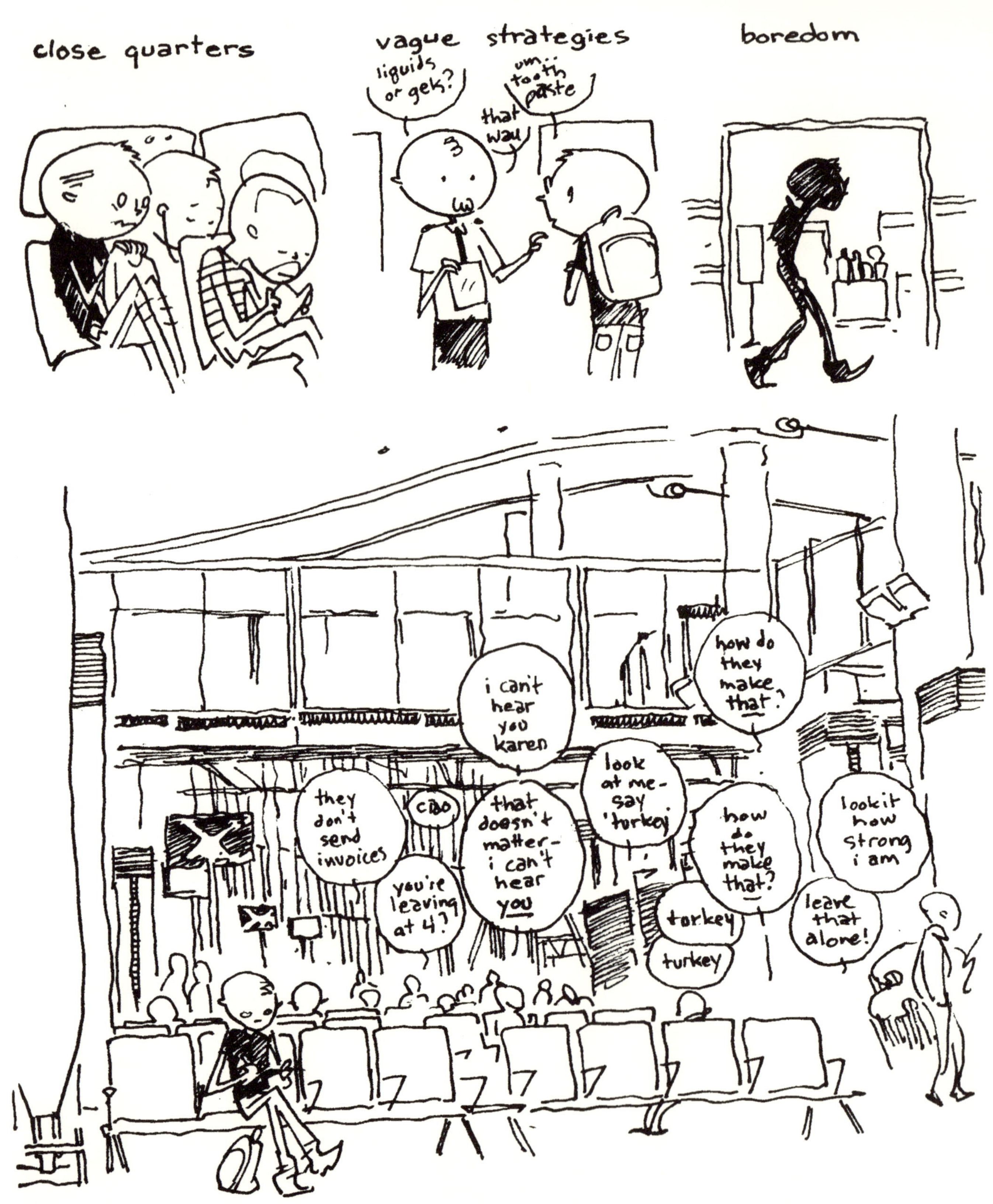

and the loneliness of placeless location

10 11 07

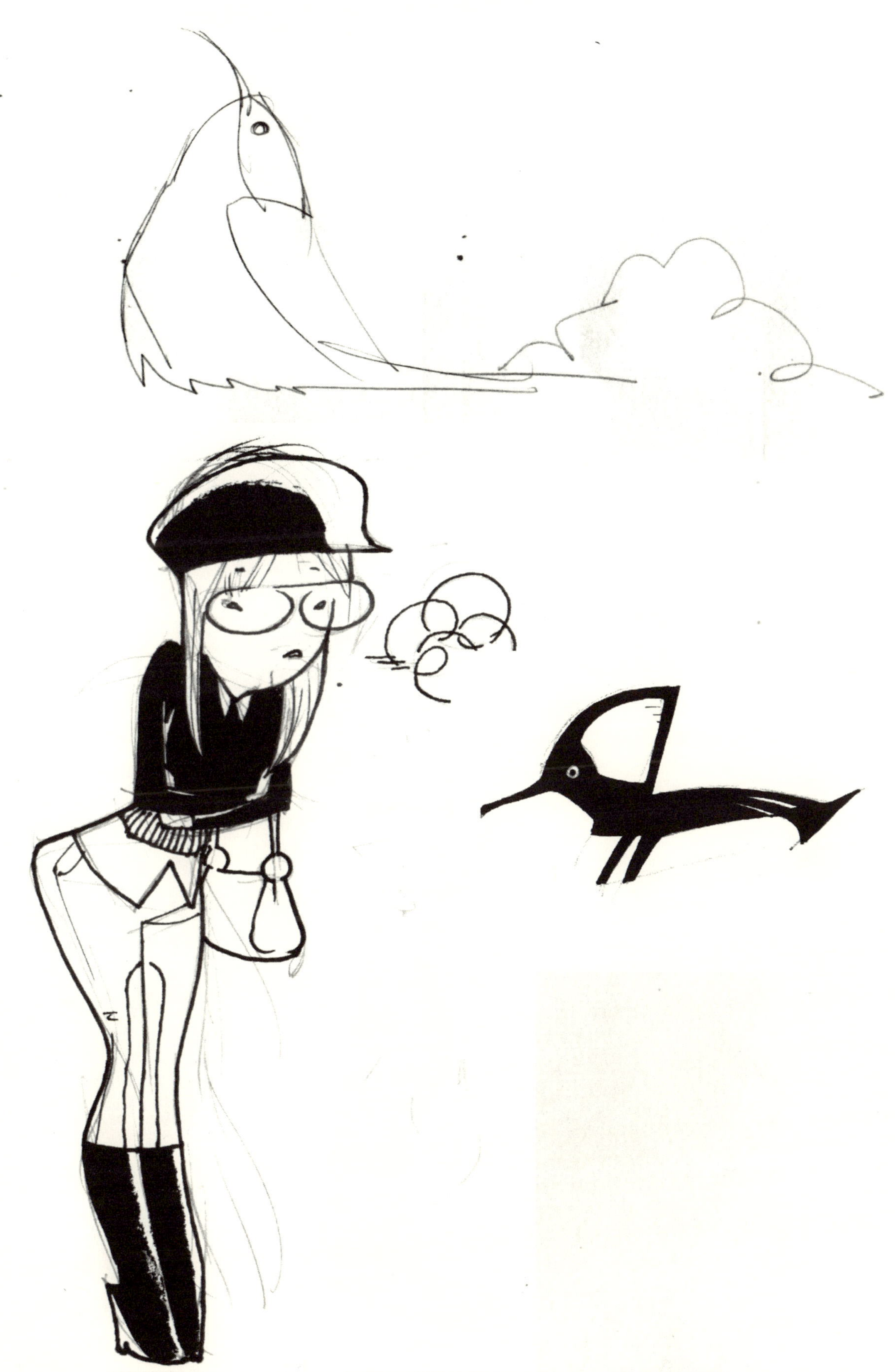

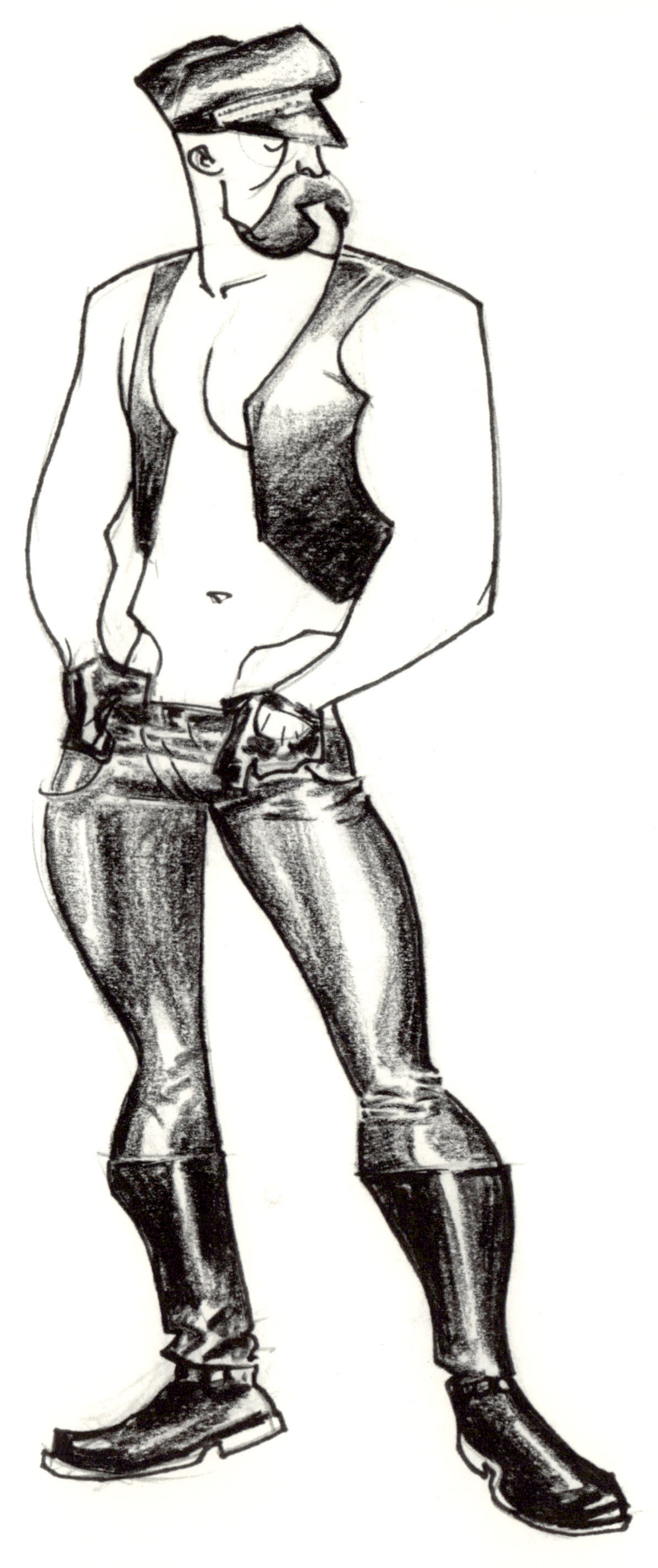

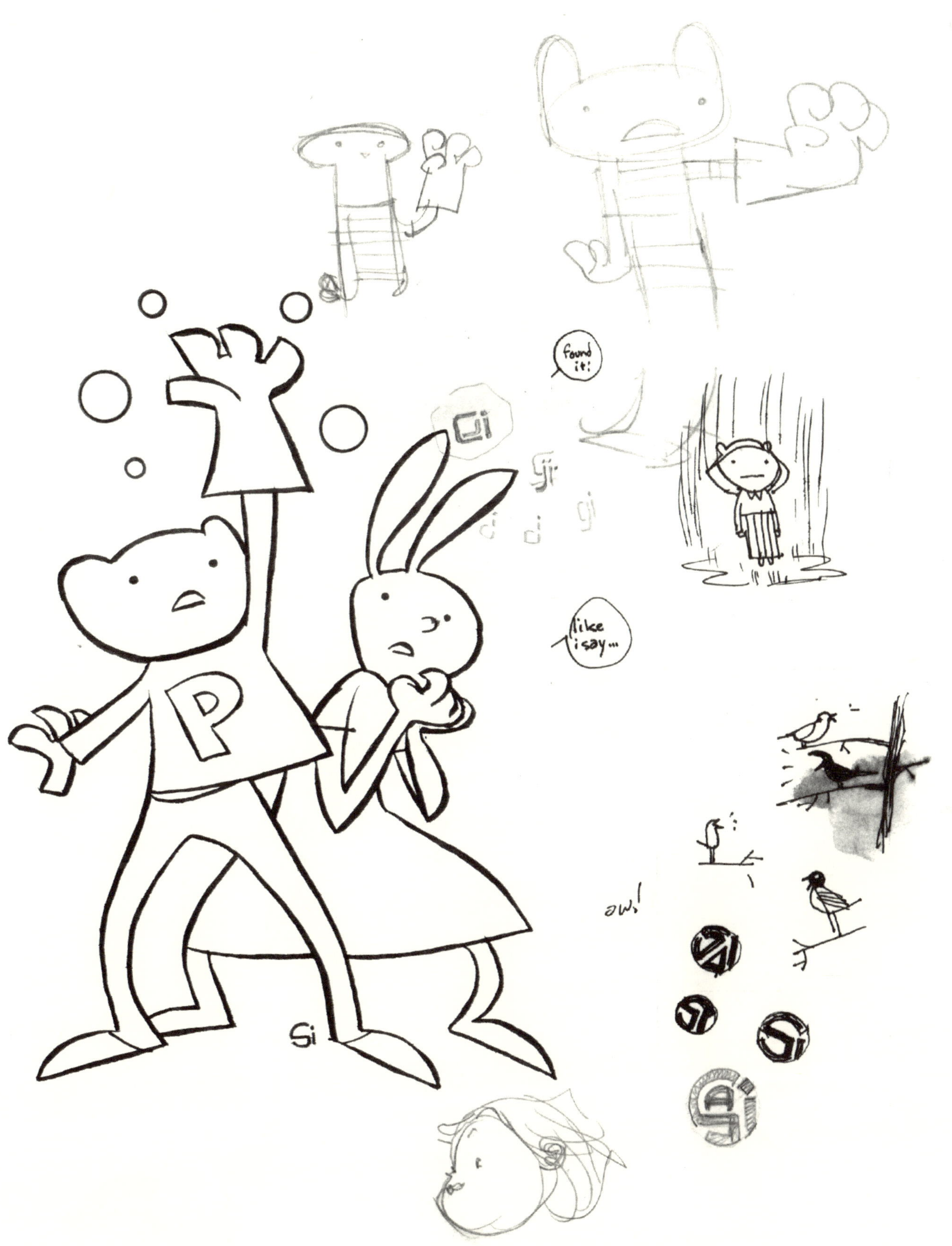
found it!
like i say...
aw!
Si

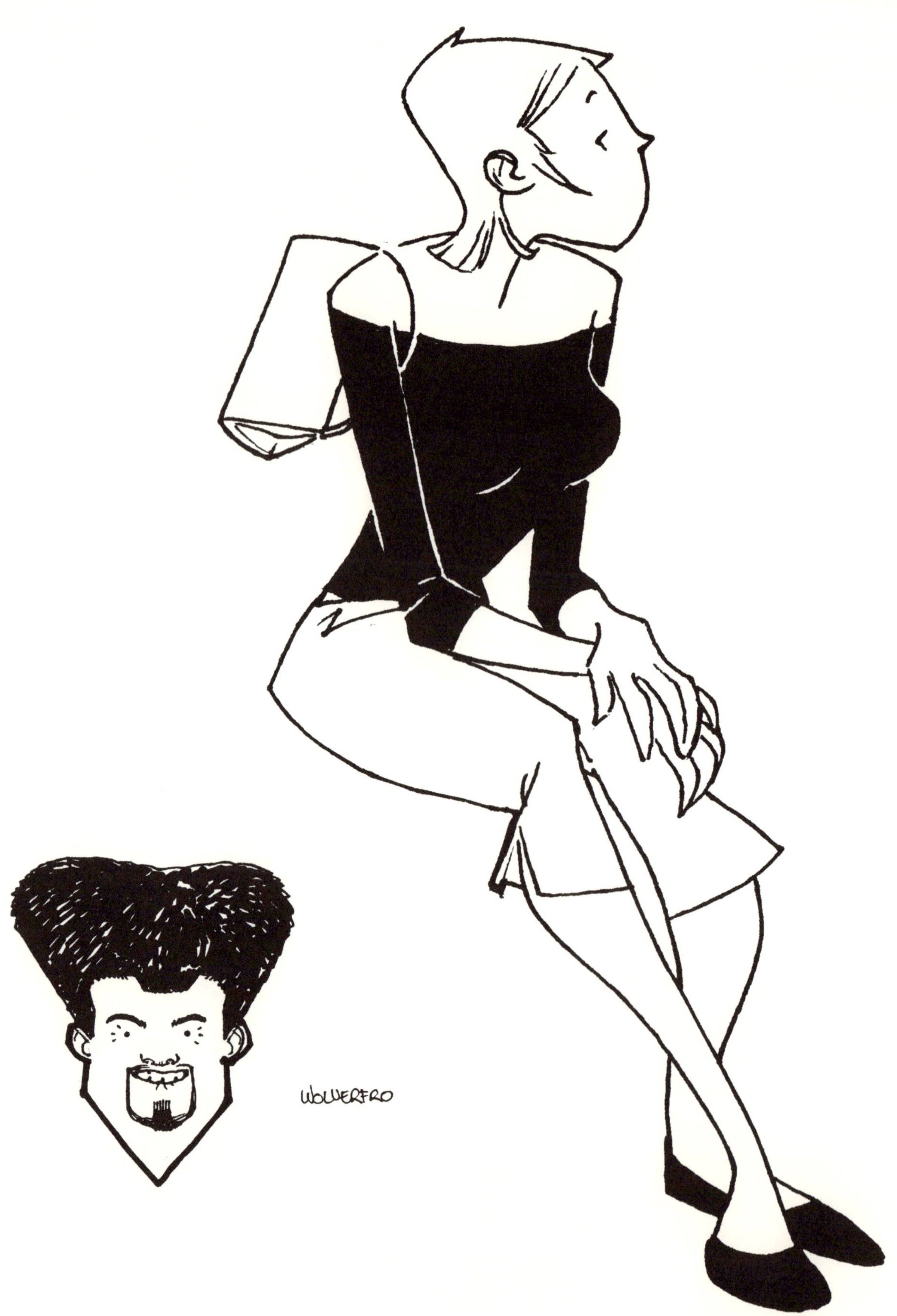
WOLVERFRO

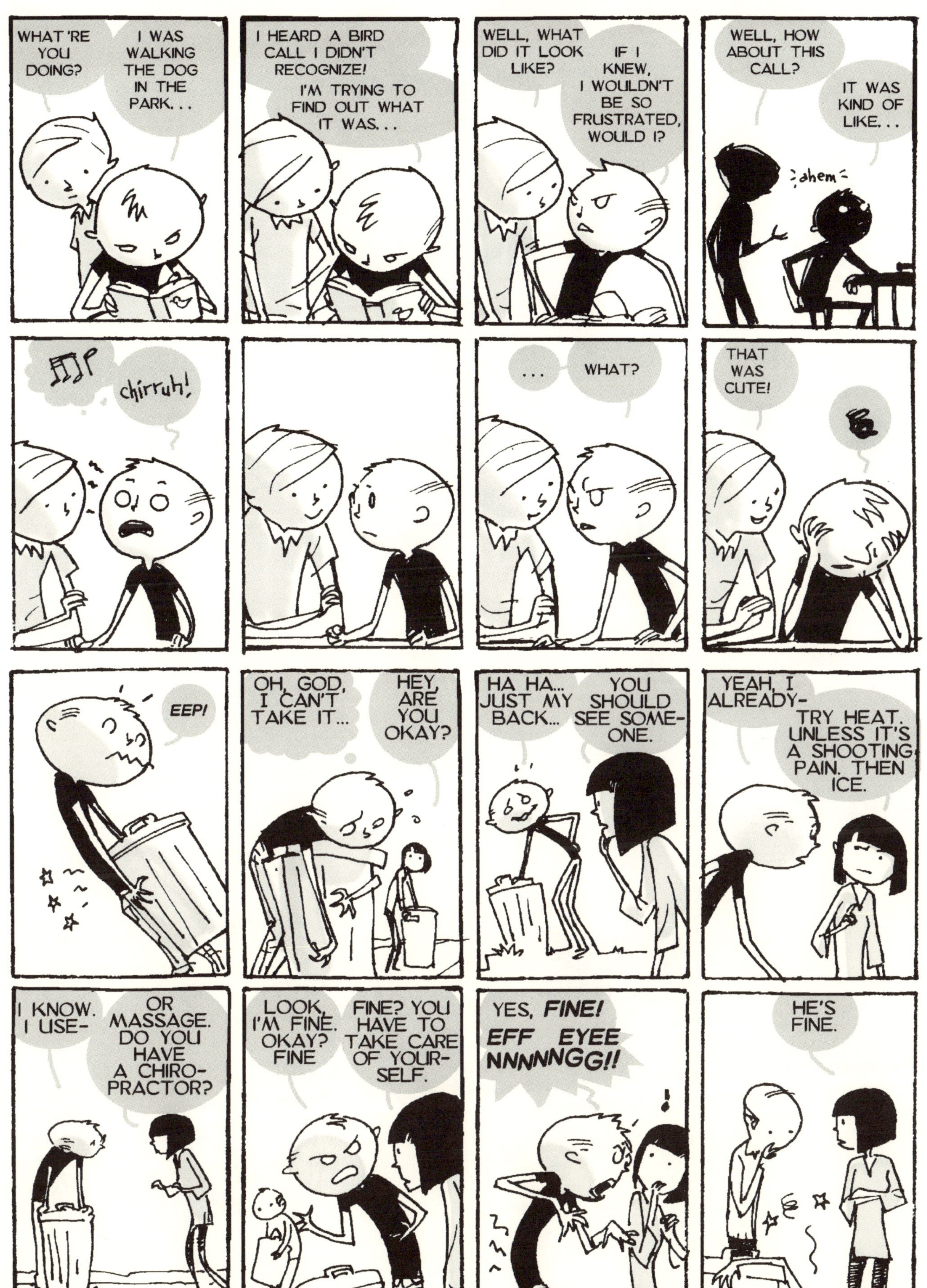
WHAT'RE YOU DOING?
I WAS WALKING THE DOG IN THE PARK. . .
I HEARD A BIRD CALL I DIDN'T RECOGNIZE!
I'M TRYING TO FIND OUT WHAT IT WAS. . .
WELL, WHAT DID IT LOOK LIKE?
IF I KNEW, I WOULDN'T BE SO FRUSTRATED, WOULD I?
WELL, HOW ABOUT THIS CALL?
IT WAS KIND OF LIKE. . .
ahem
chirruh!
. . .
WHAT?
THAT WAS CUTE!
EEP!
OH, GOD, I CAN'T TAKE IT...
HEY, ARE YOU OKAY?
HA HA... JUST MY BACK...
YOU SHOULD SEE SOME-ONE.
YEAH, I ALREADY-
TRY HEAT. UNLESS IT'S A SHOOTING PAIN. THEN ICE.
I KNOW. I USE-
OR MASSAGE. DO YOU HAVE A CHIRO-PRACTOR?
LOOK, I'M FINE. OKAY? FINE
FINE? YOU HAVE TO TAKE CARE OF YOUR-SELF.
YES, FINE!
EFF EYEE NNNNNGG!!
HE'S FINE.

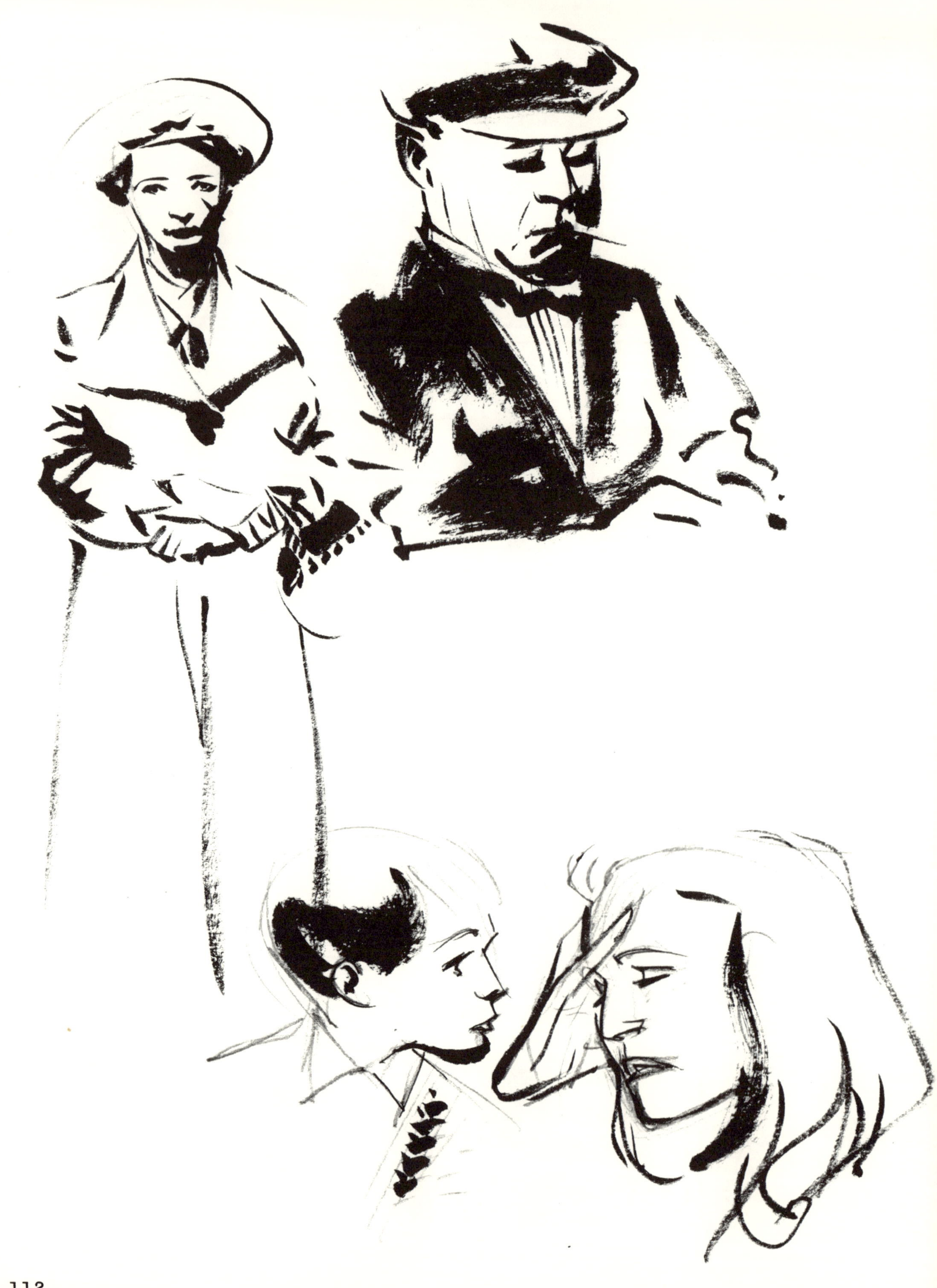

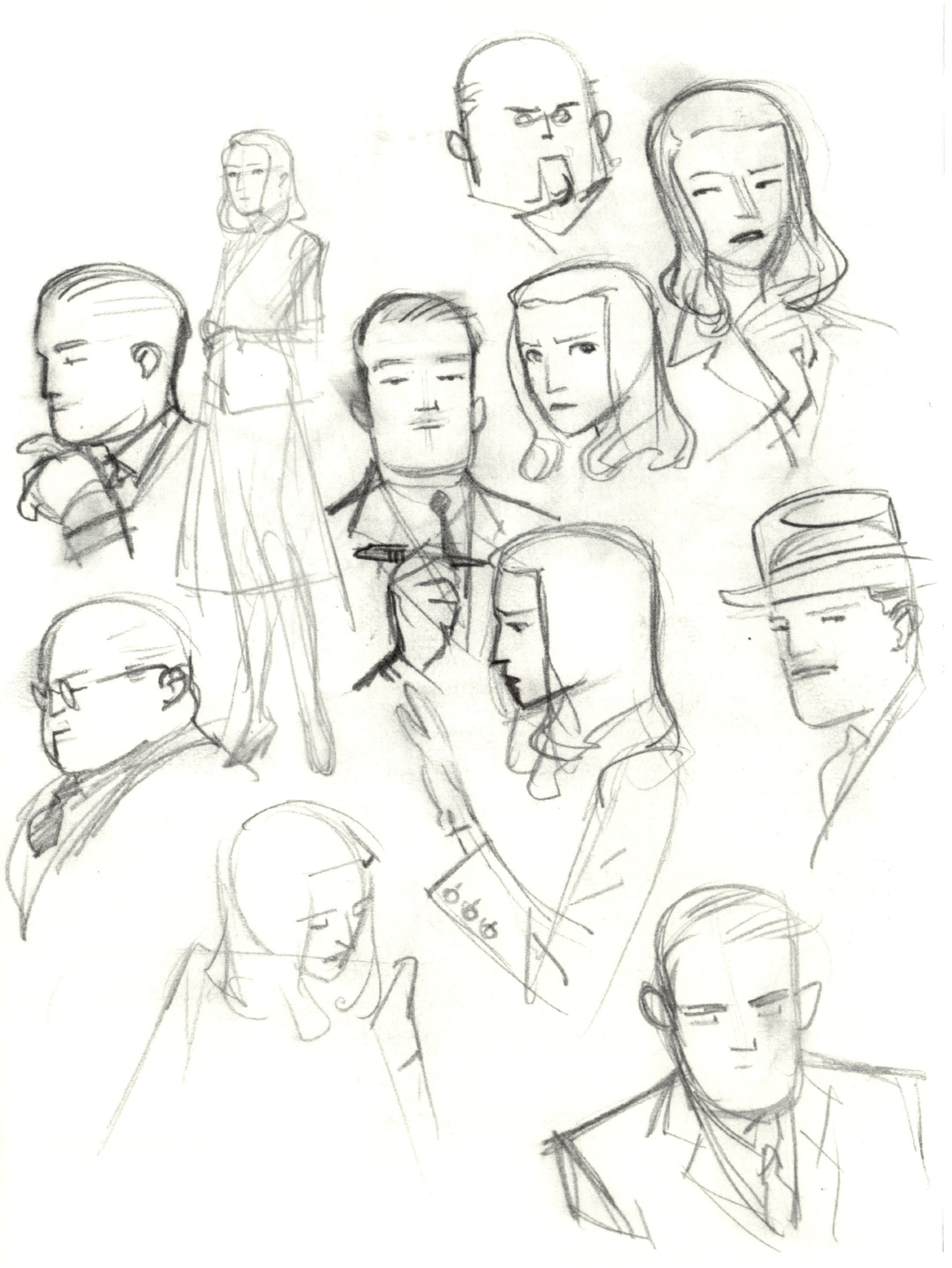

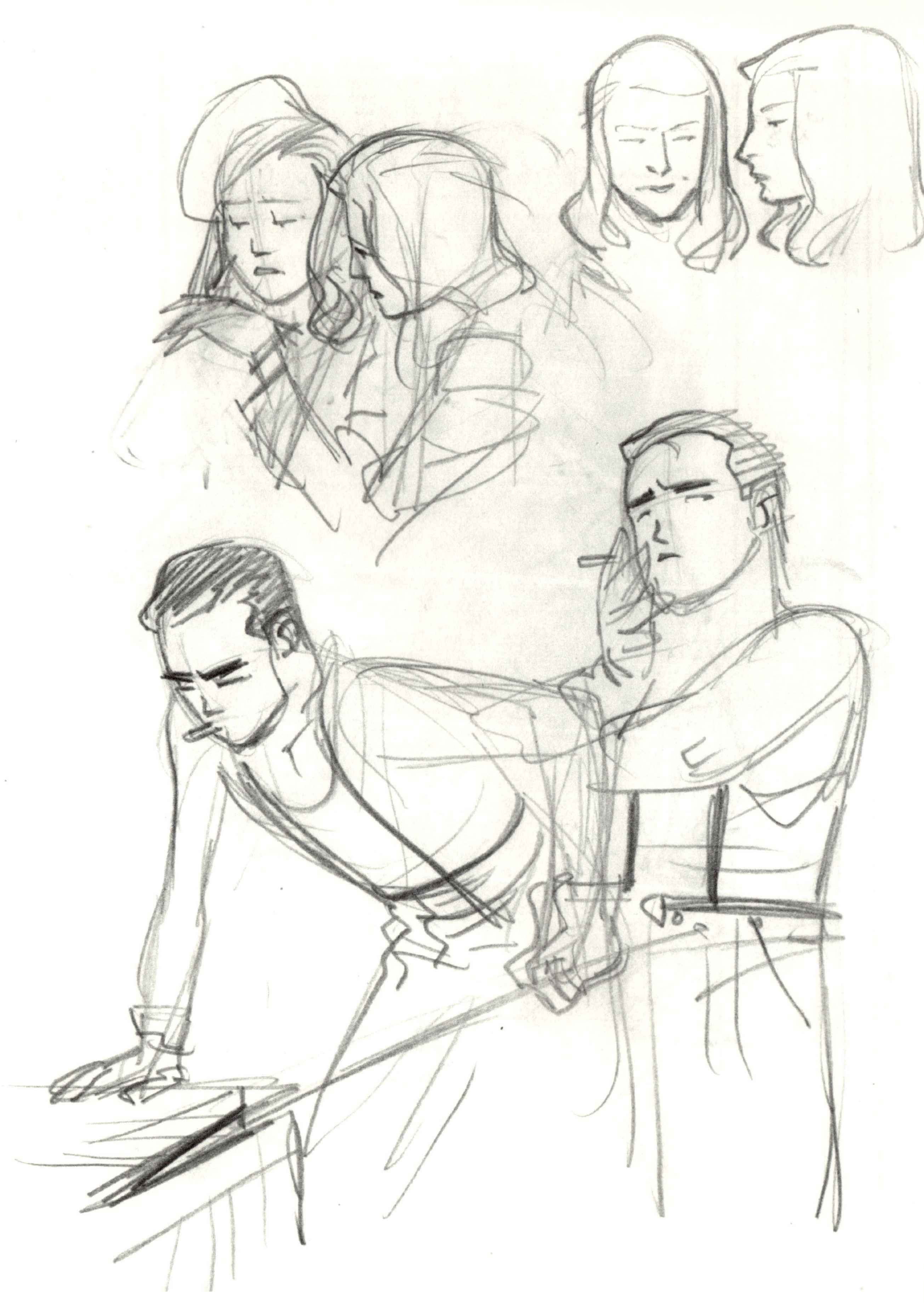

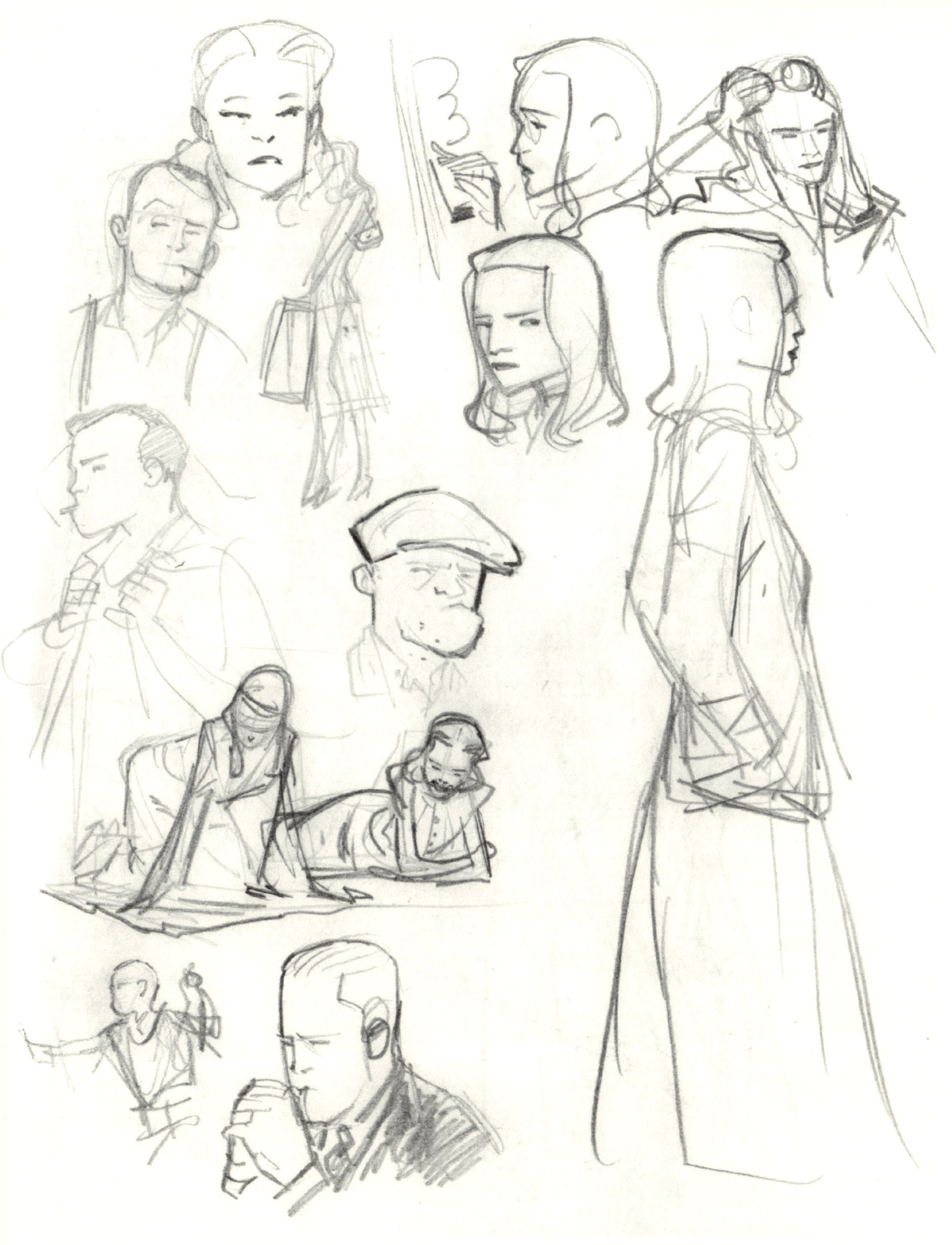

MP 52 P4

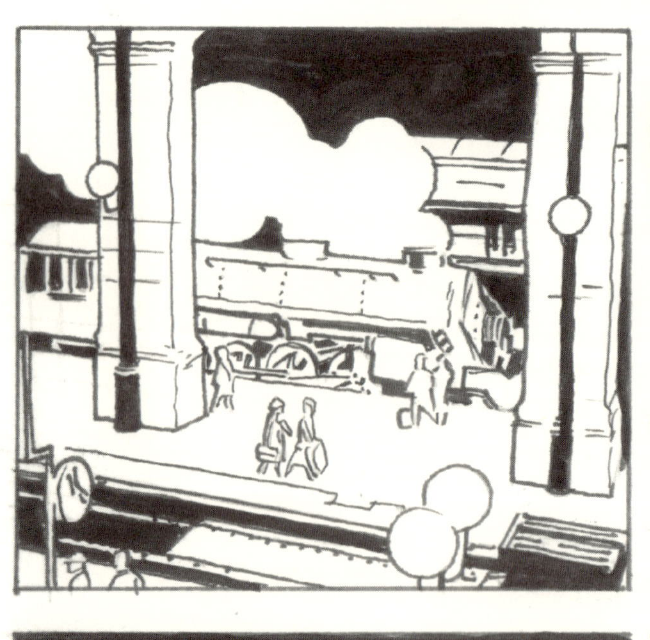

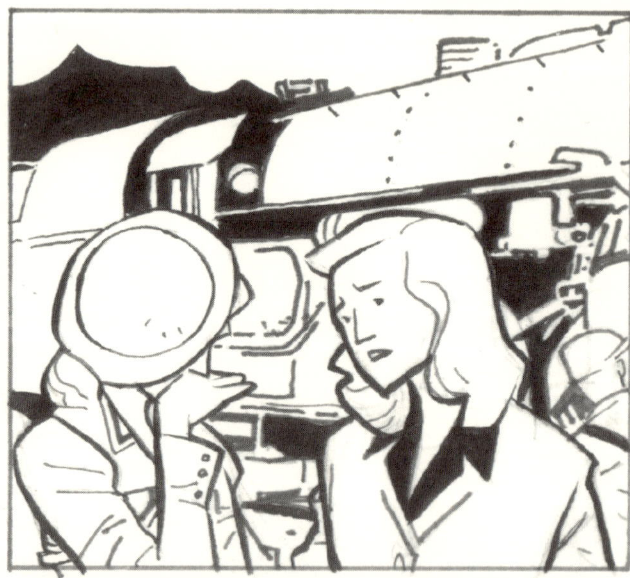

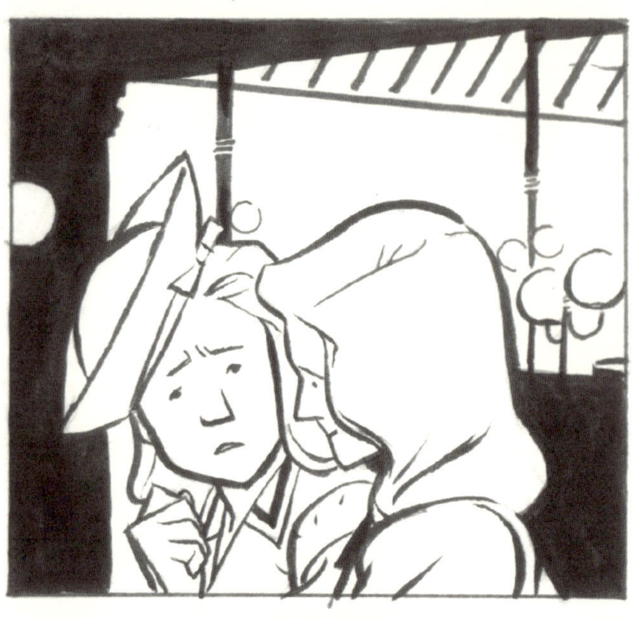

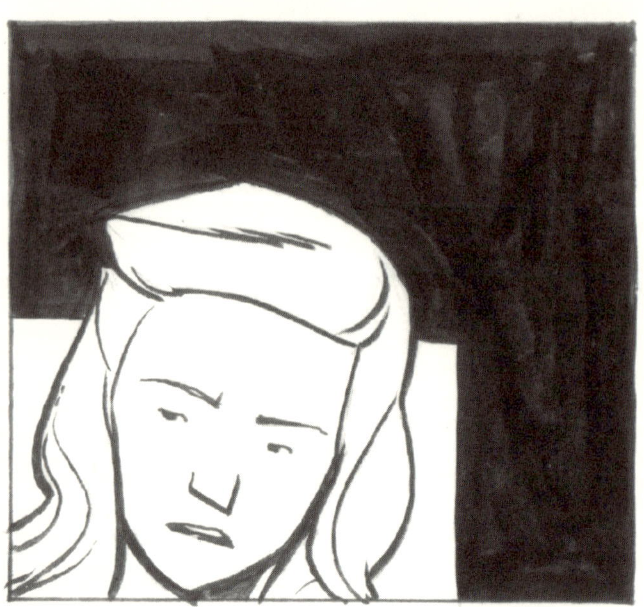

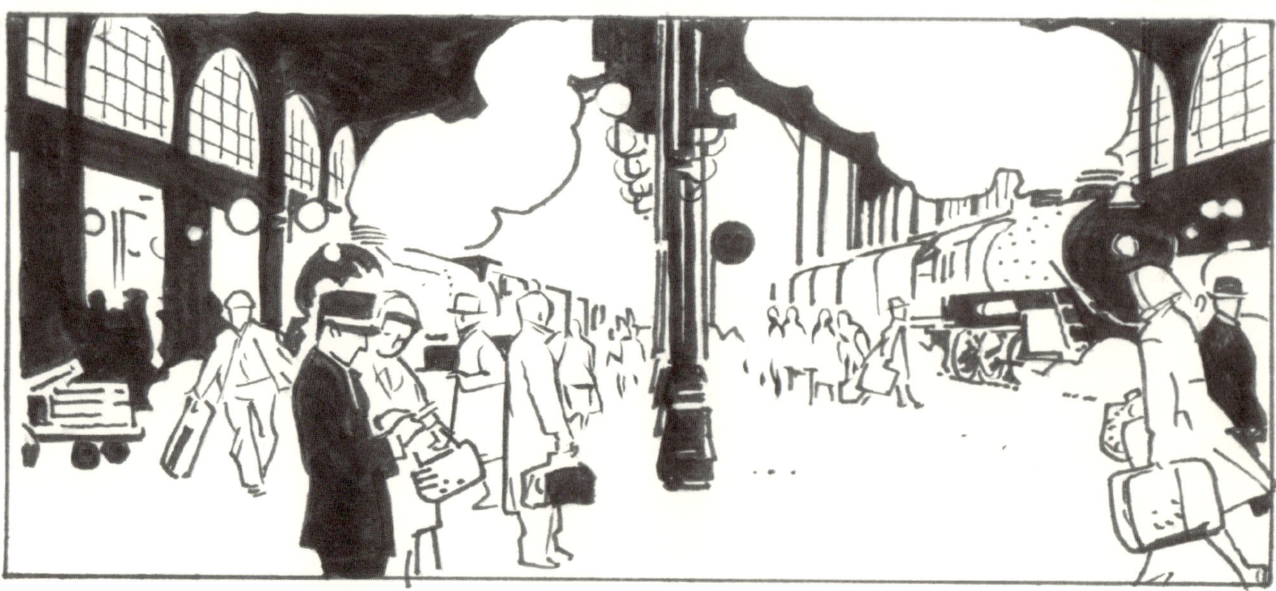

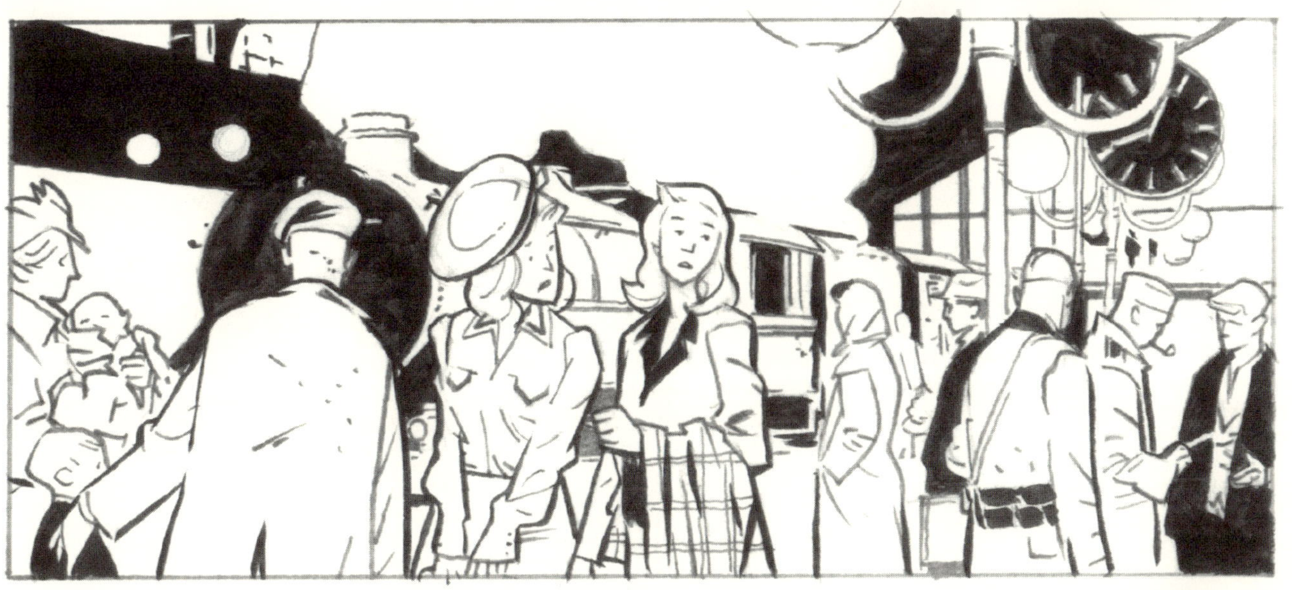

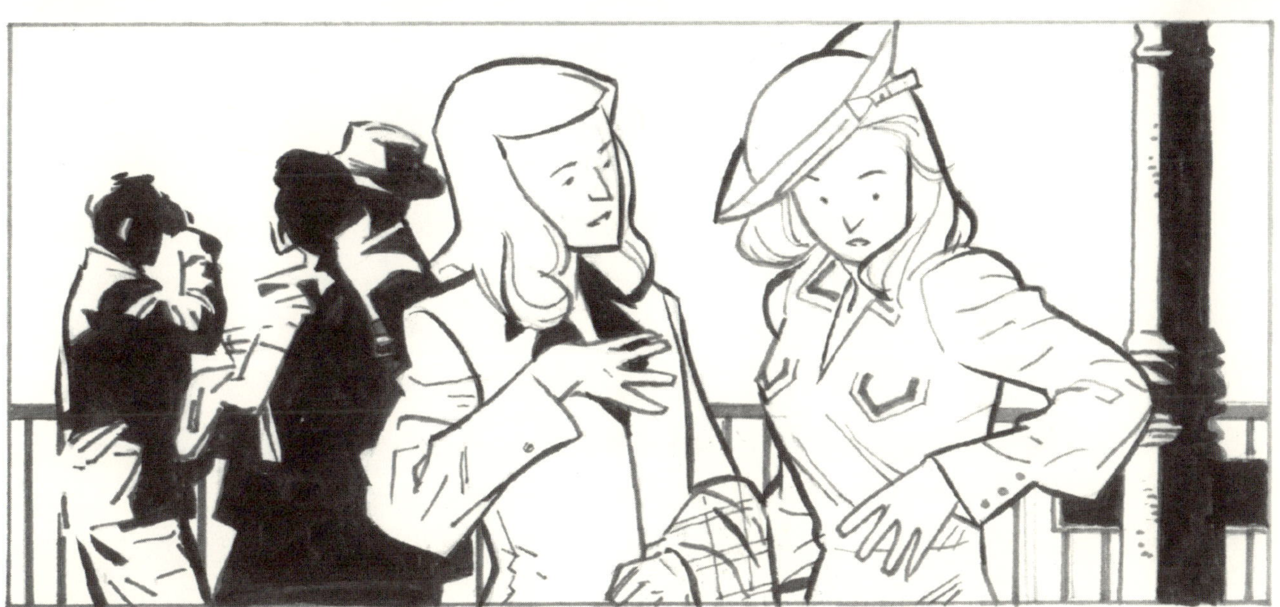

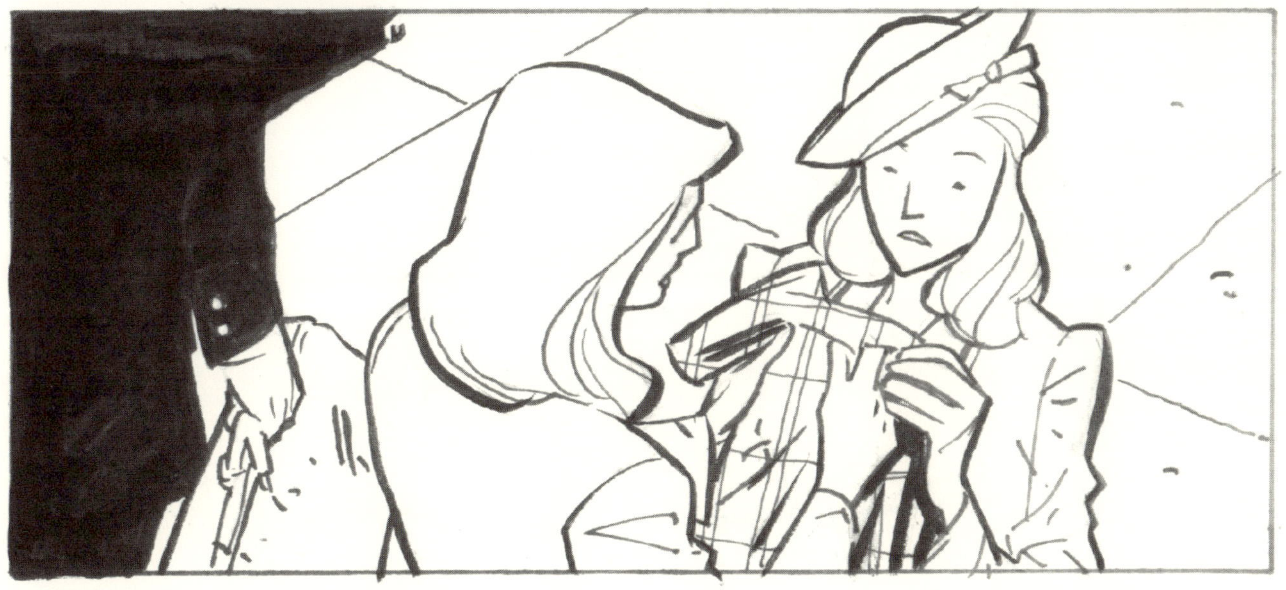

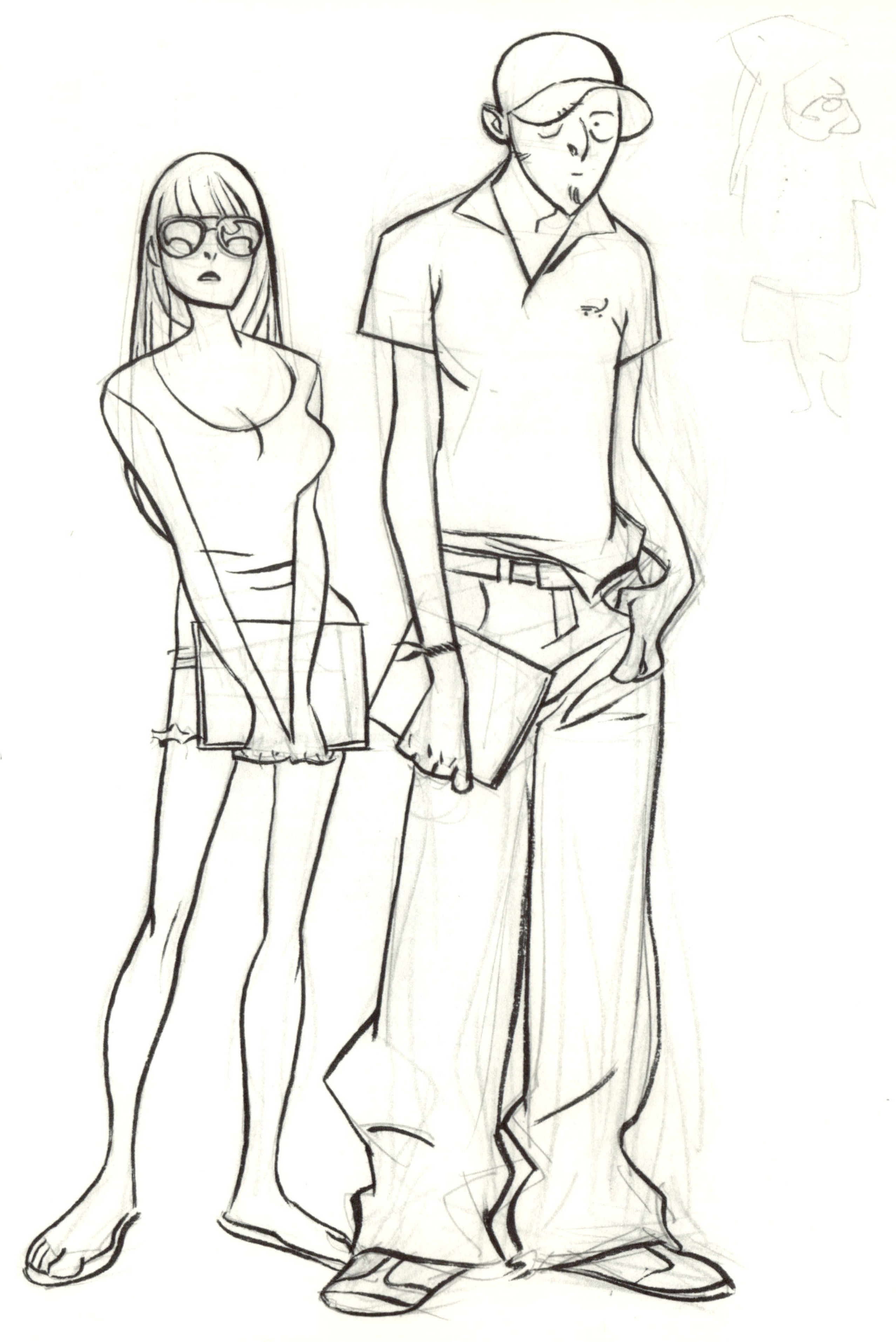

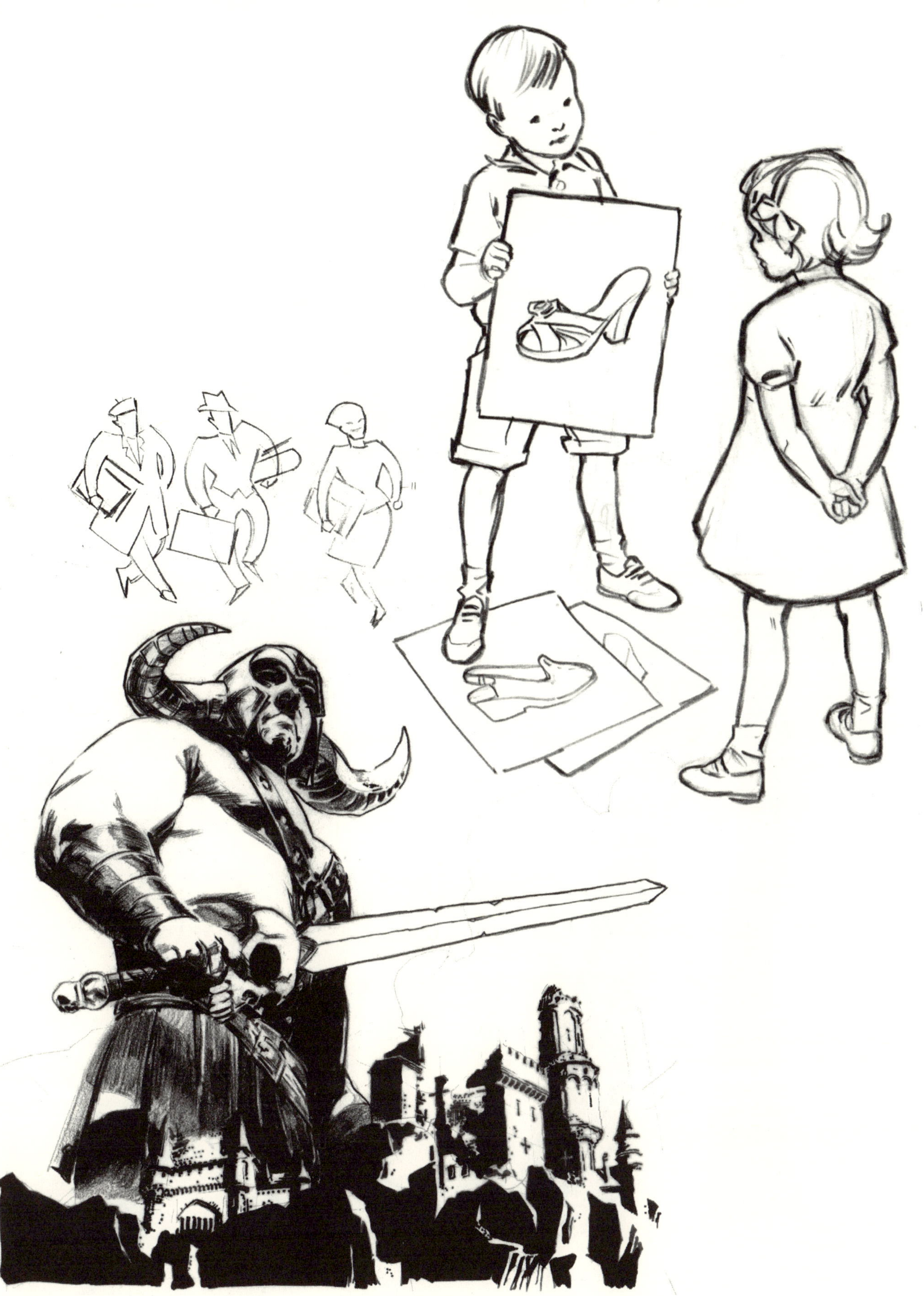

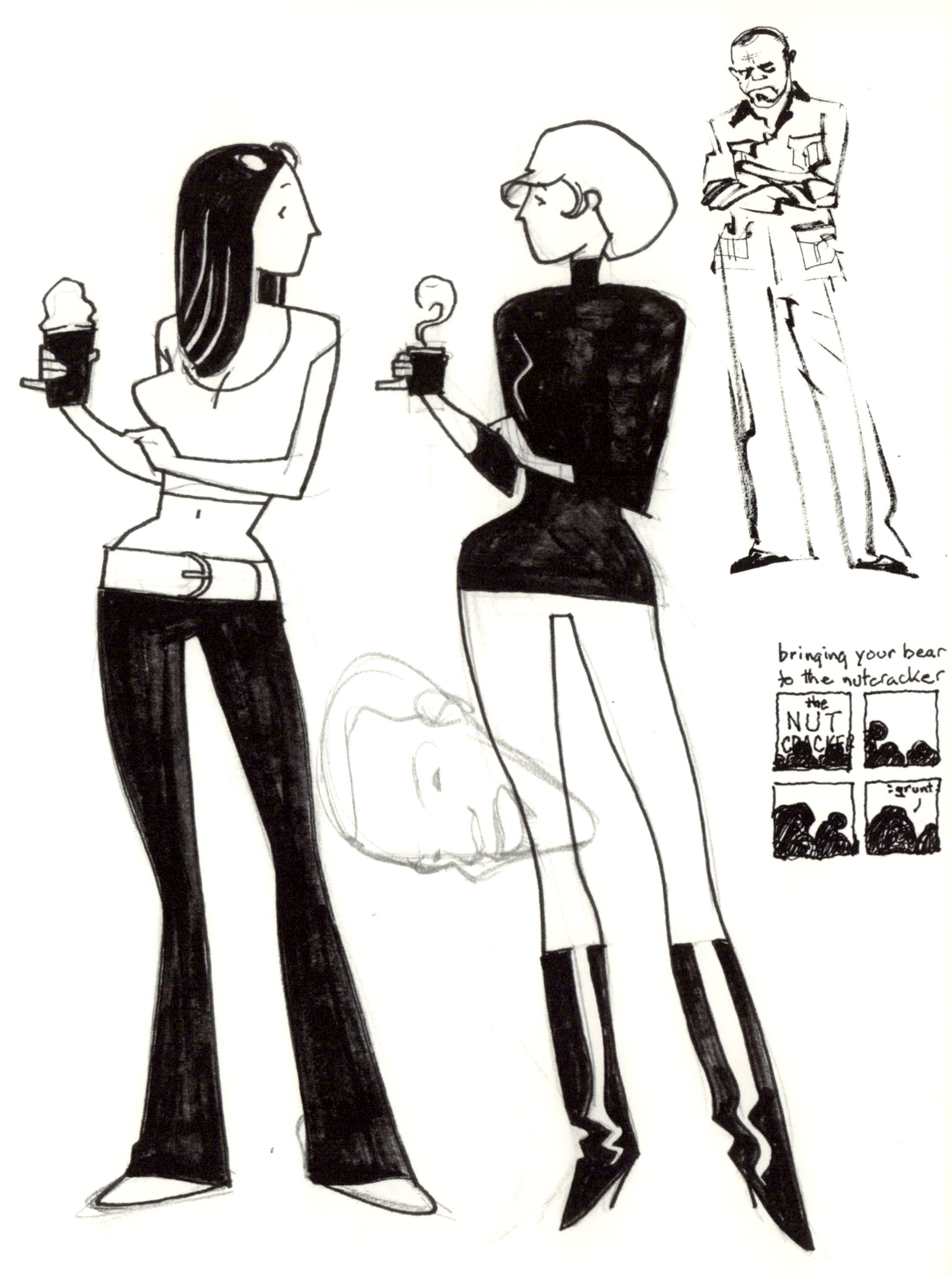
bringing your bear
to the nutcracker
the
NUT
CRACKER
grunt

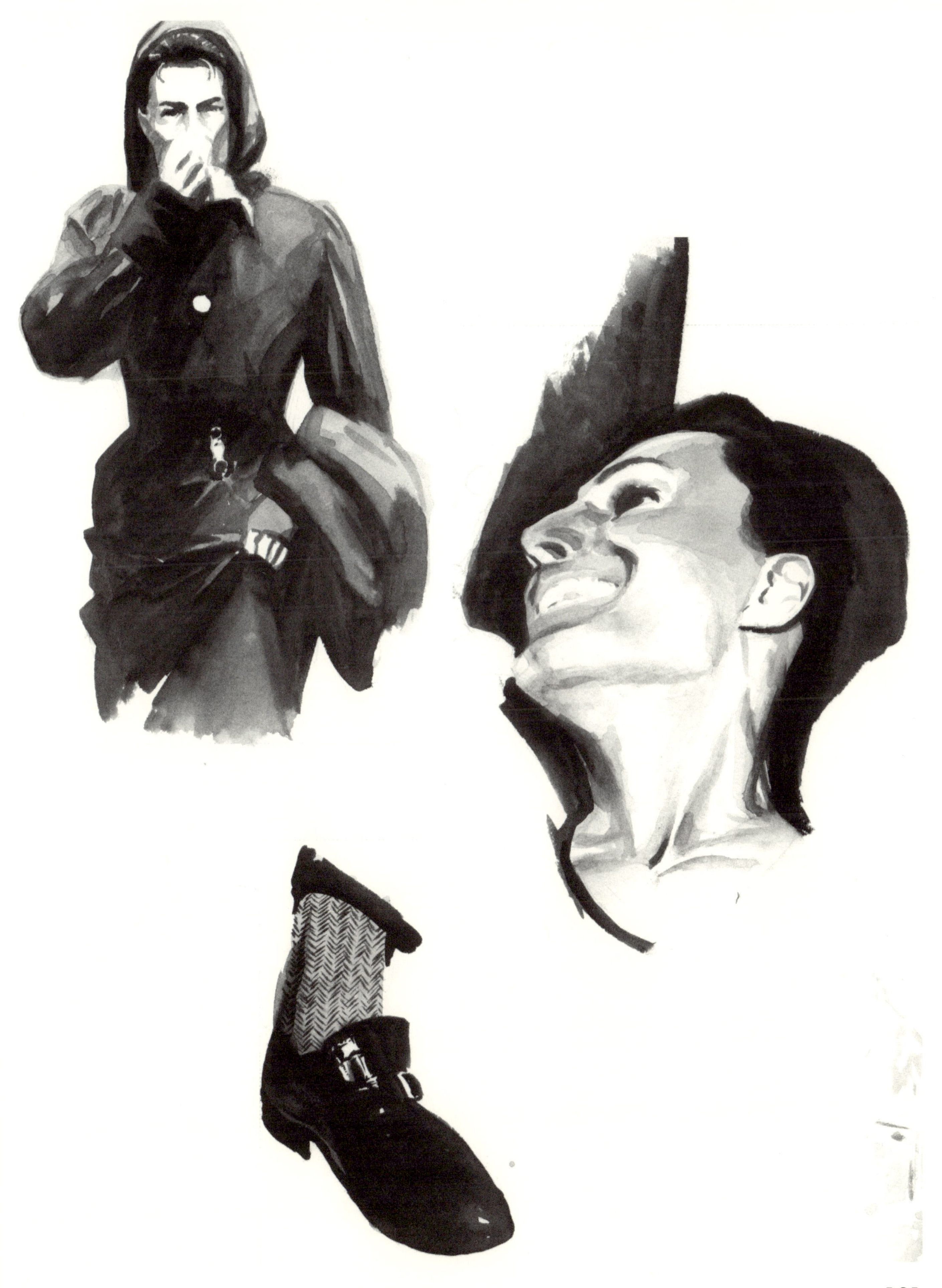

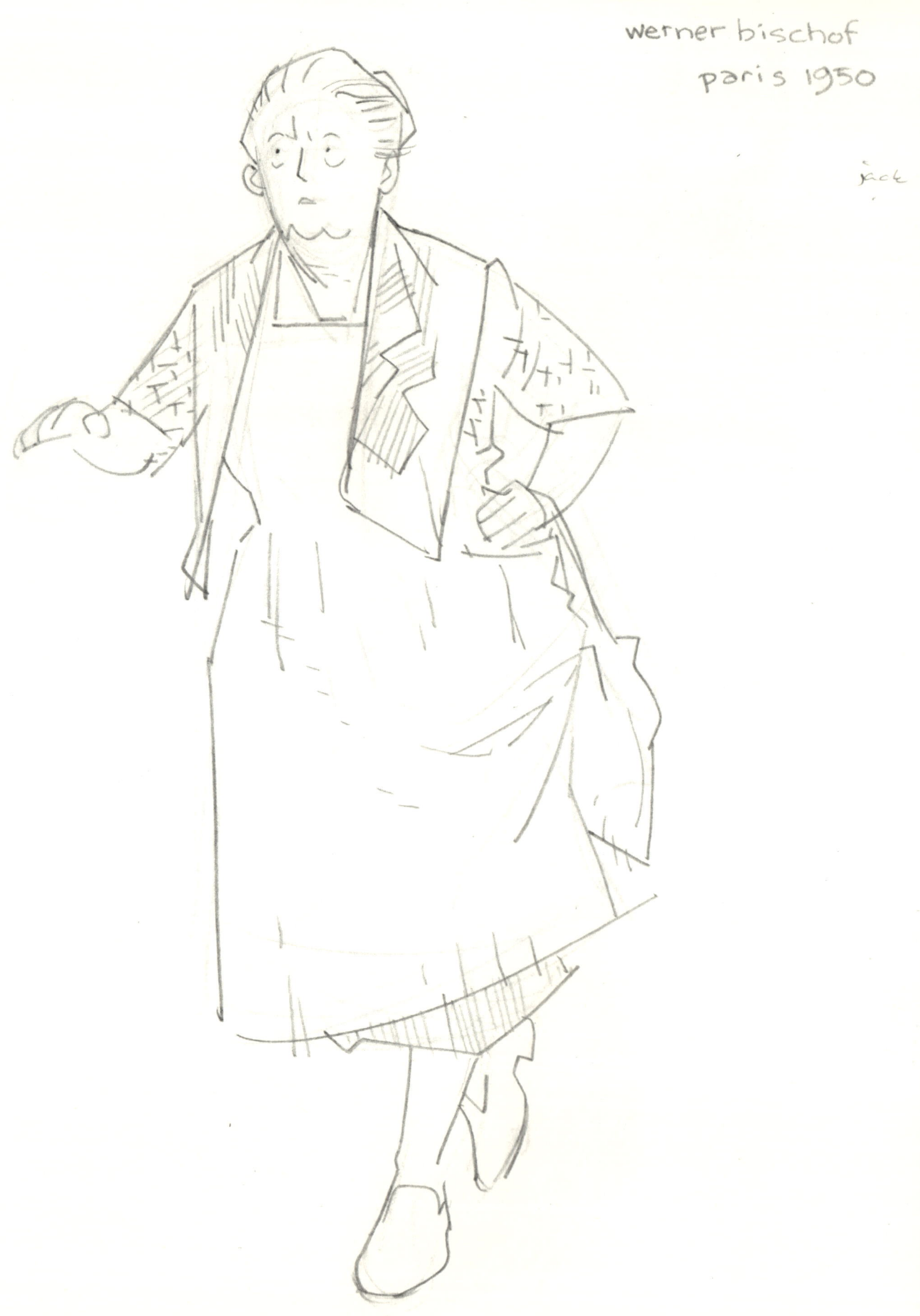
werner bischof
paris 1950
jack

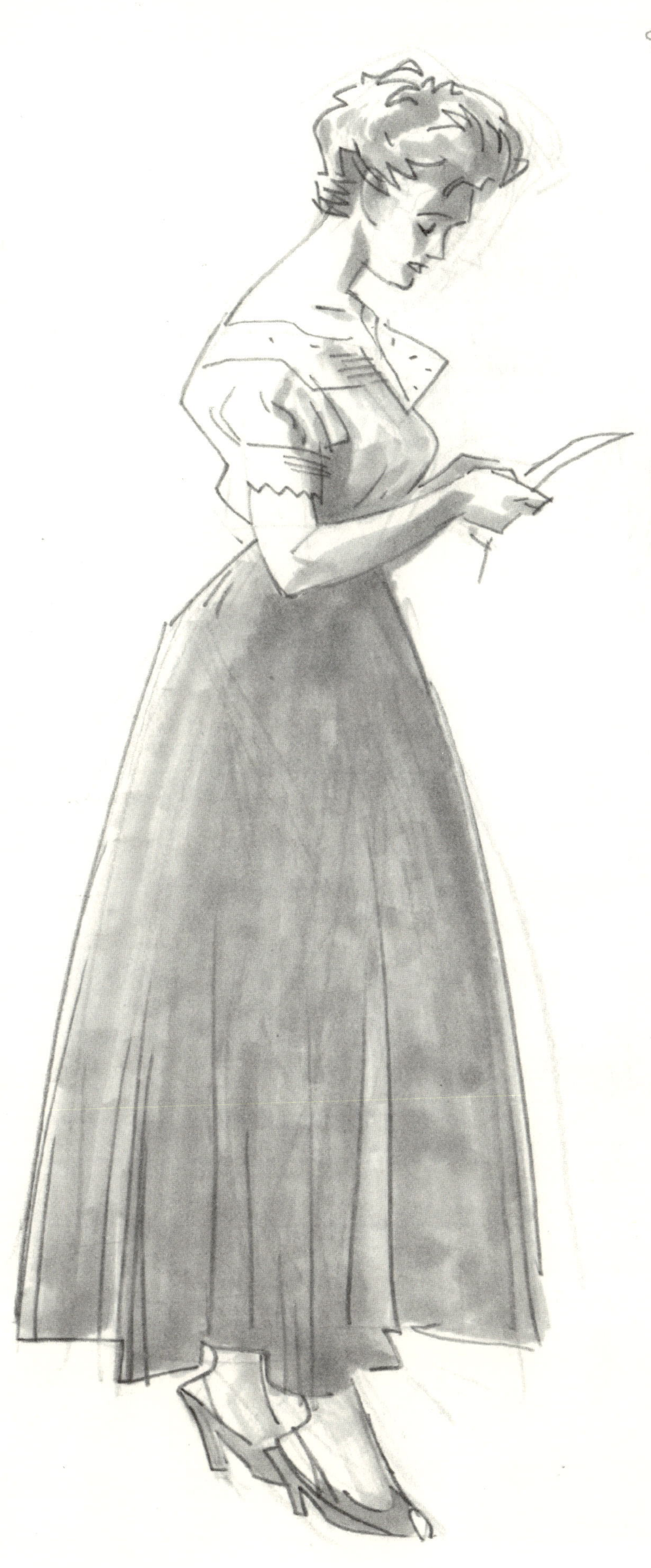

girl reading
a menu
boulevard st·michel
paris 1954

Robert Capa

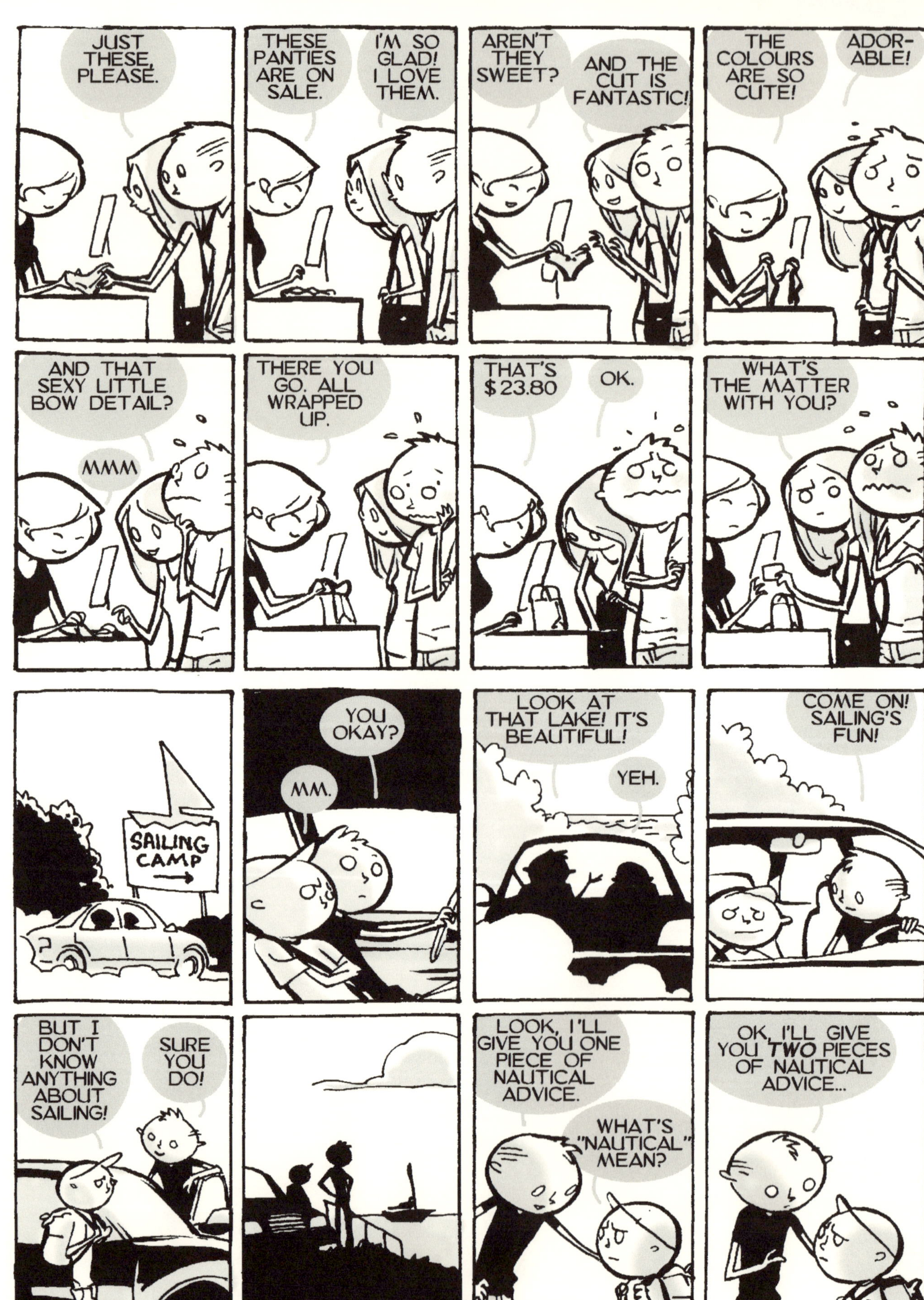
JUST THESE, PLEASE.
THESE PANTIES ARE ON SALE.
I'M SO GLAD! I LOVE THEM.
AREN'T THEY SWEET?
AND THE CUT IS FANTASTIC!
THE COLOURS ARE SO CUTE!
ADOR-ABLE!
AND THAT SEXY LITTLE BOW DETAIL?
MMM
THERE YOU GO. ALL WRAPPED UP.
THAT'S $23.80
OK.
WHAT'S THE MATTER WITH YOU?
SAILING CAMP
YOU OKAY?
MM.
LOOK AT THAT LAKE! IT'S BEAUTIFUL!
YEH.
COME ON! SAILING'S FUN!
BUT I DON'T KNOW ANYTHING ABOUT SAILING!
SURE YOU DO!
LOOK, I'LL GIVE YOU ONE PIECE OF NAUTICAL ADVICE.
WHAT'S "NAUTICAL" MEAN?
OK, I'LL GIVE YOU TWO PIECES OF NAUTICAL ADVICE...

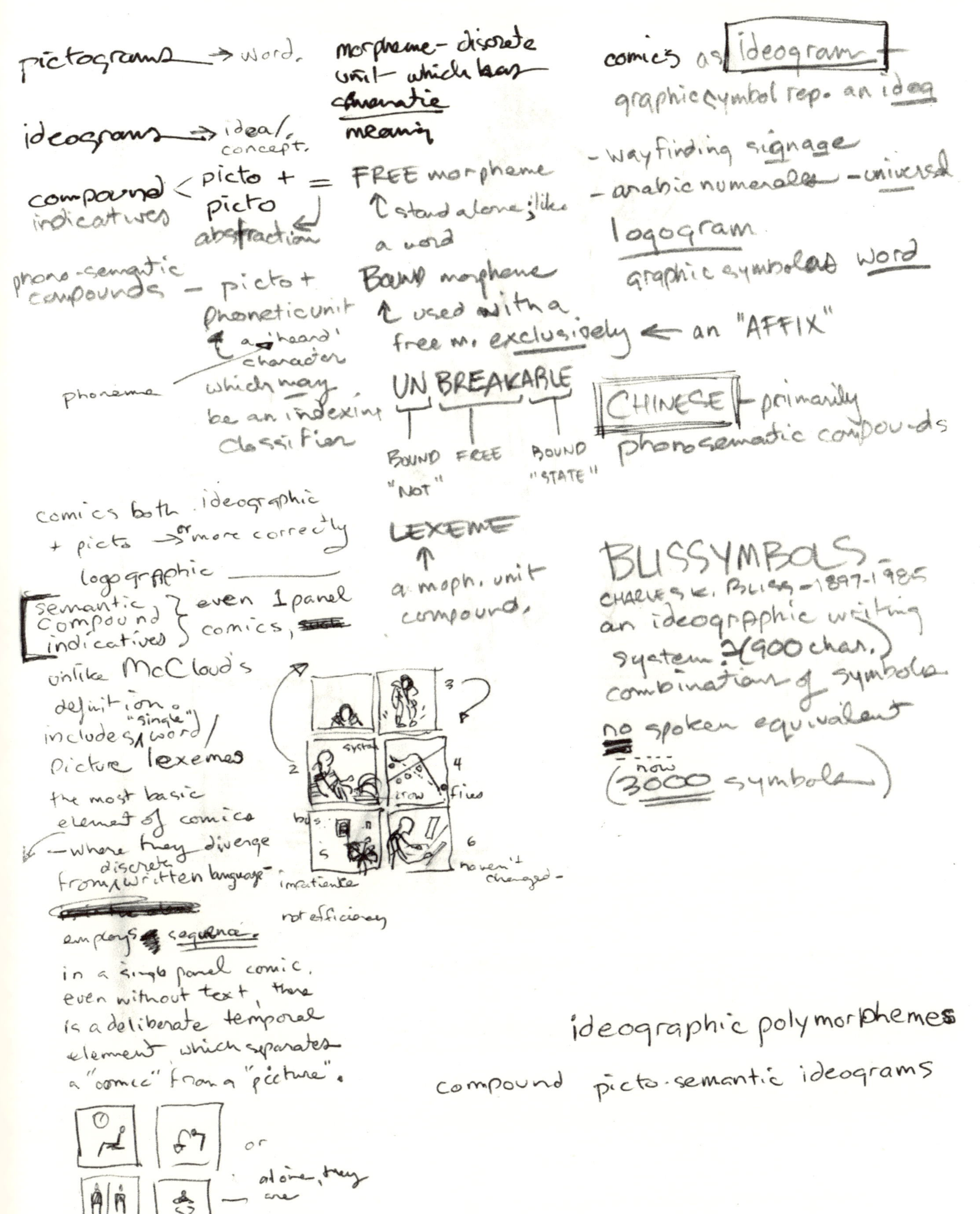
pictograms → word.
ideograms → idea/concept.
compound indicatives < picto + picto = abstraction
phono-semantic compounds – picto + phonetic unit
a 'heard' character which may be an indexing classifier
phoneme
morpheme – discrete unit which has semantic meaning
FREE morpheme
stand alone; like a word
BOUND morpheme
used with a free m. exclusively ← an "AFFIX"
UN BREAKABLE
BOUND "NOT"
FREE
BOUND "STATE"
LEXEME
a morph. unit compound.
comics as ideogram
graphic symbol rep. an idea
– wayfinding signage
– arabic numerals – universal
logogram
graphic symbol as word
CHINESE – primarily phonosemantic compounds
BLISSYMBOLS
CHARLES K. BLISS – 1897-1985
an ideographic writing system. (900 char.)
combination of symbols
no spoken equivalent
now (3000 symbols)
comics both ideographic + picto → or more correctly logographic
semantic compound indicatives } even 1 panel comics,
unlike McCloud's definition, includes "single" word / picture lexemes
the most basic element of comics
– where they diverge from discrete written language –
employs sequence
in a single panel comic, even without text, there is a deliberate temporal element which separates a "comic" from a "picture".
impatience
not efficiency
haven't changed –
or
alone, they are
ideographic polymorphemes
compound picto-semantic ideograms

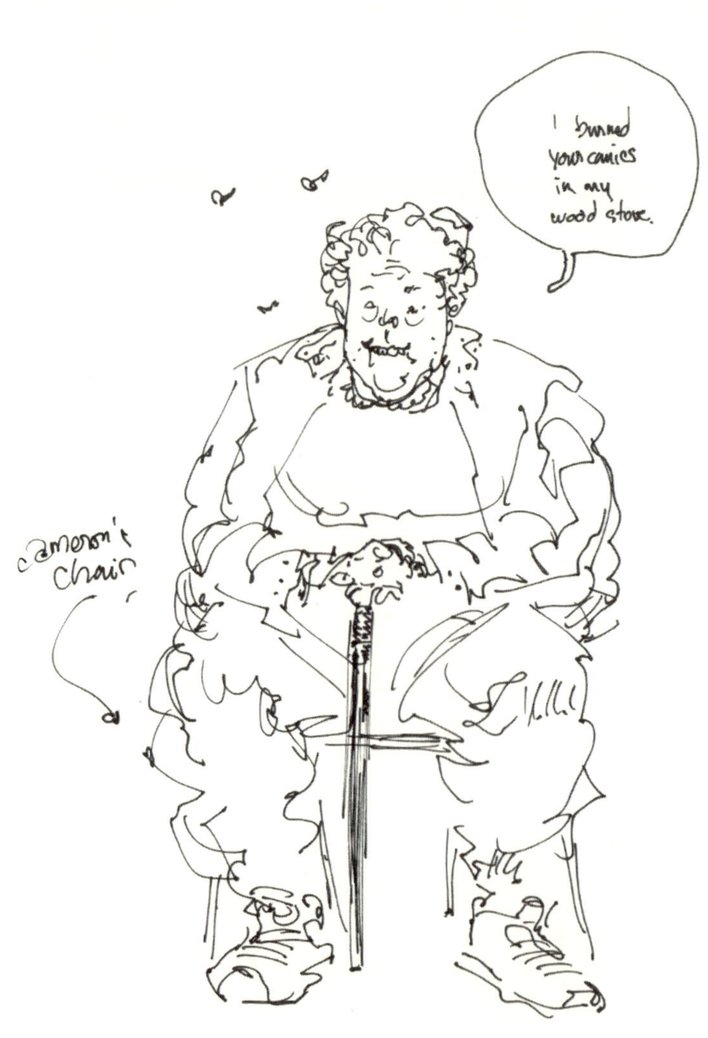
I burned your comics in my wood stove.
cameron's chair

Also from One Horse Leadworks:

50 REASONS TO STOP SKETCHING AT CONVENTIONS
by Stuart Immonen

NEVER AS BAD AS YOU THINK
by Kathryn & Stuart Immonen

CRIMINAL INSECTS
by Kathryn & Stuart Immonen

COMING SOON:

RUSSIAN OLIVE TO RED KING
by Kathryn & Stuart Immonen

www.immonen.ca

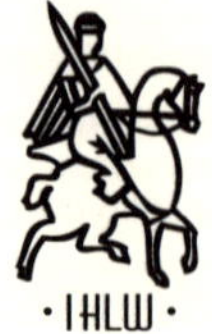